CONSUMING PL

Why do places differ from one another? Why do some places attract visitors and others investors? Why do some places repel? How are places consumed by those visiting? How does consumption affect local people and the environment?

John Urry has been discussing and writing on these and similar questions for the past fifteen years. In *Consuming Places* he gathers together his most significant contributions. Urry begins with an extensive review of the connections between society, time and space. He goes on to examine the concept of 'society', the nature of 'locality', the significance of 'economic restructuring', and the concept of the 'rural' in relationship to place. The book then considers how places have been transformed by the development of service occupations and industries. Concepts of the service class and post-industrialism are theoretically and empirically discussed. Attention is devoted to the ways in which places are consumed and particular attention is given to the visual character of such consumption and its implications for places and people. The implications for nature and the environment are also explored in depth. Finally, the author explores the changing nature of consumption and the tensions between commodification and collective enthusiasms in the context of the changing ways in which the countryside is consumed.

This wide-ranging book will be required reading for students and academics in sociology, geography, leisure studies, urban and regional studies and cultural studies.

John Urry is Professor of Sociology at Lancaster University. He is the author of numerous books including *The Tourist Gaze* (1990) and *Economies of Signs and Space* (1994, with Scott Lash).

INTERNATIONAL LIBRARY OF SOCIOLOGY

Founded by Karl Mannheim

Editor: John Urry

Lancaster University

CONSUMING PLACES

John Urry

London and New York

First published 1995
by Routledge
11 New Fetter Lane, London EC4P 4EE

Simultaneously published in the USA and Canada
by Routledge
29 West 35th Street, New York, NY 10001

© 1995 John Urry

Typeset in Times by
Ponting–Green Publishing Services, Chesham, Bucks
Printed in Great Britain by
TJ Press (Padstow) Ltd, Padstow, Cornwall

British Library Cataloguing in Publication Data
A catalogue record for this book is available for
the British Library

Library of Congress Cataloging in Publication Data
Urry, John.
Consuming places / John Urry.
p.   cm. – (The International library of sociology)
Includes bibliographical references and index.
ISBN 0–415–11310–5: $55.00.
ISBN 0–415–11311–3 (pbk.): $15.95
1. Consumption (Economics) – Social aspects.
2. Consumer behavior. 3. Tourist trade – Social aspects.
I. Title. II. Series.
HC79.C6U77 1994
306.3–dc20   94–28911
CIP

ISBN 0–415–11310–5 (hbk)
ISBN 0–415–11311–3 (pbk)

CONTENTS

TABLES

PREFACE

This book could not have been produced without the enormous stimulation
of many colleagues at Lancaster University, particularly over the past ten to
fifteen years. Partly this stimulation has been centred within various formal
groups and centres, including the Lancaster Regionalism Group, the Centre
for the Study of Cultural Values, the Centre for the Study of Environmental
Change and the Faculty of Social Sciences. But it has also resulted from the
tremendous range of more informal discussions that have occurred in and
around the Lancaster Sociology Department. Such discussions in cafés, bars,
common rooms and pubs have helped to concretise an immensely fruitful
research culture and to have made the Department an unusually creative kind
of place. This book is about some other makings of place.

John Urry
Lancaster
April 1994

1

TIME AND SPACE IN THE CONSUMPTION OF PLACE

INTRODUCTION

For many years I have been fascinated by what one could describe as the sociology of place. This developed out of a concern with how people actually experience social relations, both those which are relatively immediate and those which are much more distant, and how these intersect. But this concern is not in any simple sense empiricist because places are not clear and obvious entities. The understanding of place cannot be undertaken without major theoretical endeavour. To know something as apparently simple as the social relations of place and its consumption is to have to engage with a sophisticated array of social theorising. Indeed almost all the major social and cultural theories bear upon the explanation of place in one way or another. However, such theories have not begun to explain the diversities of place, and this is because they have not engaged with the sociologies of time and space, the relations between the social *and* the physical environment, and the interdependencies between the consumption of material objects and of the natural and built environments.

I thus seek to establish three arguments in this book: first, that the understanding of place is a complex theoretical and empirical task requiring a range of novel techniques and methods of investigation; second, that most social theories deal unsatisfactorily with the nature of place because they have not known what to do about time, space and nature; and third, that places are partly at least 'consumed' and that the mode of such consumption remains relatively underanalysed, involving as it does a range of human senses.

This book is entitled *Consuming Places*. This title is intended to indicate four claims. First, places are increasingly being restructured as centres for consumption, as providing the context within which goods and services are compared, evaluated, purchased and used. Second, places themselves are in a sense consumed, particularly visually. Especially important in this is the provision of various kinds of consumer services for both visitors and locals. Third, places can be literally consumed; what people take to be significant about a place (industry, history, buildings, literature, environment) is over

1

time depleted, devoured or exhausted by use. Fourth, it is possible for localities to consume one's identity so that such places become almost literally *all-consuming* places. This can be true for visitors, or for locals or for both. This can produce multiple local enthusiasms, social and political movements, preservation societies, repeat travel patterns, the pleasures of strolling around and so on. It is the contradictions and ambiguities revealed by these four dimensions of the consumption/place relationship that I shall principally examine in this book (see Sack 1993, for a related examination of place and consumption).

I am also concerned with the changing analysis of place, and especially with the notion of 'restructuring'. The use of this term signifies the shift in understanding of place that occurred from the late 1970s onwards. This was the result of two processes: the extraordinary economic transformations of almost every place that occurred in the late 1970s and 1980s; and the concurrent revival of political economy approaches within the social sciences which brought out the need to theorise and to research the rapidly changing economic base of place. Later in this chapter I will examine in more detail the intellectual shifts in the 1970s and early 1980s that transformed our understanding of place. I will also go on to consider how in the later 1980s the sense of restructuring changed, as politics and culture came also to be seen as central to the structuring and experience of place. In particular I will concern myself with the consumption of place, especially visually, and I will endeavour to link some notions in the analysis of the consumption of goods and services to the consumption of place.

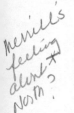

The turn towards culture was prompted by two further conceptual transformations. First, much more attention was paid to how one's sense of place is not simply given but is culturally constructed. Second, attention has also been directed to the economic bases of such cultural transformations, to what elsewhere I have termed the 'economy of signs' (Lash and Urry 1994). This has led many studies to be concerned with the so-called culture industries – arts, tourism, leisure – which have become crucial to the economic and cultural transformation of different places.

Paralleling these innovations have been some changes in the perceived relationship between society and nature. Sociology, as the study of society, was premised upon the radical distinction between society and nature. This reflected the transformation of nature and its conceptualisation as a realm of unfreedom to be tamed or mastered by humankind, by society. But in recent years this sense of nature as 'out there' and subject to control and mastery has been subject to both intellectual and practical critique (again see Lash and Urry 1994: Ch. 11). The environmental movement in particular has transformed our comprehension of nature, which in many recent formulations is to be regarded as embracing both society and the physical environment, what can be characterised as an 'integral nature'.

In this chapter I shall be concerned mostly with time and space, issues that

I have been investigating for some years now (see Urry 1981b; Gregory and Urry 1985). In this chapter I shall show that these are centrally significant notions within contemporary social theory, but that they have not always been so. The history of social theory in the twentieth century has in some ways been the history of their singular absence. But it will also be shown that this was an absence that could not be entirely sustained. Here and there time and space broke through, disrupting pre-existing notions which were formed around distinctions which had served mainly to construct an a-temporal and an a-spatial sociology. Societies were typically viewed as endogenous, as having their own *social* structures which were neither temporal nor spatial. Furthermore, societies were viewed as separate from each other and most of the processes of normative consensus, structural conflict or strategic conduct were conceptualised as internal to each society, whose boundaries were coterminous with the nation-state. Apart from aspects of urban and rural sociology there was limited recognition of the processes of internal differentiation across space. What was therefore investigated by much twentieth century sociology was a system of independent societies whose social structures were viewed as consistent over space, and where there is little analysis of diverse social times or that places and organisations are in important senses timed.

It has also been argued that this academic neglect was more marked in the case of space than time. Soja notes the paradox that in the 30 or 40 years around the turn of the twentieth century there was a series of sweeping technological and cultural changes which transformed the spatial underpinnings of contemporary life (1989). These included the telegraph, the telephone, X-ray, cinema, radio, the bicycle, the internal combustion engine, the aeroplane, the passport, the skyscraper, relativity theory, cubism, the stream-of-consciousness novel and psychoanalysis (see also Kern 1983). But Soja argues that these changes were not reflected in much social theory at the time. Such spatial changes mainly came to be the province of a separate and increasingly positivist science of geography which set up and maintained a strict demarcation and academic division of labour from its neighbours. Soja suggests that an historical consciousness became inscribed within social theory such that the 'historical "imagination" seemed to be annihilating the geographical' (1989: 323). And yet in fact this historical imagination, reflected in much twentieth century Marxism, remained relatively impervious to the precise significance of time and especially to how social relations are irreducibly temporal, and to the fact that there are different social times implicated within particular social structures.

In the first part of this chapter I shall provide relatively brief summaries of some of the early twentieth century writings on time and space. In the second part of this chapter I show what it was in the 1970s and 1980s that changed all this, that brought space and time into sociology and social theory more generally. In the last section, analysis will be provided of the 1980s

3

emergence of what one could describe as a research programme of 'time-space' sociology and social theory. Attention will be directed to some of the main works which have taken on board how social structures and cultural processes are necessarily timed and spaced; and how these timings and spacings are intrinsic to the powers and impact of such structures and processes.

A BRIEF HISTORY OF TIME AND SPACE

I will begin here with sociological approaches to the investigation of time. Although the very word time designates disparate concepts most sociological accounts have presumed that time is in some sense social. They have adopted a version of the 'French' school's approach, following Durkheim. He argued in *Elementary Forms* that only humans have a concept of time and that time in human societies is abstract and impersonal and not simply individual (1968). Moreover, this impersonality is socially organised; it is what Durkheim refers to as 'social time'. Hence, time is a 'social institution' and the category of time is not natural but social. Time is an objectively given social category of thought produced within societies and which therefore varies as between societies.

A similar emphasis upon the qualitative nature of social time was developed in Sorokin and Merton (1937). They distinguish between societies based on whether there is a separate category of clock-time, over and above social time. The Nuer for example do not have a sense of time as a resource. Time is not viewed as something that passes, that can be wasted, that can be saved (Evans-Pritchard 1940). Where there are expressions of time, these take place by reference to social activities based on cyclical ecological changes. Those periods devoid of significant social activity are passed over without reference to time. It has also been noted that while most societies have some form of 'week' this may consist of anything from three to sixteen days (Colson 1926). In many societies such divisions reflect some particular social pattern. The Khasi, for example, have an eight-day week since they hold a market every eight days.

Modern societies are generally viewed as being more reliant on clock-time than are pre-modern societies. Time in modern societies is not principally structured in terms of social activities. Clock-time is central to the organisation of modern societies and of their constitutive social activities. Such societies are centred around the emptying out of time (and space) and the development of an abstract, divisible and universally measurable calculation of time. It is clear that the first characteristic of modern machine civilisation was temporal regularity organised via the clock, an invention that was in many ways more important even than the steam engine. Thompson famously argued that an orientation to time becomes *the* crucial characteristic of industrial capitalist societies (1967). People were viewed as having shifted from an orientation to task to an orientation to time although the historical evidence now suggests that this distinction was less clear cut than Thompson suggested, since some features of a 'modern' time consciousness pre-dated industrialisation.

Thompson's argument depended upon the classical writings of Marx and Weber. Marx showed that the regulation and exploitation of labour time is the central characteristic of capitalism. The exchange of commodities is in effect the exchange of labour times. Capitalism entails the attempts by the bourgeoisie either to extend the working day or to work labour more intensively, as Marx says: 'man is nothing; he is, at most, the carcase of time' (Marx and Engels 1976: 127). If the working class is not able to resist such pressures, competition will compel capitalists to extend the work period beyond its social and physical limits. There will be 'over-consumption' of labour-power and it will be in the interests of the bourgeois class as a whole to introduce limits on continuous extensions of the working day. However, this collective need does not ensure that reductions on the length of the working day will in fact be realised. Capitalist competition has to be constrained in its own interests (and in those of the workforce). Hence during the history of the first industrial power, Britain, factory hour legislation, the intervention of the state, was particularly important in preventing continuous extensions of the working day and heralded the shift from the production of absolute surplus-value to relative surplus-value production. And it is this form of production, with what Marx calls 'denser' forms of work as compared with the more 'porous' longer day, that led to the staggering increases in productivity that have mostly characterised capitalist industry since the mid-nineteenth century.

However, what Marx did not pursue further is how this dominance of clock-time transforms people's subjectivities. Various processes in modern societies constitute people as temporal subjects, as having both an orientation *to* time, and being disciplined *by* time. Weber provided the first sociological analysis of such processes. He said of the Protestant ethic:

> Waste of time is thus the first and in principle the deadliest of sins. The span of human life is infinitely short and precious to make sure of one's own election. Loss of time through sociability, idle talk, luxury, even more sleep than is necessary to health . . . is worthy of absolute moral condemnation.
>
> (1930: 158)

The spirit of capitalism adds a further twist to this: as Benjamin Franklin maintained 'time is money' – to waste time is to waste money. People therefore have taken on the notion that it is their duty to be frugal with time, not to waste it, to use it to the full and to manage the time of oneself and that of others with the utmost diligence. Not only work but also leisure is often organised in a similar fashion. It is planned, calculative, sub-divided and worthwhile, 'rational recreation' in other words.

Alongside this rationalist analysis there has developed a more phenomenologically oriented social theory of time. Heidegger was concerned to demonstrate the irreducibly temporal character of human existence. He stresses in *Being and Time* that philosophy must return to the question of 'Being', something that had been obscured by the Western preoccupation with epistemology (1962). And central to Heidegger's ontology of Being is that of time, which expresses the nature of what subjects are. Human beings are fundamentally temporal and find their meaning in the temporal character of human existence. Being is made visible in its temporal character and in particular the fact of movement towards death. Being necessarily involves movement between birth and death or the mutual reaching out and opening up of future, past and present. Moreover, the nature of time (and space) should not be confused with the ways in which it is conventionally measured, such as intervals or instants. Measurable time–space has been imposed on time–space relations in Western culture.

There are somewhat similar themes in Bergson. For him, time proper is the time of becoming. He argues against a spatialised conception of time and maintains that time or duration must be viewed as 'temporal' (1910). People should be viewed as in time rather than time being thought of as some discrete element or presence. Furthermore, time is inextricably bound up with the body. People do not so much think real time but actually live it sensuously, qualitatively. Bergson further argues that memory should not be viewed as a drawer or store since such notions derive from incorrectly conceptualising time spatially. Memory must be viewed temporally, as the piling up of the past on the past which has the effect that no element is simply present but is changed as new elements are accumulated from the past. In Bergson's analysis time is viewed qualitatively but space as abstract and quantitative. In the critique of the 'spatialised' conception of memory as a 'drawer', Bergson privileges time over space and views the latter as abstract (see Game 1994).

Mead also adopts a consistently 'temporal' viewpoint. He focuses upon how time is embedded *within* actions, events and roles, rather than seeing time as an abstract framework (1959; Adam 1990). Mead regards the abstract time of clocks and calendars as nothing more than a 'manner of speaking'. What is 'real' for Mead is the present, hence his major work on time is called *The Philosophy of the Present*. What is in the past is necessarily reconstructed in the present, each moment of the past is recreated afresh. So there is no 'past' out there, or rather back there. There is only the present, in the context of which the past is being continually recreated. It has no status except in the light of the emergent present. It is emergence which transforms the past and gives sense to the future. This emergence stems from the interaction between people and the environment, humans being conceived by

6

Mead as indissolubly part of nature. This emergence is always more than the events giving rise to it. Moreover, if the present is real, the past and future are ideational or representational. They are only open to us through the mind. Mead's view is fully twentieth century in that he emphasises the relative nature of time. There is no universal time standard but any standard is viewed as relative to the organism undergoing the measuring. However, as Adam (1990) notes, his rejection of abstract time means that he reproduces the distinction between *durée* and time (by concentrating on the former) rather than trying to overcome it as some more recent writers have endeavoured to do.

I now turn to a short history of space. The sociological classics dealt with space but in rather cryptic and undeveloped ways. Marx and Engels were obviously concerned with how capitalist industrialisation brought about the exceedingly rapid growth of industrial towns and cities. Engels' *The Condition of the Working Class in England* (1969) provides an illuminating urban sociology of 1840s' England. More generally in *The Manifesto of the Communist Party* (1848) Marx and Engels describe how fixed, fast-frozen relations are swept away, all newly formed relations become antiquated before they can ossify; all that is solid melts into air, all that is holy is profaned. Marx and Engels argue *inter alia* that capitalism breaks the feudal ties of people to their 'natural superiors'; it forces the bourgeois class to seek markets across the surface of the globe and this destroys local and regional markets; masses of labourers are crowded into factories so concentrating the proletariat and producing a class-for-itself; and the development of trade unionism is assisted by the improved transportation and communication that capitalism brings in its wake. In his later works Marx analyses how capitalist accumulation is based upon the annihilation of space by time and how this consequently produces striking transformations of agriculture, industry and population across time and space.

Some similar processes are analysed by Durkheim although the consequences are viewed quite differently. In *The Division of Labour in Society* (1984) it is argued that there are two types of society with associated forms of solidarity: mechanical (based on likeness or similarity) and organic (based on difference and complementarity). It is the growth in the division of labour, of dramatically increased specialisation, that brings about transition from the former to the latter. This heightened division of labour results from increases in material and moral density. The former involves increases in the density of population in a given area, particularly because of the development of new forms of communication and because of the growth in towns and cities. Moral density refers to the increased density of social interaction. Different parts of society lose their individuality as people come to have more and more contacts and interactions. This produces a new organic solidarity of mutual interdependence, although on occasions cities can be centres of social pathology. Overall, Durkheim presented a thesis of modernisation in which

7

local geographical loyalties are gradually undermined by the growth of new occupationally based divisions of labour. In *Elementary Forms* Durkheim also presents a social theory of space (1968). This has two parts: first, since everybody in a given society represents space in the same way, this implies that the cause of such notions is social; and second, in some cases at least the spatial representations literally mirror the dominant pattern of social organisation.

It is a paradox that Max Weber made very few references to space since his brother Alfred Weber was one of the seminal contributors to the theory of industrial location. Max Weber was relatively critical of attempts to use spatial notions in his analysis of the city. He rejected analysis in terms of size and density and mainly concentrated on how the emergence of the medieval city constituted a challenge to the surrounding feudal system. The city was characterised by autonomy and it was there for the first time that people came together as individual citizens (see Weber 1958).

Undoubtedly the most important classical contributor to the sociology of space is Simmel. His classical paper on the 'metropolis' should be located within the context of his more general writings on space (see Levine 1971; Frisby 1992a, 1992b). He analysed five basic qualities of spatial forms that are found in those social interactions which turn an empty space into something meaningful. These qualities are the exclusive or unique character of a space; the ways in which a space may be divided into pieces and activities spatially 'framed'; the degree to which social interactions may be localised in space; the degree of proximity/distance especially in the city and the role of the sense of sight; and the possibility of changing locations and the consequences especially of the arrival of the 'stranger'. Overall Simmel tends to see space as becoming less important as social organisation is detached from space.

In 'Metropolis and the City' Simmel develops more specific arguments about space and the city (Levine 1971). First, because of the richness and diverse sets of stimuli in the metropolis people have to develop an attitude of reserve and insensitivity to feeling. Without the development of such an attitude people would not be able to cope with such experiences caused by a high density of population. The urban personality is reserved, detached and blasé. Second, at the same time the city assures individuals of a distinctive type of personal freedom. Compared with the small-scale community the modern city gives room to the individual and to the peculiarities of their inner and outer development. It is the spatial form of the large city that permits the unique development of individuals who are placed within an exceptionally wide range of contacts. Third, the city is based on the money economy which is the source and expression of the rationality and intellectualism of the city. Both money and the intellect share a matter-of-fact attitude towards people and things. It is money which produces a levelling of feeling and attitude. Fourth, in particular the money economy as reflected in modern life generates a concern for precision and punctuality. This is so both in the general sense that the money economy makes people more calculating about their activities and relationships; and in the specific sense that people have to schedule activities in precise ways and that there needs to be accurate time-keeping, punctuality and a prohibition on spontaneity.

Thus Simmel does not so much explain urban life in terms of the spatial form of the city. His work is more an early examination, paralleling Marx and Engels in the *Communist Manifesto*, of the effects of 'modern' patterns of mobility on social life wherever it is to be found (see of course Berman 1983; Frisby 1992a, 1992b). Simmel analyses the fragmentation and diversity of modern life and shows that motion, the diversity of stimuli and the visual appropriations of places are centrally important features of that experience.

Unfortunately, however, such analyses were not then followed by the academic speciality that arose to investigate such metropolises, namely 'urban sociology'. This was established in the inter-war period at the University of Chicago. Much of this work involved the attempt to develop ecological approaches to the study of the city such as the concentric ring theory, although other studies were concerned to develop the ethnographic method. Theoretically the most important contribution was Louis Wirth's 'Urbanism as a way of life' (1938) followed by Redfield's 'The folk society' (1947). Wirth argued that there are three causes of the differences in social patterns between urban and rural areas: size, which produces segregation, indifference and social distance; density, which causes people to relate to each other in terms of specific roles, for urban segregation between occupants of such roles, and greater formal regulation; and heterogeneity, meaning that people participate in different social circles, none commanding their total involvement, which means that they have discrepant and unstable statuses. Wirth (and Redfield) thus claim that the organisation of space, mainly in terms of size and density, produces corresponding social patterns. It is therefore a position significantly different from that of Simmel.

Nevertheless it has been Wirth's analysis that provided the basis for research in urban sociology and Redfield's for research in rural sociology. Much effort was spent on testing the hypothesis that there are two distinct ways of life and that these result from the respective size, density and heterogeneity of urban and rural areas. However, the research has largely shown that there are no such simple urban and rural patterns. *Inter alia* it is clear first, that urban areas contain some often close-knit social groups, such as the urban villages of Bethnal Green or the immigrant ghettos in north American cities, or mining communities more or less anywhere. More generally Gans has questioned the thesis that most city dwellers are isolated, individualised and autonomous (1986). Cities are more diverse than this and some inner-city areas can be centres of a complex sociality focused around, for example, gentrification. Other city areas can be much more suburban, where the focus of activity is the home and where the main forms of activity

9

are car-based. In such cases it is the forms of mobility that are important and less the size and density of the urban area. Suburban patterns of life can be found in urban and rural areas.

Furthermore, rural life is not simply organised around farm-based communities, where people frequently meet each other, are connected in diverse ways and tend to know each other's friends (see the reporting of the classic studies in Frankenberg 1966). Studies of rural communities have shown that there may be considerable conflict and opposition in such places, especially around status, access to land and housing and the nature of the 'environment'. In Britain many rural areas have become increasingly populated not by those employed in farming but by urban newcomers who have pushed out existing poorly paid farm labourers or their children. Newby argues that:

> The newcomers often possess a set of stereotyped expectations of village life which place a heavy emphasis on the quality of the rural environment . . . many newcomers hold strong views on the desired social and aesthetic qualities of the English village. It must conform as closely as possible to the prevailing urban view – picturesque, ancient and unchanging . . . [this has led] many newcomers to be bitterly critical of the changes wrought by modern farming methods.
>
> (1985: 167)

Williams also showed just how seductive are these conceptions of the countryside as an unchanging idyllic way of life defined by contrast with the dirt, danger and darkness of the urban (1973). To a significant extent sociology took over such deceptively easy contrasts in its endeavour to construct a spatially determined analysis of the rural way of life.

One theoretical issue has concerned the concept of 'community'. Bell and Newby (1976) have usefully distinguished between the three different senses of this concept (see also Savage and Warde 1993: 104). First, there is its use in a simply topographical sense, such as to refer to the boundaries of a particular settlement; second, there is the sense of community as a local social system implying a degree of social interconnection of local people and institutions; and third, there is 'communion', a particular kind of human association implying personal ties, a sense of belonging and warmth. Bell and Newby point out that the last of these is not necessarily produced by any particular settlement type and indeed it could also result from a complete lack of routine propinquity. It should also be noted that community can be understood in a fourth sense, as ideology, where efforts are made to attach conceptions of communion to buildings, or areas, or estates, or cities and so on, in ways which conceal and help to perpetuate the non-communion relations actually to be found there.

Finally here, it should be noted that much of the existing literature has tended to reproduce not just the distinction in popular discourse between the countryside and the city but also Tönnies' (1955) opposition of *Gemeinschaft* and *Gesellschaft*. Such binary distinctions are not helpful and Schmalenbach's (1977) concept of the *Bund*, a kind of community which people choose to join and can leave, is an important additional notion. Cities and rural areas differ in their capacity to generate a wide array of *Bund*-like associations. Some urban areas have particularly facilitated the proliferation of such *Bund*-like social groupings, the gay culture of San Francisco being a good example (see Hetherington 1990).

It is clear that the spatial concepts of size, density and heterogeneity do not explain how and why places develop different *Bund*-like patterns of social and cultural life. In the next section I will firstly outline the 1970s' Marxist critique of this social theory of the urban and rural that was mounted by Castells and others. Following this I will detail a whole variety of intellectual and social processes which brought urban sociology in from the cold but forced it to reject these simplistic notions as a social theory of time and space began at last to be developed in the academy in the 'West' in the 1980s.

THE 1970s CRITIQUE

In this section I will outline a number of social and intellectual shifts in the late 1970s/early 1980s which significantly challenged existing theories of time, and especially, of space.

First, the writings of Castells served to crystallise a number of objections to the existing 'sociology of space' which, as shown in the previous section, had been organised around attempts to theorise and research the 'urban' and the 'rural', including so-called 'urban managers' (Pahl 1975). By the early 1970s these topics had become intellectually impoverished and little or no innovative work was being developed. Castells, drawing partly on the 1968 events in Paris and elsewhere on the 'structuralist' innovations of Louis Althusser, argued that any scientific discipline needed a properly constituted 'theoretical object' (1977, 1978). He argued that urban sociology (and by implication rural sociology) did not possess such a theoretical object; there was a wide variety of merely common-sense concepts such as town, city, community, the urban and so on. Castells argued that such an object should be developed and this would be based on a distinctive 'structuralist' analysis of the unfolding contradictions of capitalist relations. Such relations are increasingly organised on an international basis. This gives a particular role to towns and cities which have become centres no longer of production but of 'collective consumption', that is, of services generally provided by the state and which are necessary for the 'reproduction' of the energies and skills of the labour force. There are two reasons why collective consumption (of transport, education, planning, health, etc.) has come to be organised by the state within towns and cities: first, because of the historical concentration of the labour force within urban areas; and second, because there has been a long-term tendency for these activities to be unprofitable when provided by the private sector.

Castells, having identified a proper 'theoretical object' for urban sociology, namely 'collective consumption', then seeks to use this to explain particular kinds of spatially varied politics. He argues that these forms of collective consumption cannot be provided unproblematically since states are rarely able (and willing) to raise sufficient taxation revenues. All sorts of disputes arise over the forms and levels of provision, such as the quality of public housing, the location of health care, the nature of public transport and so on. Each of these services becomes 'politicised' because they are provided collectively. Thus what emerges is a sphere of urban politics which is focused in and around these forms of collective consumption. Castells devotes particular attention to analysing 'urban social movements'. These normally comprise a number of different urban groups but because they are all concerned with the reproduction of labour-power tend to come under the dominance of working-class organisations, to become in effect a new kind of class politics. Thus he argues strongly against efforts to understand the urban in terms of either 'culture'/'way of life' or in terms of a spatial determinism. Cities have become centres of new kinds of politics because of changes in the *social* relations of production which have generated the requirement for labour-power to be reproduced through forms of collective consumption. In this account the 'spatial' form taken by patterns of urban protest is seen as explicable in terms of the changing social relations of production.

Castells' writings rapidly generated a whole set of new debates and controversies. Among other things critics argued that there are in fact many conservative responses to issues of collective consumption – in the US and the UK these have led to marked spatial inequalities through, for example, sustaining much lower housing densities in richer areas. It was argued that many services, especially housing, are not *necessarily* provided 'collectively' and can and should be privatised and individualised; that services are not necessarily 'urban' and as populations have undergone counter-urbanisation it has been realised that some of these can be located elsewhere; that what develops is a sociology of services which would have little to do with developing an 'urban' sociology; that the spatial distribution of activities is not to be regarded as determined by the social structure; and that the urban is in fact also crucially affected by changing relations of production, not just of collective consumption (Castells 1977, 1978, 1983; Dunleavy 1980; Saunders 1980, 1982, 1990).

In an influential later work Castells examines a number of urban movements, especially the gay and Latino movements in San Francisco and the citizens' movement in Madrid (1983). He then derives a model from these studies to explain their relative degree of success. The movement must work on three fronts: collective consumption, community culture, and political self-management; it must define itself as an *urban* social movement; it must make use of the media, professionals, and parties; and it must be organisationally independent of such parties (see discussion in Pickvance 1985). One problem about this schema is that the notion of the urban is presumed to be self-evident. In fact Pickvance suggests that there are three important characteristics of the urban: collective consumption (as in Castells); local-level political processes; and spatial proximity. Existing formulations are unsatisfactory because they only focus upon one of these. Pickvance further argues that Castells' model ignores some centrally significant contextual factors: rapid urbanization, state responses to the demands of the movements, political context, the role of the middle class in resource mobilization and its objective work and residential situation, and the general economic and social conditions which affect the general disposition to political activism (Pickvance 1985: 39–44).

A second aspect of the 1970s critique developed the last point in detail. While sociology had organised its understanding of space around the urban/rural distinction, geography's particular spatial focus had been on the 'region'. However this was similarly critiqued in the late 1970s by Massey. She argues that 'space matters':

> The fact that processes take place over space, the facts of distances, of closeness, of geographical variation between areas, of the individual character and meaning of specific places and repair – all these are essential to the operation of social processes themselves.
>
> (Massey 1984: 14)

Spatiality then is taken by Massey to be an integral and active feature of the processes of capitalist production; it has various aspects besides that of region including distance, movement, proximity, specificity, perception, symbolism and meaning; and space makes a clear difference to the degree to which, to use realist terminology, the causal powers of social entities (such as class, the state, capitalist relations, patriarchy) are realised (see Gregory and Urry 1985; Sayer 1992).

Specifically, Massey argues that there are a number of distinct spatial forms taken by the social division of labour; that there is no particular historical ordering in the emergence of each of these forms of restructuring; that which develops depends upon the specific struggle between capital and wage-labour; that one important pattern of spatial restructuring involves the relocation of certain more routine elements of production away from head-quarters and R. & D. functions; that these diverse patterns of spatial restructuring generate new patterns of inequality, which are not just social but also spatial; and that the once relatively coherent regional economies begin to dissolve as more diverse economic and social structures emerge at the local level. On this account a particular locality is to be seen as the outcome of a unique set of 'layers' of restructuring dependent upon different rounds of accumulation. How these layers combine together in particular

13

places, and especially how international, national and local capitals combine together to produce particular local social and political effects became the subject of a major research programme in Britain in the 1980s (see Cooke 1989, in general; and Bagguley *et al.* 1990).

One important effect of this emphasis upon spatial differentiation within sociology has been to challenge the notion that social class is an unproblematically *national* phenomenon, that classes are essentially specified by the boundaries of the nation-state. The emphasis within the restructuring literature on local/regional variation has led analysts to rethink social classes through this prism of space (later gender and ethnicity were subject to similar analyses). Thus it has been argued that there are international determinants of the social class relations *within* a nation-state; that there are large variations in local stratification structures within a society so that the national pattern may not be found in any particular place at all; that the combination of local, national and international enterprises may produce locally unexpected and perverse commonalities and conflicts of class interest; that there are marked variations in the degree of spatial concentration of class; that some class conflicts are in fact caused by, or are displaced onto, spatial conflicts; and that in certain cases, localities emerge with distinct powers to produce significant social and political effects, whether these be socialist (inter-war Nelson), anti-black (Los Angeles), conservationist (Cheltenham) and so on (see MacIntyre 1980; Davis 1990; Cowen 1990, respectively).

Further, attention was increasingly paid to how production had been internationalised since the end of the Second World War. Specifically, the 'new international division of labour' thesis involved a sophisticated attempt to theorise this new spatial form (Fröbel *et al.* 1977; Savage and Warde 1993: Ch. 3). It was argued that three factors in particular enable a newly internationalised division of labour to develop. The first is the rapid improvement in the productivity of parts of agriculture in the developing world – this has the effect that significant numbers of landless labourers become available for work in the cities. Second, there are technical and organisational changes in the production process of certain industrial products which enable the organisational and spatial separation of 'conception' and 'execution'. Third, there are developments in communications technology, especially the telephone line and the computer, which facilitate instantaneous flows of information to occur internationally, so enabling distant parts of a globalised company to be informed, surveyed and controlled. The reaction to these factors is that a much more complex spatial division of labour develops with significant parts of the routine manufacturing employment shifting from the 'First' to the 'Third' World, although research and management functions remain in the First World. Three effects of this new spatiality are the massive collapse, the de-industrialisation, of manufacturing employment in many First World cities; increasing manufacturing employment in some newly industrialising countries, albeit with wage rates, conditions of work and trade union organisation far inferior to those experienced by First World workers; and heightened competition between places to attract and keep the increasingly mobile capital which because of new communications technology can be located anywhere.

Various empirical criticisms have been made of this approach (particularly over the probable scale of the phenomenon) but in terms of a social theory of time and space there are three points to note in conclusion. First, it was seen that the instantaneity of time involved in the transmission of information (as well as of other signs) transforms nation and place which are necessarily incorporated into a set of globalising processes. Such processes undermine the coherence of individual 'societies'. The instantaneity of time transforms space and the maintenance of apparently separate spaces (see Chapter 14). Second, the thesis under-emphasises the role of agency in generating changes in the spatial form. In particular it ignores the extraordinary flows of people into parts of the developed world, a process particularly marked in the USA. An appropriate theory would have to explain the relationship *between* the flows of international capital, the flows of information, and the flows of people, and one factor affecting the last of these is the flows of images (especially of Western consumerism; see Lash and Urry 1994, on 'flows'). Finally, the thesis over-emphasises economic determinants in the generation of new spatial forms and ignores social, political and cultural factors which structure space. It is a thesis similar to others developed in the 1970s which emphasise the changing political economy of time and space. Harvey is particularly known for theorising the way in which capital may move into the 'secondary circuit' of land and the built environment, so as to compensate for 'over-accumulation' and falling profits in the primary circuit of capitalist production (1982).

The last main set of writings was produced by Giddens, his theory of time and space appearing in the late 1970s and 1980s (see 1981, 1984, as well as 1990). Drawing on Heidegger, Giddens elucidated five ways in which, because of their temporal character, human subjects are different from material objects. First, only humans live their lives in awareness of their own finitude, something reinforced by seeing the death of others and how the dead make their influence felt upon the practices of the living. Second, the human agent is able to transcend the immediacy of sensory experience through both individual and collective forms of memory; through an immensely complex interpenetration of presence and absence. Third, human beings do not merely live in time but have an awareness of the passing of time, which is embodied within social institutions. Furthermore, some societies develop an abstract concept of rational, measurable time, radically separable from the social activities that it appears to order. Fourth, the time-experience of humans cannot be grasped only at the level of intentional consciousness but also within each person's unconscious in which past and present are indissolubly linked. Fifth, the movement of individuals through time and space is to be grasped via the interpenetration of presence and absence, which results from the location of the human body and the changing means of its interchange with the wider society. Each new technology transforms the intermingling of presence and absence, the forms by which memories are stored and weigh upon the present, and the ways in which the long-term *durée* of major social institutions is drawn upon within contingent social acts. In order to investigate particularly these latter processes more fully, Giddens also draws upon the work of 'time-geography' (see Gregory 1985).

Giddens develops a battery of concepts by which to think through just how the life processes of individuals, including their daily, weekly and monthly paths, are linked to the *longue durée* of social institutions. First there is regionalisation, the zoning of time-space in relationship to routinised social practices. Rooms in a house are, for example, zoned both spatially and temporally. Second, there is the concept of presence-availability, the degree to which, and the forms through which, people are co-present within an individual's social milieu. Communities of high presence-availability include almost all societies up to a few hundred years ago. Presence-availability has been transformed in the past century or two through the development of new transportation technologies and especially the separation of the media of communication from the media of transportation. Third, there is Giddens' concept of time-space distanciation: the processes by which societies are 'stretched' over shorter or longer spans of time and space. Such stretching reflects the fact that social activity increasingly depends upon interactions with those who are absent in time-space. Fourth, there are time-space edges, the forms of contact or encounter between types of society organised according to different structural principles. It is essential to investigate *inter*-societal systems, the time-space edges by which, for example, a tribal society is confronted by a class-divided society. The fifth concept here is that of power-containers, what Giddens calls the storage capacity of different societies, particularly storage across time and space. In oral cultures human memory is virtually the sole repository of information storage. In class-divided societies the city, especially with the development of writing, becomes the primary crucible or container of power. By contrast, in capitalist societies it is the territorially bounded nation-state that is the dominant time-space container of power. The city loses its distinctiveness as such (the walls come tumbling down!). Finally, there is the disembedding of time and space from social activities, the development of an 'empty' dimension of time, the separation of space from place, and the emergence of disembedding mechanisms, of symbolic tokens and expert systems which lift social relations out of local involvements. Expert systems bracket time and space through deploying modes of technical knowledge which are valued independently of the practitioners and clients who make use of them. Such systems depend on *trust*, on a qualitative leap or commitment related to absence in time and/or space. Trust in disembedding mechanisms is vested not in individuals but in abstract systems or capacities and is specifically related to absence in time and space (see Boden 1994, on trust).

Although this constitutes an impressive argument a number of deficiencies have been identified. First, there is little analysis of the specific time-space organisation of particular places or societies, all traditional and all industrial societies being seen as more or less the same. There is a tendency to regard the organisation of time and space as given, somehow embedded within the structuring of rules and resources that characterise modern societies in general.

It has also been noted that Giddens does not conceptualise time as a resource. Time is seen by him as a measure of chronological distance and stacked information, a measure of stretching across societies. But time in modern societies also functions as a centrally important resource. Indeed Adam argues that time is only conceptualised as a resource in societies like ours; societies which have not only created clock-time, but relate to that creation as *being* time and organise their social life by it (1990: 120). Or as Lefebvre suggests, with modernity lived time disappears. It is no longer visible and is replaced by measuring instruments, clocks, which are separate from social space. Time becomes a resource, separate from social space and is consumed, deployed and exhausted (1991: 95–6). The emergence of time and space as relatively independent resources is one of the defining characteristics of modern society.

This in turn relates to a further gap in Giddens' account, namely, the importance of the use of time and space for travel. He provides no analysis of why people travel and hence why saving 'time', or covering more 'space', might be of 'interest'. One obvious reason for travel is for pleasure – it enables people to visit other environments, places and people and to do so in particular stylised kinds of way (Urry 1990). Travel is a performance and some categories of aesthetic judgement may be pertinent to its comprehension (see Adler 1989b on travel as 'performed art'; Lash and Urry 1994: Ch. 10). Furthermore, a key aspect of many kinds of travel is that one enters a kind of liminoid space where some of the rules and restrictions of routine life are relaxed and replaced by different norms of behaviour, in particular those appropriate to being in the company of strangers. This may entail new and exciting forms of sociability and playfulness, including what one might call 'temporal play' while on holiday (see Shields 1991). It is necessary to investigate how time-space changes will often have the consequence not merely of heightening distanciation, but also of encouraging anticipation, resistance, opposition, pleasure, autonomy or a sense of deprivation.

Thus I have suggested that four sets of writings consecrated the temporal and spatial turns in the later 1970s and early 1980s: these can be summarised in terms of the concepts of 'collective consumption' and the city; 're-structuring'; the 'new international division of labour'; and 'time-space distanciation'. These concepts laid the foundations for the construction of a new discourse of 'time-space social analysis' that took root in the 1980s. It is noteworthy just how the infrastructure for such a development was laid, through the formation of a number of key journals and organisations. In the English-speaking world these included: the *International Journal of Urban and Regional Research*; *Antipode*; *Environment and Planning*, especially *D: Society and Space*; *Theory, Culture and Society*; *Association for Social Studies of Time*; *Time and Society*; *Ecumene. A Journal of Environment, Culture, Meaning*.

TIME-SPACE SOCIAL ANALYSIS

I will begin here with the sociology of time. It has recently been argued that much of the conventional understanding of time in the social sciences is rooted in out-dated and inappropriate notions. When Durkheim, Sorokin, Merton and the like insisted on the radical distinction between natural time and social time, this was based on an inadequate understanding of time in nature. Adam has recently argued that it is necessary to undertake a thorough re-examination of time, incorporating the insights and arguments from contemporary physical and biological sciences which have transformed the notion of 'natural time' (1990).

Adam argues that we should dissolve the distinction betwen natural time and social time (and also the distinctions between subject and object and nature and culture). Most of what social scientists have seen as specifically human is in fact generalised throughout nature. The one aspect which is not generalised through nature, clock-time, is paradoxically the characteristic which social science has thought to be the defining feature of natural time. Social science has operated with an inappropriate conception of time in the natural sciences, an almost non-temporal time invented by certain human societies. It can be described as Newtonian and Cartesian. It is Newtonian because it is based on the notion of absolute time, that from 'its own nature, [it] flows equably without relation to anything eternal . . . the flowing of absolute time is not liable to change' (cited in Adam 1990: 50). Such absolute time is invariant, infinitely divisible into space-like units, measurable in length, expressible as a number and crucially reversible. It is time seen essentially as space, as invariant measurable lengths which can be moved along, forwards *and* backwards. It is Cartesian space because it is premised upon the dualisms of mind and body, repetition and process, quantity and quality, form and content, subject and object and so on. In such a notion of time it seems that the great edifices of science would all appear to work equally well with time running in reverse.

Four scientific 'discoveries' developed in this century have transformed the understanding of time in nature: as Einstein demonstrated, there is no fixed time which is independent of the system to which it refers – time is a local, internal feature of the system of observation; again as Einstein showed, time and space are fused into four-dimensional space-time entities and such a fused space-time is curved under the influence of mass; chronobiologists have demonstrated that rhythmicity is the crucial principle of nature, and in particular that humans are not just affected by clock-time but are themselves clocks; and scientists of evolutionary processes have emphasised that the time of one's body should be extended to include the entire evolutionary history of humans – 'the time of our body is not exhausted by our finitude but arrives within it our entire evolutionary history' (Adam 1990).

The implication of all of this is that nature is intrinsically temporal; and that there are many different times in nature. Especially important is the way that physical time is now conceptualised as irreversible and directional. The clearest example of this can be seen in the process by which the universe has expanded – through the cosmological arrow of time following the extra-ordinary singularity of a 'big bang'. Laws of nature should thus be viewed as historical and hence it is incorrect to construct a simple dichotomy between nature as time-free or time-less or having a reversible concept of time and society as fundamentally temporal. Moreover, biologists have shown that it is false to assert that only human beings experience time or organise their lives through time. Biological time is not confined to ageing but expresses the nature of biological beings as temporal, dynamic, and cyclical – humans as having a life-cycle. Thus Adam argues for a notion of time which is non-spatialised, non-reversible, multi-faceted, and where no strong distinction is drawn between the times of nature and those of humans.

This kind of formulation is then reflected in more recent analyses in the sociology of time. Two areas of research are noteworthy. First, there is what is known as the historical sociology and geography of time, much of it concerned to debate the E. P. Thompson thesis that industrial capitalism ushers in a transformation from an orientation to *task* to an orientation to *time* (1967). Thrift in particular analyses the 'making of a capitalist time con-sciousness' in Britain suggesting a greater complexity of development than this simple dichotomy suggests (1990). In the period up to the sixteenth century daily life was task-oriented, the week was not a very important unit of time, and the seasons and related fairs and markets and the church calendar were the bases for temporal organisation. Between the sixteenth and eight-eenth centuries this began to change with the following developments: some growth in the ownership of domestic clocks; the increasing use of public clocks and bells; the growth of schooling for the upper and middle classes where activities began to be timetabled; the efforts by Puritans to organise work on a weekly basis; the increasing development of a cash economy which implied the need to calculate days of work and rates of pay; and the introduction of the term 'punctuality' into the popular vocabulary. By the eighteenth century time had become more clearly 'disembedded' from social activities. Partly this was due to innovations within the world of work concerned to instil a new time discipline for the emerging industrial work force. But it was also to do with changes within the leisured English upper class which developed visiting and social patterns of Byzantine temporal complexity. There were also developments outside work, the growth of Sunday Schools, of rational leisure and of Greenwich Mean Time. The last of these, a mathematical fiction signalling the total disembedding of time from social activity, developed so as to facilitate new kinds of social practice, namely mass travel and mobility, not just within a city as Simmel discussed, but between cities and from the later nineteenth century between countries (also see Lash and Urry 1994: 228–9). Overall the spreading of the paradigm of 'clock-time' occurred more unevenly than Thompson's thesis suggests; it involved more diverse social practices than those of industrial capitalism; and it came to operate on a much wider spatial scale.

It should also be noted that there are interesting connections analysed between the emergence of this kind of clock-time and the shift from a mainly oral to a mainly written culture (see Ong 1982). Much nineteenth century culture was written. There was a huge growth of cheap books, with daily newspapers doubling every fifteen years or so; an increase in the general use of time-keeping records; widespread written documentation of citizens through the registration of births, deaths, marriages, travel, and later of the passport; a proliferation of transport timetables; and an increased general employment of written signs to indicate routes, location, leisure facilities, tourist sites and so on (see Lash and Urry 1994: Ch. 9, on modernity and travel).

The second area of theoretical debate has concerned the significance of time and space for the development of a supposed postmodernism. I will highlight three aspects here relating to place (otherwise see Harvey 1989; Soja 1989; Lash 1990b; Jameson 1991; Crook *et al.* 1992). First, it is argued that the predominant written culture is under threat from a more visual and aesthetic culture, one which comes to be appreciated in a less detached, formal and distanced manner. Indeed the postmodern can itself be viewed as a post-cultural condition if culture is taken to imply that aesthetic or moral standards are imposed by and through an elite. Thus it is further argued that the symbolic boundaries between art, high culture and the academy, on the one hand, and everyday life and popular culture on the other, are dissolving. Specifically in relationship to spaces, Venturi famously wrote that architecture should 'learn from Las Vegas', it should develop a playful and pastiched style of 'roadside eclecticism' and break with the idea of buildings as exemplifying good taste or moral authority (1977).

Zukin (1992a, 1992b) has particularly explored this merging of the urban landscape and the vernacular. She points out that increasingly we sense there is a difference in how we organise what we see in the city. The visual consumption of space and time is both speeded up and abstracted from the logic of industrial production. This has led to the city being predominantly

20

reconstructed as a centre for postmodern consumption – the city has become a spectacle, a 'dreamscape of visual consumption' (1992b: 221). She shows how property developers have self-consciously sought to construct these new landscapes of power, which are stage-sets within which consumption can take place. These dreamscapes pose significant problems for people's identity which has historically been founded on place, on where people come from or have moved to. Yet postmodern landscapes are all about place, such as Main St in EuroDisney, world fairs or Covent Garden in London. But these are simulated places which are there for consumption. They are barely places that people any longer come from, or live in, or which provide much of a sense of social identity. Somewhat similarly Sennett argues that in the contemporary city different buildings no longer exercise a moral function – the most significant new spaces are those based around consumption and tourism (1991). Such spaces are specifically designed to wall off the differences between diverse social groups and to separate the inner life of people from their public activities.

Second, it is argued that the postmodern ushers in much more open and fluid social identities as compared with the traditionally fixed and unchanging identities of the modern period (particularly those centred around work, career and family). It is argued that the rapid speeding up of time and space in the postmodern period dissolves any sense of identity at all. One particular activity, watching TV, is seen as central to these claims. TV changes the temporal and spatial organisation of social life. The 'TV self is the electronic individual *par excellence* who gets everything there is to get from the simulacrum of the media: a market identity as a consumer in the society of the spectacle' (Kellner 1992: 145). In postmodern TV it is argued that the signifier has been liberated and image takes precedence over narrative, the aesthetic is dominant and the viewer is seduced by the free play of an excess or bombardment of images. It is argued that this produces a waning of affect, that postmodern selves are without depth or substance, and there is no self beyond appearances. Such decentred selves are particularly likely to be seduced by the postmodern urban environments described by Zukin.

Third, more specifically with regard to time it is argued that clock-time is partly being replaced by what can be described as 'instantaneous time'. It is suggested that the future is dissolving into the present, that 'we want the future now' has become emblematic of a panic about the future and a search for instantaneous gratification (Adam 1990). This is seen as partly resulting from how TV brings geographically distant events often of an appallingly tragic character into people's everyday lives. There is almost literal time-space compression as a collage of disconnected stories, with no coherent geographical patterning, intrudes and shapes social life. This temporal and spatial fragmentation is reinforced by the emergence of a so-called 'three-minute' culture, in that those watching TV/VCR tend to hop from channel to channel and they rarely spend time following through a lengthy or

21

complex programme. The result is that watching TV becomes much more of a private matter since programmes can be stored, repeated, broken up. Little sense remains of the shared collective watching of a particular key programme. And increasingly many programmes and especially advertisements are made to mimic such a pattern of instantaneously produced fragments. They consist of a collage of disconnected visual and aural images, each lasting a very short time and having little or no connection with those coming before or after (this might be caricatured as a shift from BBC to MTV). It is also suggested that this speeding up and fragmenting of an increasingly visual media, the growth of 'fast capitalism', makes it increasingly unlikely that people will have the concentration and stamina to read complex books from beginning to end (see Chapter 14 for more detail on time).

The most systematic attempt to place these developments within a conceptual framework has been Harvey's notion of 'time-space compression' (1989). Like many other analysts he begins with Berman's account of the modern world:

> To be modern is to find ourselves in an environment that promises adventure, power, joy, growth, transformation of ourselves and the world. . . . Modern environments and experiences cut across all boundaries of geography and ethnicity, of class and nationality, of religion and ideology . . . it pours us all into a maelstrom of perpetual disintegration and renewal.
>
> (Berman 1983: 15)

Harvey though tries to give a more detailed historico-geographical analysis of such developments (1989). In particular he is concerned with how capitalism entails different spatial fixes pertaining to different historical periods. By this he means that within each capitalist epoch, space is organised in such a way as best to facilitate the growth of production, the reproduction of labour-power and the maximisation of profit. It is through the reorganisation of time-space that capitalism is able to overcome its periods of crisis and lay the foundations for a new period of accumulation. In particular, Harvey examines Marx's thesis of the annihilation of space by time and attempts to demonstrate how this explains the complex shift from 'Fordism' to the flexible accumulation of 'Post-Fordism'. The latter involves a new spatial fix and most significantly new ways in which time and space are represented.

Central in this analysis is 'time-space compression':

> the processes that so revolutionize the objective qualities of space and time that we are forced to alter . . . how we represent the world to ourselves. . . . Space appears to shrink to a 'global village' of telecommunications and a 'spaceship earth' of economic and ecological interdependencies . . . and as time horizons shorten to the point where

the present is all there is . . . so we have to learn how to cope with an overwhelming sense of *compression* of our spatial and temporal worlds.

(Harvey 1989: 240)

More specifically, this compression involves the accelerating turnover time in production; the increased pace of change and ephemerality of fashion; the greater availability of products almost everywhere; the increased temporariness of products, relationships and contracts; the heightened significance of short-termism and the decline of a 'waiting culture'; the greater importance of advertising and rapidly changing media images to social life, the so-called 'promotional culture'; the increased availability of techniques of simulation, including buildings and physical landscapes; and the extraordinary proliferation of new technologies of information and communication which transcend space instantaneously, at the speed of nanoseconds (Harvey 1989: Ch. 17; Adam 1990; Lash and Urry 1994). Brunn and Leinbach in particular have detailed the nature and consequences of such a 'collapsing space and time' (1991). Postmodernism then is the outcome of the disorientation and fragmentation generated by this compression of time and space; it results in a dystopic nightmare, which in the view of some theorists results in the very disappearance of time and space as materialised and tangible dimensions of social life.

But Harvey argues this is not all there is to the postmodern. The collapse of many spatial boundaries does not mean that the significance of space decreases. As spatial barriers diminish so we become more sensitised to what different places in the world actually or appear to contain. Moreover, there is increasing competition between places to present themselves as attractive to potential investors, employers, tourists and so on, to promote themselves, to sell themselves as service- and skill-rich places (see Kearns and Philo 1993). Harvey notes the paradox: 'the less important the spatial barriers, the greater the sensitivity of capital to the variations of place within space, and the greater the incentive for places to be differentiated in ways attractive to capital' (1989: 295–6), and we might add to migrants and tourists.

This reinforcement of place does however remain a sub-theme in Harvey's account and is relatively underanalysed. Other writers have endeavoured to theorise the nature of place and locale, drawing on alternative traditions of social theory. Particularly influential in the early 1990s have been certain much earlier texts from Bachelard, Benjamin and Lefebvre. These have recently been rediscovered and located within the emergent discourse surrounding place. I will briefly summarise these contributions.

I noted earlier that one deficiency of Bergson's analysis is that he conceptualised space as overly abstract and quantitative, and hence his account of duration remains disembodied and abstract. Bachelard (1969) endeavours to remedy this failing by developing a conception of space as qualitative and heterogenous, and central to the Bergsonian comprehension

23

of time. There are three points to make here (see Game 1994). First, Bachelard argues that phenomenology is concerned with experiencing an image in its 'reverberations', not in terms of its visual impact. He thus employs an aural rather than a visual metaphor. This notion of reverberation points to a movement between the subject and object which disrupts any clear distinction between the two. The metaphor of reverberation implies immediacy.

Second, Bachelard specifically considers the nature of the house and argues that it is not to be seen purely as a physical object. Spaces, such as the house in which one is born, are not simply given, but are imbued with memory traces. Moreover, the very duration of time which is Bergson's concern is itself dependent upon such spatial specificity. Space is necessary to give quality to time. Or as Game neatly expresses it: 'Space transforms time in such a way that memory is made possible' (1994: 16). Thus a space such as a house plays a particularly significant role in the forming of memory. In particular, it shelters day-dreaming, it is a metaphorical space within which Bergsonian time operates.

Third, Bachelard presents a notion of memory as embodied. Our bodies do not forget the first house we encounter. Its characteristics are physically inscribed in us. Memories are materially localised and so the temporality of memory is spatially rooted for Bachelard. Houses are lived through one's body and its memories.

Benjamin (1979) draws on similar themes in his more wide-ranging analysis of how people 'read' the city (see also Buck-Morss 1989; Savage and Warde 1993). This is not a matter of intellectual or positivistic observation, rather it involves fantasy, wish-processes and dreams. The city is the repository of people's memories and of the past; and it also functions as a receptacle of cultural symbols. These memories are embodied in buildings which can then take on a significance very different from that intended by their architect. However, this is not simply a matter of individual interpretation since buildings demonstrate collective myths. Understanding these myths entails a process of unlocking or undermining existing interpretations and traditions and of juxtaposing conflicting elements together. Even derelict buildings may leave traces and reveal memories, dreams and hopes of previous periods. Wright's *A Journey Through Ruins* (1992) is a recent demonstration of Benjamin's method; he begins his journey with an old toilet in Dalston Lane in East London.

Benjamin was also concerned with the similarities between artistic perception and the reading of the urban text. The former can be absorbed through 'concentration' or 'distraction'. Benjamin suggests that buildings are normally appreciated in passing, in a state of distraction, as people are moving on elsewhere. This is by contrast with people's 'concentrated' absorption of paintings in a gallery. And this distracted perception helps to disrupt conservative cultural traditions. Most famously Benjamin examined the role of the *flâneur*, the stroller, who wandered around the city sampling life in a distracted and unpremeditated form (see Buck-Morss 1989). The voyeuristic and distracted nature of the encounter with the urban means that memories of the past can be ignited by some current event. It is only with distracted perception that this kind of chance linking of past and present can take place and undermine the oppressive weight of past traditions. Benjamin also analyses those places concerned only with entertainment, such as the expositions in Paris; they transform visitors to the level of the commodity as they enter a truly 'phantasmagorical world'.

The third social theorist that I will consider here is Lefebvre. Although much of his work was produced some decades ago he has only really come to exert recent influence through *The Production of Space* (1991). He argues that space is not a neutral and passive geometry. Space is produced and reproduced and thus represents the site of struggle. Moreover, all sorts of different spatial phenomena – land, territory, site and so on – should be understood as part of the same dialectical structure of space or spatialisation. While conventionally these different phenomena are separated as a result of fragmented discipline-based analyses, they need to be brought together in a unified theoretical structure. This structure comprises three elements. First, there are 'spatial practices'. These range from individual routines to the systematic creation of zones and regions. Such spatial practices are concretised over time in the built environment and in the landscape. The most significant spatial practices are those of property and other forms of capital. Second, there are representations of space, the forms of knowledge and practices which organise and represent space particularly through the techniques of planning and the state. Third, there are the spaces of representation, or the collective experiences of space. These include symbolic differentiations and collective fantasies around space, the resistances to the dominant practices and resulting forms of individual and collective transgression.

Lefebvre is particularly concerned with the production of space under capitalism. Different forms of space succeed each other through time. There is succession from natural to absolute to abstract space, the effect being progressively to expel nature from the social. Abstract space is the high point of capitalist relations leading to the quite extraordinary 'created spaces' of the 'end of the millennium'. But he wants to show that in each period it is necessary to investigate the interplay between these different spatialities conceptualised above.

A creative employment of Lefebvre's approach has been Shields' analysis of social spatialisation (1991). He uses this term to designate the fundamentally social construction of the spatial, both at the level of specific interventions in the environment and of the social imagination. He suggests Lefebvre's main interest is not in space itself but in the processes of production of cultural notions and practices of space. It is this cultural construction of space that Shields seeks to examine, particularly via the further concept of the place-myth which in turn comprises a number of place-images. Place-myths are moreover contested and changeable and often a number of myths overlie each other, pertaining to different social spaces. He employs this battery of concepts to examine the changing social spatialisation of the beach, as it went from a medical zone to a pleasure zone; the social construction of the place-myths of Brighton and Niagara Falls; the construction of the 'north' and 'south' of Britain; and the contested space myths of the north of Canada (see Chapter 13 for further discussion).

Finally, I will mention briefly some remaining topics for debate in the 1990s which bear upon the production and consumption of place. The first concerns the connections between time-space and the social relations of gender and ethnicity. The following are some of the crucial arguments which have been developed from a feminist perspective: the spatial distribution of paid and unpaid labour of men and women varies greatly and much social science has incorrectly focused upon male paid labour; men and women have different relations to the 'city' which is often dominated by male interests and the main forms of representation, such as monuments, commemorative buildings, historic sites and so on, predominantly record male activities; there are huge spatial variations in the resistances and social and political organisation of different genders; it is important to understand that landscapes and townscapes should not be viewed as neutral objects on which to gaze but as irreducibly gendered; urban design is particularly significant for the safe dwelling and mobility of men and women (see Wolff 1987; Wilson, E. 1991; Ardener 1993).

Similar arguments have been developed with respect to ethnicity, although there are two further points to note. First, much focus has been placed on showing the changing spatial distribution of different ethnic groups and especially the development of a black underclass in the USA (see Wilson, W. 1978, 1987). Wilson argues that this has resulted from the spatial mobility of the black middle class which in very large numbers left the black areas. This has helped to undermine the bases of community life, at the same time that such areas have been devastated by massive de-industrialisation as jobs moved south and west and out to the suburbs. So although American blacks have become strikingly better educated they have experienced greater poverty, unemployment and underemployment as they have been locked into the poorer areas of 'de-industrialised cities'. Elsewhere we have described these processes as the 'emptying out of the ghetto' or the 'impacted ghetto' (Lash and Urry 1994: Ch. 6; Wacquant 1989). Second, and related to this, all sorts of ethnic groups have come to be constructed as peculiarly prone to commit certain kinds of crime, especially theft, mugging and various drug-related offences. This has led to research interest in the social and spatial patterning of the fear of crime. Certain areas in towns and cities have come to be viewed as having very high rates of crime, where the fear of crime is particularly marked. This has led to analysis of the changing social geography of towns and cities in which certain ethnicities and certain crimes are believed to cohere together within certain places. There has been the 'racialisation' of the phenomenology of the urban; and this works partly in England through the contrasting high valuation which is placed upon the English countryside which is taken to be predominantly white (see Chapters 12 and 13).

Further, these insights have led to an increased comprehension of the multiple and contradictory ways in which national and other identities (ethnic, regional or local and so on) are inextricably bound up with particular townscapes or landscapes (see Smith 1986; Wright 1992; Carter *et al.* 1993). Such places are often taken to be definitive signifiers of identity, although of course people's memories of place are subject to incalculable distortion. A number of points about this intertwining of memory, identity and place have recently come to the theoretical foreground. It has been well established that memories are not to be seen as simply physically locatable in some part of the brain and merely waiting for appropriate activation (see Arcaya 1992). Many branches of the human sciences have shown the diverse and para-doxical ways in which memories are irreducibly social: that people basically remember together; that the production of a shared memory of an event, place or person necessitates cooperative work; that such cooperation may involve acts of institutional commemoration which silence alternative memories of the past; that there is a complex rhetoric involved in the articulation of a discourse of memory; that communities are often united only by memories and little else; that forgetting is also socially structured and of equal significance as remembering; that memories are often organised around artefacts such as buildings, rooms, machines, walls, furniture and so on; and that social groups, institutions and whole societies all presuppose multiple and often contradictory memory practices (see especially Middleton and Edwards 1990; Lash and Urry 1994: 238–41). Later chapters in this book examine how such social practices of memory are embedded in place and how many places exemplify exceptional levels of contestation. Particular attention will be devoted to various tourist practices which presuppose the commodification of memory, most strikingly around the so-called 'heritage' industry. Contestation occurs over who has claims to a given place and within such claims it is socially organised memories that are invoked as authoritative sources of being able to speak a place.

However I also discussed earlier the arguments of Bergson and Bachelard that would lead us to 'remember' that memories are embodied. Part of what is remembered are ways of sitting and standing, looking and lounging, hearing and hoping, ruminating and recollecting, which are embodied. There are, Connerton suggests, both incorporating and inscribing practices, that sediment memories in bodily postures of those living in particular societies (1989). So memories involve an array of senses. The past is 'passed' on to us not merely in what we think or what we do but literally in how we do it. Places are not just seen, as in the scopic regime of the 'sightseer', but are

27

understood through the diverse senses that may make us ache to be some-where else or shiver at the prospect of having to stay put (Jay 1992; Urry 1992, on the ocularcentrism of the tourist). Proust brilliantly conveys this embodied character of memory, 'our arms and legs are full of torpid memories' (cited in Lowenthal 1985: 203).

This brings us onto a further agenda for social theory, namely how and in what ways nature is itself to be understood since it is in many ways itself a social and cultural construction. What indeed is nature and should it not include the social as well as the apparently physical environment? What kind of social theory of space and time would be appropriate to a unified nature of that sort? Indeed in some ways the analysis of space-time is currently repositioning itself around issues of nature and the environment. This raises very significant theoretical questions which will assuredly fix space-time as central to the developing social theory of 'nature'. Elsewhere I have argued that a properly constituted sociology of 'nature' would concern itself with the following topics: the historic diversity of different concepts of 'nature'; the way in which any such nature can only be understood in its relationship with the concepts of God and society; the intricate connections between the natural and market relations; social variation in the reading and interpretation of 'nature' and of threats or damage to the environment; the causes and consequences of the recent emergence of 'environmental identities'; and the interrogation of the environmental sciences themselves in the light of the sociology of knowledge (see Macnaghten and Urry 1994; and Chapters 12, 13 and 14 in this book on the connections between tourism/leisure and the environment).

Finally, I will return to the issue of consumption – this book is after all about *consuming* places. I will not have much to say about the changing patterns of consumption of goods and services (although see Chapter 8, as well as Keat *et al.* 1994). However, it is worth noting some of the complex ways in which the consumption of place and the consumption of goods and services are interdependent, and that these interdependencies have been under-researched. First, images of place are routinely used in the symbolic location of products and services. Particular images include capital cities (Paris), the countryside (the Cotswolds), the north of England and so on. Second, living in or visiting particular places often entails certain kinds of other con-sumption, such as hotel beds in Brighton, theatre tickets in London, funfair rides in Blackpool, mintcake in Kendal and so on. Third, certain products and services can *only* be obtained by visiting a particular place, although the likelihood of this has been reduced through national and international markets. Examples include Paris fashion items, seeing a Broadway musical, visually consuming the Matterhorn and so on. Finally, images of place are themselves significantly constructed out of particular products and services which are or have been available in particular places. Examples here would include popular music in Liverpool, wine in the Loire, haggis in Scotland and so on. Thus there are complex interdependencies between consuming goods, services and places, and what links them together are the patterns of social life organised in and through particular places. Such patterns are significantly commodified but there is generally a complex mixing of both commodification and collective enthusiasm.

The chapters in this book are reproduced in rough chronological sequence, reflecting the evolution of my own interests and those of British social science. Thus Part I derives from debates in the early 1980s concerning the relations between space and society, the nature of the concepts of the social and of society, and the characteristics of collective action. This part of the book also deals with the argument that sociology enjoys a distinct discursive organisation which makes it peculiarly open to theorising and research undertaken in neighbouring disciplines.

Part II stems from the mid-1980s research programme of 'restructuring'; in particular, I examine its relevance both for rural societies and for the significance of service industries. I also consider the changing social location of the service class which emerges out of the struggles between capital and labour and has had major effects upon the overall dynamics of especially American society.

Part III concerns topics which came onto the agenda around 1990. These include the nature of tourism as a form of consumption, the interconnections between modernity, identity and travel and the significance of heritage, including industrial heritage, in the making and remaking of place. Many of my examples are drawn from the north-west of England.

Part IV reflects debates in the 1990s which have been concerned with the construction of a sociology of nature. Topics examined here include the relationship between tourism and the environment; changes in the nature of time and identity; and the making of landscape and nature.

In the penultimate chapter I analyse some of the literary and artistic bases for the very making of the English Lake District. In particular, I show that its place-myth can only be explained in terms of the role of Romanticism in the emergence of the canon of English literature. This reflects a much more general trend of the 1990s, namely the ways in which the sociology of place increasingly incorporates the analysis of various cultural outputs, industries and images into its examination of place and place-myth. As such this further de-differentiates the social sciences and the humanities as we approach the end of the millennium. Recent examples of such work would include Bhabha on 'narrating the nation' (1990), Davis' excavation of a 'city of quartz' (1990), Wright on a 'journey through ruins' (1992), Anderson and Gale on 'inventing places' (1992), A. Wilson's examination of 'the culture of nature' (1992), Barnes and Duncan's analysis of 'writing worlds' (1992), Carter and others on theories of identity and location (1993), Bird and others on 'mapping the futures' (1993) and Chambers on 'migrancy' and identity (1994).

Taking place seriously means taking writing, architectural designs, paintings, guide books, literary texts, films, postcards, advertisements, music, travel patterns, photographs and so on seriously. We have in the analysis of place travelled a long way from the typologies of the urban and the rural, or indeed from concepts of economic restructuring.

Part I
SOCIETY AND SPACE

2

SOCIOLOGY AS A PARASITE
Some vices and virtues*

INTRODUCTION

I think that Giddens is wrong in suggesting that there are only four myths in the history of sociology – there is a further myth, namely, that there is an essence to sociology, that it has some essential characteristics that give it and its practitioners a unity, coherence and common tradition (Giddens 1977). Giddens of course is well aware of the ambiguous nature of sociology as a subject – but he leaves its character merely as uncertain through the employment of terms like 'social thought' rather than 'sociology'. In this chapter I want to consider the status of the subject in more detail: just what kind of academic discourse is it? It is only by carrying out such an investigation that we can see exactly what we are defending when, for example, we argue against cuts in sociological teaching and research. In particular, I want to make sense of an interesting contradiction which first led me to this problem. On the one hand, it is commonly argued in public debate that there is no such subject as sociology, that you can make it up since there is not a rigorous structure of learning, research and content, that since everyone knows about society there is no need for a specific subject to study it. On the other hand, sociologists generally perceive that their subject is both important and difficult, that most people are sociologically ignorant, that a long period of training is involved and that it is more complex and worthwhile than most of the other social sciences. Sociologists generally get round this contradiction by rejecting or even ridiculing the first view, that of public opinion, and by adopting the latter. However, I think there is something mistaken about this – there is more to the public opinion view than we are normally willing to acknowledge. What this exactly is I shall try to indicate below.

In particular, I want to consider one aspect, namely, that sociology is a parasitic subject since it has no essence, no essential unity. In a sense it feeds

* This first appeared in P. Abrams, R. Deem, J. Finch, P. Rock (eds) (1981) *Practice and Progress*, London: Allen & Unwin. I have partly amended it here and removed the original footnotes.

off developments in neighbouring disciplines to an extraordinary degree. To illustrate this, consider three BSA conferences on the state, culture and ideology, and law (see Littlejohn *et al*. 1978 and Barrett *et al*. 1979, on the 1977 and 1978 conferences). How much of the content of these conferences could be described as 'sociology' – indeed, how many 'sociologists' attended, how many gave papers or made substantial oral contributions, how much sociological material was referred to in these papers? In each case the answer is 'relatively few' or 'relatively little'. The developments in these three topics have been appropriated *within* sociology, but sociology *per se* has not contributed much to such developments, except in a rather special sense as we shall see. In the first part of this chapter I shall consider one such area in particular, namely the state, and I shall show that most recent developments in its analysis have occurred outside mainstream sociological discourse. I shall then consider in the following section some important implications of this for the social and intellectual organisation of sociology. In particular, it will be seen first that sociology develops in part through *appropriating* theoretical and empirical work conducted in neighbouring disciplines and related social movements; second, that it can never be understood in terms of the idea of a paradigm, or even of a scientific community, or communities (Kuhn 1970); and third, that its intellectual strength predominantly lies in its parasitism, its openness and relative lack of authority and control. It is perhaps the only scientific community to resemble Popper's ideal precisely because it is not organised like other natural or social scientific subjects (see Popper 1970). This might suggest of course that it does contain some essence which produces these distinctive characteristics. But this is only so in one sense, that it has a particular organisation as *an academic discourse* and this is because its central concepts neither generate a discursive unity nor demarcate it in a strong sense from neighbouring subjects which may well employ similar concepts (but not necessarily the same terms). I shall conclude the chapter with some more general comments on the virtues of sociology's parasitic character.

Three provisos should be made before I proceed. First, although some of my argument rests on implicit comparisons with other social sciences, I am not claiming that sociology is unique among such sciences. It may well be that certain social sciences are also in part parasitic – 'politics' is the most obvious example. However, I would still want to argue for the greater parasitism of sociology, and hence, as we shall see, for its greater virtue. Second, most of my discussion is related to recent developments in British sociology. Yet there is little doubt that in Britain sociology has generally enjoyed a more marginal academic status than in the United States or Western Europe, and this has increased its tendency here to feed off and incorporate the more established (and 'respectable') social sciences. This is, however, only a question of degree. Indeed, for reasons that I shall discuss, this parasitism is particularly important in a period of advance within sociology and British sociology since the mid-1960s has been advancing. It is thus worth exploring for this particular reason. Third, the term 'sociological discourse' refers to the set of social practices characteristic of the members of such a discourse – such practices being structured in terms of common concepts, beliefs, theories, traditions, institutions, methods, techniques, exemplars and so on. In most cases those individuals who happen to bear the official label 'sociologist' are agents who are part of, and contributors to, this on-going set of reproducible social practices known as 'sociological discourse'. However, this is not always the case, in part precisely because of sociology's parasitic and hence rapidly changing nature. There is thus an important disjuncture between 'sociological discourse'/practitioners of 'sociology' – the latter may not be agents of the former.

SOCIOLOGY AND THE STATE

At the beginning of the collection of papers from the BSA conference on power and the state (Littlejohn *et al.* 1978) it is said to be a good thing that sociologists have at last begun exploration of the nature of the state. However, what is not pointed out is that most of the interesting parts of this collection, in relation to the state, were produced as a result of developments outside sociology, most noticeably because of debates within Marxism and within feminism. It is agreed that many contributors recognised the value of alternative disciplines and paradigms (Littlejohn *et al.* 1978: 3), but no indication is given as to what their value actually was. It is further implied that there is an authentic sociological tradition to which these alternative paradigms (ignoring the typically slip-shod use of that much-maligned term) happened to give added value. By contrast in this section I shall suggest that there is no authentic, essential contribution made by sociology to our understanding of contemporary capitalist states. The important contributions have been produced outside the mainstream of sociological discourse and by non-practitioners of 'sociology'; those notions have then been taken up and discussed within that discourse.

Before showing this in a little detail I will initially deal with an obvious objection that might be made to these claims. It could be said that the case of the state is a rather special one and that what may be true of the state is not necessarily true of any other area of sociological inquiry. After all, sociology only really developed after the conceptual separation between the state and the civil society had been effected. So while politics studies the former, sociology and the other social sciences study the latter. Hence, it could be claimed, there is no particular reason to expect that sociology would study the state. This is in fact a weak argument since the distinction between these spheres of influence has never been consistently maintained. All those authors typically treated as part of the classical tradition in sociology addressed themselves to the political, and in more recent years the growth of 'political sociology' indicates how the area designated by the term 'state' has been part of sociological discourse. However, my claim is that sociological writing on the state failed to produce any distinctive insights, and that much of the important work on the capitalist state developed in neighbouring disciplines. Such claims will obviously be contentious; indeed some may argue that such judgements cannot be made at all. I shall simply assume here that we have to make such judgements about the relative worth of different pieces of academic work.

In short then, the major contributions to the recent analysis of the capitalist state are the texts related to first, the Miliband/Poulantzas debate; second, the critical theory tradition in the Federal Republic of Germany; third, the *Staatsableitung* debate also in the FRG; fourth, American controversy over the suggested fiscal crisis of the state; and fifth, writings within political science on the corporatist state.

The first set of texts are those best known in Britain – to some degree the controversy on the state has been a debate about the respective merits of Miliband/Poulantzas, with Laclau as a kind of arbitrator (Miliband 1970, 1973; Poulantzas 1969, 1976). This debate within Marxist discourse (of a neo-Gramscian variety) has revolved around whether the capitalist state is to be viewed as the instrument of the economically dominant class, or whether it is to be seen as the general factor of social cohesion in capitalist social formations and hence is relatively autonomous of the economy as such. These texts have all been criticised for ignoring the form of the state and for having related the state only to classes in struggle and not to the nature of capital and the requirements of accumulation (see amongst others, Holloway and Picciotto 1978).

The second main set of texts derive from the critical theory tradition, the best known being Habermas (1976) and Offe (1972 and 1975). Here there is a more systematic attempt to relate the state to the economy and to establish the changing political conditions under which the state can effectively intervene. In Habermas (1976) there is discussion of the nature of legitimation crisis, while Offe analyses contradictions encountered in the employment of different political mechanisms necessary to sustain capital accumulation. These texts are in part sociological, but are also heavily influenced by debates within both systems theory and Marxism.

The third set of texts have been in part developed through a critique of some of the earlier work of Offe and Habermas. Much work has revolved around exactly how the nature of the capitalist state can be derived from capital. There have been four main approaches to the derivation of the state form: first, from the sphere of circulation (Flatow and Huisken 1973); second, from the crisis character of late capitalism; third, from the nature of capital as individual capital units (Altvater 1973a and 1973b); and fourth, from the capital relation as one of class domination (Hirsch, J. 1978; Holloway and Picciotto 1978). These texts have been produced from within a fairly fundamentalist Marxist discourse; while the fourth set of texts derives more from a neo-Ricardian perspective. The main text here is O'Connor's *The Fiscal Crisis of the State* (O'Connor 1973) which is an attempt, albeit ultimately unsuccessful, to explain the persistent tendency for the expenditures of contemporary states (divided into social capital, social consumption and social expenses) to outrun revenues. Particular emphasis is placed upon the interaction between monopoly capital and the state. The importance of class struggle, although still problematic, has begun to be extensively confronted within this and other Marxist works.

Finally, there are many texts now written on the theme of corporatism, some written from within Marxist discourse (Jessop 1978), others which treat corporatism as a new economic system (Winckler 1977). But the main discourse here has been that of political science and the counterposing of corporatism to pluralism, with the tendency to reproduce some of the errors of the latter within the former (see Panitch 1978, for discussion and criticism of these different formulations). Corporatism, in this view, is seen as a system of interest intermediation in which the different units are

> organised into a limited number of singular, compulsory, non-competitive, hierarchically ordered, and functionally differentiated categories, recognised or licensed (if not created) by the state and granted a deliberate representational monopoly within their respective categories in exchange for observing certain controls on their selection of leaders and articulation of demands and supports.
>
> (Schmitter 1974: 9)

Thus far I have suggested that there are five main sets of texts which, since the mid-1960s, have advanced discussion, debate and understanding of the capitalist state. Indeed there seems to have been considerable theoretical advance. Sociology's contribution to these five has been very limited and discussions in sociology have seen the taking-up and then the elaboration of notions already advanced within these other discursive formations. So sociology has been parasitic. Its discussions have fed off, and made relatively little initial contribution to, the original theoretical ideas. This is clear, for example, from considering the material produced for the 1977 BSA conference, or for the BSA State and Economy Group. Generally speaking, then, sociology has been parasitic upon certain neighbouring discourses, particularly that of Marxism and political science.

However, there is one sense in which sociology has been important and thus is in providing a site in which these different texts have been placed in critical confrontation with each other. They have been taken up within sociological discourse and some of the respective merits and deficiencies have become clarified. Of course this has also happened within Marxism, in political science and economics – but it would seem that the debates have been very widespread and productive in sociology. Issues discussed have included: the nature of, and relationship between, competing 'problematics'; the relevance of empirical evidence to theoretical claims regarding the economy and the state; the relevance of the concept 'élite' to a 'ruling class' analysis; the importance of class 'fractions' in the analysis of class relations between capital and labour; the degree to which the analysis of a 'power bloc' is relevant; and the extent to which capitalist societies are broadly similar or are to be analysed in their diversity.

This discussion has supported my claim that there is something distinctive about the organisation of sociology as a discourse. In the following section I shall consider this in more detail. In conclusion here I will mention one or two of the differences between the discursive organisation of sociology and of Marxism. First of all, the latter is a relatively unified discourse, or as some would argue, a pair of related discourses. This unity is based upon the central concepts of capitalism, alienation, class, surplus-value, exploitation, politics, the state, ideology, the dictatorship of the proletariat and so on. Sociology is not unified – we shall see below that the central term, 'society', may denote a number of quite different and opposed concepts. This means that when Poulantzas, in his famous debate with Miliband, talks of contrasting 'problematics', this conveys a misleading impression (Poulantzas 1969). The organisation of the two problematics is not isomorphic, they are not equally unified. It is very doubtful if sociology can be seen as a 'problematic' at all. But furthermore, it is equally incorrect to treat Marx and Marxists as simply one element of *sociology*. For Marxist texts to be treated as sociological requires appropriation – which stems from sociology's parasitic character. But this in a sense only occurs after the theoretical work has taken place *within* Marxist discourse.

THE ORGANISATION OF SOCIOLOGICAL DISCOURSE

The parasitic character of sociology can not only be seen in the analysis of the state. Consider, for example, how the sociology of the family has recently been transformed, not because of the debate between sociologists on the relationship between industrialisation and the extended family, but because of the incorporation of arguments, insights and research material produced within both the anti-psychiatry and the women's movements (see Morgan 1975, for very helpful discussion). Likewise, the sociology of development was greatly changed through the incorporation of work produced outside sociology, namely, certain texts of Frank on the manner in which development produces underdevelopment (see Frank 1969, for example). Similarly, if we consider BSA conferences, the debates on culture and ideology in 1978 very largely reflected the theoretical and empirical insights of semiology, psychoanalysis and neo-Gramscian Marxism (Barrett *et al.* 1979). Also the sociology of law, as in the 1979 conference, has been transformed through critical confrontation with Pashukanis' by now historic attempt to relate the

38

legal subject to the commodity form (Pashukanis 1978; and see, for example, Fine *et al.* 1979). Even if we consider Bottomore and Nisbet's massive and authoritative *A History of Sociological Analysis*, many of the texts which are referred to were produced within philosophy, economics, politics and so on (Bottomore and Nisbet 1979). What is the explanation of sociology's parasitic character? I will try to answer this by considering Bottomore and Nisbet's 'Introduction' to this collection, which I will take as an authoritative statement about the history of sociology.

They argue that there is 'now a single discipline, a realm of scientific discourse outside of which sociological analysis cannot properly be pursued at all', and this 'constitutes a relatively autonomous sphere' (Bottomore and Nisbet 1979: xiv–xv). What, though, provides the basis of this unity, around what central concepts or principles is this discourse organised? They say that this unity is provided by the 'more precise conception of society as an object of study', this being a concept separate from both the state and politics, and from vaguer notions of civilisation or mankind (Bottomore and Nisbet 1979: viii). The concept of 'society' has constituted sociology as a scientific discipline. This has then developed in a fairly normal manner, first, through the continued elaboration of alternative paradigms and theoretical controversy among adherents, second, through the accumulation of an ordered body of knowledge 'directed' by one or other paradigm, and third, through the 'specialisation of research' (Bottomore and Nisbet 1979: viii–ix). However, they also say that there have been three unsatisfactory features of sociological development: that there has been a multiplicity of paradigms such that no particular theory ever dies and no new theory ever becomes dominant; that sociological knowledge is too close to everyday common-sense knowledge; and that there has been a failure to progress in important areas.

What are the deficiencies of Bottomore and Nisbet's interpretation? First, they imply that sociology is like any other science in being characterised by alternative paradigms and theoretical controversy. Since they quote Kuhn they must be employing the term 'paradigm' in his sense (Kuhn 1970; Masterman 1970). Yet for Kuhn it is the crucial fact of science that there are *not* alternative paradigms except in the limited periods of scientific revolution. If a particular discourse is, during normal periods, characterised by inter-paradigmatic competition, then it is not, as yet, a fully fledged science. But what Bottomore and Nisbet have done is to construct a spurious teleology, to view all kinds of earlier social thought as somehow contributing to the end-state – the present organisation of sociology oriented around particularly the concept of 'society'. Yet it is clear that this structuring of history is largely a fiction – the history has no such unity, purpose or direction. This is implied by them when they refer to the three unsatisfactory characteristics of sociology – but they cannot have it both ways. If these three characteristics are important then sociology is not a conventional science comprehensible through even a minimally accumulationist model of its development. I will

39

now try to show that these features are both correct and so important that they undermine Bottomore and Nisbet's attempt to suggest that we have already achieved a systematic, unified, sociological discourse. In particular, I shall argue that the term 'society' does not provide the sought-for unity, that sociology cannot be demarcated adequately from the common-sense, and that there is little in the way of sociological progress, except in a highly paradoxical sense.

First, then, let me consider the concept 'society' in relationship to the main perspectives incorporated within sociology. There are eight such perspectives, not necessarily similar in organisation, structure or intellectual coherence. They are: critical theory, ethnomethodology, functionalism, interactionism, Marxism, positivism, structuralism and Weberianism (see Urry 1980, for more details). There is no common external object 'society' which brings together these disparate perspectives into a unified discourse. This can be seen from the following where I set out the central notion of society specific to each of these various perspectives:

critical theory: society as a form of alienated consciousness judged by the criterion of reason

ethnomethodology: society as the fragile order displayed by the common-sense methods members use in practical reasoning

functionalism: society as the social system in which all the parts are functionally integrated with each other

interactionism: society as social order negotiated and renegotiated between actors

Marxism: society as the structure of relations between the economic base and the political and ideological super-structures

positivism: society as the structure of relations between observable (generally measurable) social phenomena

structuralism: society as the system of signs generated from fundamental structures in the human mind

Weberianism: society as the relations between different social orders and of the social groupings present within each order.

Obviously particular writers may disagree with these formulations – but in general this list indicates the diverse concepts of 'society' which are employed within perspectives generally taken to be part of sociological discourse.

Second, it has been plausibly argued by Bachelard that the objective of science is to create something which is in a radical discontinuity with the world of common sense (see the discussion in Lecourt 1975). There has to be a discontinuity between the two and this provides one of the guarantees of scientific progress. Even if this is broadly true of natural science, it is clear that sociology is organised differently. Sociology is thoroughly contaminated with common-sense terms, concepts and understandings and most of the attempts to create and sustain a separate, purely academic, discourse have been unsuccessful. One reason for this has been the manner in which contemporary political and social movements affect sociology more than most of the other social sciences, let alone the natural sciences. In recent years, the students', black, and women's movements have all become, in a sense, part of sociological discourse, juxtaposed and assessed within that discourse. I have already mentioned how the previously dormant sociology of the family has been revitalised through incorporating the common-sense understandings and theoretical reflections of women seeking to develop alternative forms of social relations between the sexes.

Third, there is little that can be described as sociological progress in the sense understood by that notion within science. Bottomore and Nisbet point out that specific theories are rarely worked through sufficiently to establish whether a particular research programme is progressive (see Lakatos 1970, on this notion in science). There is considerable emphasis placed upon novelty – on making sociological reputations through developing and employing a new theory. Progress is thus generally achieved and indicated not primarily by working through existing theory, not by the puzzle-solving practices of normal science – it rather follows from the generation of new theories and of the critical discussions engendered through these. This is not, incidentally, to be arguing for that well-worn cliché in sociology, for theory rather than empirical research. It is rather that in sociology 'progress' seems to take the form of theoretical innovations – and these may derive from many sources which include empirical research, philosophical speculation or the incorporation of, or juxtaposition of, contributions made from outside sociological discourse. This emphasis upon the making of theoretical innovations means that there is a tendency for the cyclical repetition of theories, rather than for one wholly to replace that already in existence. This is not entirely the case – Parkin suggests, for example, that Lloyd Warner is unlikely ever to make a come-back (1979: 603). But there is nevertheless a tendency for new theories to bear strong similarities with those once discarded. He also points out that most of what counts as important and interesting in the field of class and stratification analysis is almost entirely derived from the competing theoretical perspectives of Marx/Engels, Weber and Pareto/Mosca (Parkin 1979: 599).

I will conclude this section by relating the discussion of sociology to Kuhn's account of how a scientific discourse is organised (Kuhn 1970; Lakatos and Musgrave 1970). Kuhn presumes at least during normal science that there is a unity of the discourse which results from the role of the paradigm as exemplar. Sociology is obviously not organised in this manner, since sociological change and development does not result from the working through of the paradigm until anomalies arise. I am not presuming that Kuhn's account of change and revolution is philosophically correct – in

41

particular he requires sociological categories to do too much epistemological work. But sociologically there are great differences between his account of the discourse of a natural scientific community and my account of the discursive organisation of sociology. This means that attempts to employ Kuhn as providing philosophical protocols for developments in sociology are unjustified – whether these involve the non-radical advocacy of positivism as sociology's normal science or the radical advocacy of sociological revolutions and the founding of a plethora of new paradigms (see my discussion of this in Urry 1973).

THE VIRTUES OF BEING A PARASITE

I have so far argued that sociological discourse is organised as follows:

1 there is a multiplicity of perspectives with no common concept of 'society' which unifies them;
2 sociological concepts and propositions cannot be clearly demarcated from common-sense concepts and propositions;
3 it is difficult to establish that there is sociological progress – it mainly follows *theoretical* innovations;
4 one major form of such innovation results from the parasitic nature of sociology, from the fact that innovations originate in discourses outside sociology itself.

I shall now consider certain aspects of the fourth point in more detail. What, we might ask, are the circumstances that permit this parasitism to occur? Within sociology's neighbouring disciplines there is a simultaneous process of both presupposing and rejecting what I will loosely call the 'social', by which I mean the general social relations which link together individuals and groups. In these disciplines, which include economics, geography, history, Marxism, psychology and politics, these social relations are presumed to be of importance, and yet are in part ignored. The social is thus both present and absent simultaneously. Instead, in these disciplines some particular dimension or aspect of social life is abstracted for study, such as people's behaviour as agents in the market, or their distribution within space, or their behaviour in the past. But this means that each of these disciplines is discursively unstable. On occasions, certain texts will break through the limitations implied by that discourse. New understandings emerge which will involve more systematic comprehension of the general form of these social relations which will not obscure or neglect the realm of the social. How, though, does such a development in a neighbouring discipline relate to sociology? First, these other disciplines are to varying degrees discursively unified – which will mean that blocks will be placed upon the new, more 'social', interpretation. Yet, second, because there is no essence to sociological discourse, apart from a broad commitment to this idea

42

of the interdependence of individuals and social groups, sociology may attract this new 'social' interpretation. So simultaneously we encounter two likely developments: a process of at least partial repulsion from the originating discourse and attraction into sociological discourse. There are a number of examples of where both developments have occurred. I will mention one for each of the social sciences recently listed: in economics, Frank and the development of the underdevelopment thesis; in geography, analysis of the growth of multinational corporations and changes in the spatial division of labour; in history, the nature of class relations in nineteenth century Britain; in Marxism, the theorisation of the state and ideology; in psychology, the critique of the family in the anti-psychiatry movement; and in politics, the class structuring of local power structures.

Thus far I have claimed that in many social sciences there is a simultaneous presupposing and rejecting of the social. Where social relations in a sense break through, the innovation may get elaborated in part outside the originating discourse and within sociology instead. So sociology is important in permitting analysis and elaboration of aspects of the social world which are generally neglected by the other social sciences. It can thus be defined negatively – as a discourse with minimal organisation, structure or unity into which many contending developments from other social sciences get incorporated. So although it is parasitic it enjoys two crucially important features: first, to provide a site within which further elaboration of the original innovation may occur; and second, to provide the context in which a wide variety of contending social theories can be placed in juxtaposition with each other. This has the function of promoting interdiscursive debate and confrontation. I am not claiming that this is sufficient to permit a necessarily rational evaluation of such social theories – but there are nevertheless some very important positive effects of these processes which may then react back on the originating discourse.

1 *Positive overlap* In some cases it becomes clear through the juxtaposition of perspectives that there are certain shared concepts and related propositions. There can be very positive effects which follow from this juxtaposing of related perspectives in terms of producing new bases of empirical work or novel theoretical insights. A good example is the collective work which resulted in *Capitalism and the Rule of Law* (Fine *et al.* 1979) – a book which developed from the positive overlap between the 'left interactionism and conflict theory' of the National Deviancy Conference and the fairly fundamentalist Marxism of the CSE (Conference of Socialist Economists) Law and State Group.

2 *Improved rigour and precision* Because of the critical confrontation between two or more perspectives the original theory is made more specific, its referents are clarified and the logical consistency of the propositional structure is improved. This is what has happened in development studies

43

where the original Frankian thesis that 'development produces under-development' has been taken up and greatly clarified within sociological discourse, first in Laclau's critique, and then in many other texts, including some of those in the Oxaal collection (Oxaal 1975; Laclau 1979).

3 *Mutual weaknesses exposed* Through the critical confrontation of perspectives the relative deficiencies of each are brought more clearly into view. An example would be the recent debate as to the relationship between Marxism and psychoanalysis. The effort by Coward and Ellis (1977) to synthesise Althusserian Marxism with Lacanian psychoanalysis has demonstrated both that this cannot be satisfactorily achieved and that each perspective is theoretically problematic partly in ways highlighted by the other.

4 *Further empirical research* The challenge of perspectives produces increased specification of the research implications of one or both theories which then get taken up and elaborated. The theoretical debates between Marxist and neo-Weberian theories of class and stratification have produced more detailed empirical support for both: good examples, if very different, would be Nichols and Beynon (1977) and Goldthorpe (1980).

5 *Synthesis* In rare circumstances different perspectives can get incorporated into a single work and elements fused. A good example of this is Newby (1977) in which there is an effective synthesis of a number of different theoretical traditions, in particular of political economy, political sociology, labour history and industrial sociology.

These points 1–5 are not intended to be exhaustive, only illustrative of the kinds of benefits that follow from sociology's parasitic character and of how a variety of perspectives may be brought into beneficial critical confrontation. One interesting effect takes us back to the Introduction, namely that sociology is one of the most difficult social sciences because competent practitioners have to acquire familiarity with this successive range of incorporated perspectives. Recent examples of this would include the way in which Lacan, Foucault and Derrida have become part of contemporary sociological discourse. In Britain Giddens has been particularly important in providing a means by which this parasitism has been achieved (see Giddens 1976, 1977 and 1979). He has interpreted the latest foreign import for sensitive Anglo-American readers and has located it within a sociological context. Sociology in such a golden age changes very rapidly and it may be difficult for the old guard to police effectively. Indeed, although Kuhn showed that generational differences are important in natural science, this is even more marked in sociology where new tendencies have been taken up and incorporated every four or five years. It is interesting to see how this produces difficulties for established sociologists who have to run hard just to keep up with the latest fashionable foreign import.

Finally, it might be wondered what the political implications are of my position. It is obviously the case that sociology involves a large degree of political struggle over exactly which aspects of which disciplines can be incorporated within it. And this struggle is likely to be more complicated and involve more diverse interests than in the neighbouring social sciences. In the latter the lines of struggle are more clearly drawn; in economics, for example, between the orthodoxy, once Keynesian, now part-Keynesian/part-monetarist, and the Marxists, as represented in the Conference of Socialist Economists. In the site of sociology many new developments enter, and the radicals of one generation may, five years later, be the conservatives of the new generation. Thus, it is not the case that sociological discourse needs to be dominated by the left – indeed my argument would suggest that domination is difficult for any perspective. Indeed, given the present move to the right, nationally and internationally, it would be possible to expect that the next discourse on which sociology will be parasitic will be the conservative New Philosophy of the failed Parisian left. However, an even worse prospect would be that what has been a relatively golden age for sociology, especially in Britain, is coming to a close. One very important reason for this is the rapid decline in the number of young staff and graduate students in the early 1980s. It is an implication of my argument that graduates have been particularly important in effecting this parasitism. Yet with the current decline in the number of such students this will not occur to anything like the same degree, and of course this will be even more the case if most graduates are turned into deskilled research trainees. So my final claim would be that if the parasitic nature of sociology is in fact correct, and if the current main social grouping which has effected this is being decimated, then we have to consider very carefully just what kind of alternative social/intellectual structures can be devised. What are the means by which we can defend a space for sociology? What are the social preconditions for sustaining this particular discursive structure?

Incidentally, it may be wondered whether to view sociology as a virtuous parasite is the same as seeing it as the Queen of Sciences. I think that depends on whether one regards monarchs not only as parasitic but also as virtuous. For me sociology, unlike a monarch, is both parasitic and virtuous. Whether this will continue to be the case is another and equally controversial question.

3

THE NEW MARXISM OF COLLECTIVE ACTION

A critical analysis*

INTRODUCTION

The new theory of collective action has with some impact swept into the social sciences in general, and into sociology in particular. Two of sociology's foremost journals, *Theory and Society* and *Politics and Society*, have devoted entire issues to the explication and discussion of the potential of this theory. Moreover, although these journals are American, the debate has been international in character with British, Canadian, German, Norwegian and Polish contributors also taking part. Our aim in this paper is to elucidate the general coherence of this novel version of Marxism, particularly the work of Elster, Offe and Wiesenthal, to draw attention to some of its failings and then to present elements of a fundamentally altered, and we think more illuminating, approach to collective agency.

  This new theory of collective action provides a formal consecration for fundamental mutations in Marxism and in left social science that have taken place over the past half decade or so; mutations in which an emphasis on forms of agency have increasingly come to take the place of purely structural determinations. These shifts can be seen in a variety of areas of analysis. The study of the labour process, for example, has been transformed from Braverman's (1974) focus on the structural accumulation of capital accompanied by the necessary de-skilling of labour to the analysis of various strategies of class agents. The examination of politics has shifted from Poulantzas's structurally determined relative autonomy (1973) to neo-corporatist analyses (see for example Lehmbruch and Schmitter 1982), which have focused upon how trade union confederations trade their willingness to act as agencies of social control over their members, in exchange for certain forms of policy-making power. In the study of the transition from feudalism to capitalism, Brenner (1976), among others, has rejected the previous 'structural' emphases of Dobb (1976) and Sweezy (1976) in order to

* This was written jointly with Scott Lash. It first appeared in *Sociology*, 1984, vol. 18. It is reprinted here without the original footnotes. Many thanks to Scott for allowing it to be reprinted and more importantly for his inspirational collegiality.

underline the importance of class capacities and class struggles. In the field of social stratification, Przeworski (1977) has most clearly developed the argument for the centrality of class struggles which render indeterminate the outcomes of supposedly determinate social structures. More generally, there has been the development of 'structurationism' as a relatively distinctive theoretical tendency in which structures are viewed as both the medium and the outcome of the skilful and knowledgeable actions of social agents (see Giddens 1979). Even the study of ideology has shifted away from the Althusserian analysis of the structural determination of the 'ideological instance' to the post-structuralism of Foucault, whose intentional and many-faceted 'body' can potentially resist discourse-constituted structural constraints, and to the analysis of Derrida, whose 'writing' and 'text', through constitutive structuring of subjects, objects and ideas, display qualities of activity and creativity which – in contradistinction to Barthes' prison of language – are as characteristic of agency as they are of structure (1972). The renaissance of interest in Heidegger (see Rorty 1982, for example) and Nietzsche further bespeak this shift to a new theoretical *Weltanschauung*.

In a very important sense the new game-theoretic Marxism is the culmination, even a self-reflective culmination, of this sea change in social theory. With a clarity which contrasts admirably with what has been termed as today's 'theoretical babel', it claims that within game theory there is a basis, or perhaps *the* basis, to establish a micro-foundation for Marxist social science and by implication for all social science. The new collective action theorists commence from the presumption that agents typically engage in benefit-formation of collective actors in general, and of classes in particular. The effective midwife of this theory was what has become known as the Cohen–Elster debate in contemporary social theory.

Function and intention

This influential and challenging debate revolves about the nature of *explanation* in Marxism, and more generally in the social sciences. The debate began with Elster's review of Cohen's *Karl Marx's Theory of History* (Cohen 1978; Elster 1980a). Cohen had in this book used and defended functional (or consequence) explanation in order to argue for the validity of what he plausibly sees as historical materialism's two central theses. The first thesis is that the level of development of the productive forces determines the nature of productive relations. Cohen argues that this is defensible if it is taken to mean that a certain set of productive relations are to be explained by the level of development of the forces of production *only* insofar as those relations are conducive to the development of the forces. That is, as Elster notes, that an effect is explained by its disposition to further its cause. Marx's second thesis is that the economic structure ('the totality of production relations') determines the super-structures. The functional explanation involved here is that

47

the super-structural properties (again an effect) are explained by their disposition to stabilise class power in the economic structure (its cause). To speak of 'dispositional facts' is to avoid falling prey to earlier criticism of functionalism which had stressed the fallacy that an *event* was used to explain another earlier-occurring *event* (see P. Cohen 1968).

Elster has no quarrel with Cohen's use of dispositional facts or of functional (and consequence) explanations *per se*. He sees it as wholly acceptable in biology, and would accept it in sociology if a 'causal feedback loop' is present which would describe *how* the element which is to be explained contributes to the maintenance of the institution or behaviour pattern which supposedly explains it. His complaint is that such a mechanism is absent in Cohen's discussion and indeed in most contemporary Marxist and non-Marxist sociology.

Cohen's reply makes clear his argument with Elster in finding contemporary functional Marxism (Althusser, the 'capital-logic school' and so on) irredeemably flawed. For one thing such writers falsely assume that because a structure is functional for the development of the productive forces and therefore the accumulation of capital, it is therefore *explained* by its consequences. Moreover, such writers rarely even convincingly show that a structure *is* in fact functional for capital accumulation. Cohen's disagreements with Elster are, however, more fundamental. On the one hand, he does not accept Elster's counterposition of functional as opposed to causal explanation. Cohen argues (1980: 130), we think correctly, that functional explanation is one variety of causal explanation. Every causal explanation, Cohen notes, mentions 'causally relevant features'. In functional explanation this causally relevant feature is a 'dispositional fact'. This is not, as we observed above, a causal argument in which an *event* e is held to bring about a consequential event f; but one whereby an event or property of *type* E would bring about an event or property of type F.

Furthermore, Cohen finds that Elster's criteria for a successful functional explanation are too stringent. Cohen would prefer elaboration by some kind of causal mechanism, but even in the absence of such a mechanism, he argues that it is rational to accept a functional explanation (1980: 131). Or more precisely, even in the absence of a causal feedback loop 'we can support the claim that B functionally explains A ... if ... one can point to an appropriately varied range of instances in which, whenever A would be functional for B, A appears' (Cohen 1982a: 51). Cohen's retort is telling here since even many instances of intentional explanation (and for Elster all causal explanation is intentional) do not involve the specification of relevant causal mechanisms.

The other main debate between Cohen and Elster has taken place around Elster's theory of intentional explanation (see especially Elster 1982a and Cohen 1982b). Elster argues that a game-theoretic Marxism is particularly helpful in the understanding of class struggles, alliances and revolution.

48

Cohen does not disagree but maintains that these issues are basically peripheral to historical materialism's central theses. Here though we would agree with Elster that these 'peripheral' theses are of absolutely central interest to the development of contemporary historical materialism, or of a more general social science.

This is then briefly the theoretical context for the specific development of a game-theoretic Marxism. Next, we will consider the classic account of game theory as applied to the explanation of collective action.

Olson and the prisoner's dilemma

Olson employs the prisoner's dilemma game in order to analyse the nature of collective action. The paradox or contradiction of the game is that if both prisoners pursue their individual self-interest, they end up with a result that is less satisfactory than if they had in some way been able to sacrifice those individual interests. This contradiction between what Barry and Hardin call 'Rational Man' [sic] and 'Irrational Society' involves a radical critique of rational self-interest (1982). The prisoner's dilemma game demonstrates that:

> A lobbying organisation, or indeed a labour union or any other organisation, working in the interest of a large group of firms or workers in some industry, would get no assistance from the rational, self-interested individuals in that industry.
>
> (Olson 1965: 11)

The reason for this derives from the problem of the so-called 'free-rider'. Where the group to be organised is large and where the benefits from such an organisation are public and cannot be confined to particular individuals, then the group is *latent* and will fail to be so organised unless individuals are induced to cooperate through the provision of other non-collective (selective) incentives (see Olson 1965: 33, 49–50). Without such selective benefits, individuals can 'free-ride', gaining the general benefits of the organisation if any materialise, but not incurring any of the material, temporal or motivational costs of membership.

Olson maintains that large groups are likely to remain 'latent' since they have particular problems in establishing and sustaining collective organisation. They will be less able to prevent free-riders, particularly because there will be little development of the social pressures and beliefs that would otherwise induce commitment to the organisation in question. In a large group not everyone can possibly know everybody else and so each person will not ordinarily be affected if he or she fails to make sacrifices on the group's behalf (Olson 1965; Barry 1970: 25, 62). Furthermore, the advantages to the whole that each person's contribution can bring cannot but be fairly slight – hence it will not seem worthwhile for a given individual to contribute time, energy or money to the organisation in question (Olson 1965: 62). At the same time the larger the organisation the greater the costs involved in getting it off the ground and into a form whereby any of the collective goods can be obtained (1965: 48).

Perhaps the most dramatic sociological application of Olson's analysis is his critique of Marx's theory of social class (1965: 105). Generally, Marx believed that as capitalist relations became generalised throughout society individuals would increasingly act in terms of their self-interest. And this self-interest would, he thought, lead the proletariat to see that their interests would be best served by organising together as a class. Now the fact that workers have been fairly reluctant to be so organised and have generally sought relatively limited gains has caused Marxists many problems of explanation (cf., 'false consciousness', the 'labour aristocracy' and so on). Olson however has no need for such explanations. He says that 'class-oriented action will not occur if the individuals that make up a class act rationally' (1965: 105). This is because a worker who thought he would benefit from a 'proletarian' government would not find it rational to risk his life and resources to start a revolution against the bourgeois government (1965: 106), since individuals would gain the 'benefits' of class actions whether or not they actually participated. It is therefore in some sense individually irrational for workers to organise as a class. Where workers do so organise, Olson argues that: 'Class differences resulting from sociological factors might lead individuals irrationally and emotionally to act in a class-oriented way' (1965: 108).

There are a number of obvious objections to Olson's provocative and illuminating argument. It has been pointed out that 'selective benefits' cannot explain the enormous diversity and strength of actually occurring collective organisations (Barry and Hardin 1982: 28–9). This is especially relevant to explaining the existence of many groups which do not directly produce any material gains for their members, what Heath terms 'altruistic' pressure groups (1976: 126; Barry 1970: 35). These demand analysis of both 'moral incentives' and 'political entrepreneurship' which can both partly neutralise the otherwise pervasive 'free-rider' effect (Barry and Hardin 1982: 29–31).

However, the most serious problem in Olson's analysis concerns the assumption of independent individual self-interest that is involved. Barry points out that social life is analogous, not so much to a single-play prisoner's dilemma, but rather to an iterated prisoner's dilemma or 'supergame' (1965: 254–5). Where there is iteration the two players who should rationally defect (not cooperate), may in fact cooperate. This is because in many social situations people play over time what are in effect a great number of prisoner's dilemma games. They may gradually perceive by pursuing their narrow self-interest that they end up with a non-optimal collective solution. Hence, there may be a learning process through which many of the actors try out solutions to the games they play which are individually non-rational. If these actors then come to realise there are major collective gains which result from the pursuit of individually non-rational solutions, then these cooperative games may become institutionalised amongst many of the players involved. It thus becomes rational to engage in social practices which would ensure such agreement (see Gauthier 1982: 96–9 for further discussion of 'inter-dependent actions'), although Barry and Hardin suggest that even in this 'dynamic' situation the logic of collective action will militate against cooperation in very large groups (1982: 34).

THEMES IN GAME-THEORETIC MARXISM

Elster and the main thesis

Jon Elster's originality is only exceeded by his inimitability. He is an anti-naturalist and methodological individualist who at the same time endorses a scientific sociology. He is an advocate of the *Geisteswissenschaften* or *sciences humaines* who wants to understand *Wissenschaft*/science, not in the French or German, but in the Anglo-Saxon sense. In *Logic and Society* he employs symbolic logic to specify *inter alia* the different contradictions within society and the mind (1978); while in *Ulysses and the Sirens* he establishes a framework for the understanding of rational action (1979). In particular in *Ulysses* he seeks to show how human action generically differs from animal behaviour; and hence while functionalist explanation is perfectly legitimate in biology it is forbidden in the social sciences. Explanation in the latter is simultaneously causal and intentional, not functional.

The crux of his case is that organisms adapt functionally while people adapt intentionally, and that only intentional adaptation can provide for humans '*a generalised capacity for global maximisation* that applies even to qualitat-ively new situations' (1979: 16). Functional adaptation through mutation and natural selection is only normally capable of 'local maximisation' (and thus usually only small improvements). Elster uses game-theoretic notions to ground this anti-naturalism. Natural selection acts as if in a 'parametric environment', whereas people interact in a 'strategic environment', that is, only in the latter are actors treated as having variable courses of behaviour. Equally, only people not animals are capable of realising solutions to games in which there is no dominant strategy – that is, a strategy which is 'best for "me" whatever the others do' (1979: Ch. 1). Finally, only humans are so rational that even in situations where they are only imperfectly rational (e.g. in smoking, overeating, etc.) they are able to bind themselves to future courses of action which will enable them to realise these desired goals (to stop smoking, lose weight, etc.) (see 1979: Ch. 2). As Homer expressed it in *The Odyssey*, Ulysses says: 'but you must bind me hard and fast, so that I cannot stir from the spot where you will stand me . . . and if I beg you to release me, you must tighten and add to my bonds'. In other words, Ulysses, and hence all human beings, are capable of achieving by indirect means the same ends that others could realise directly. Elster argues that we need a theory of imperfect rationality, 'being weak and knowing it' (1979: 36; see also Hahn 1980).

More specifically, Elster argues for the importance of two basic premises of rational choice theory: (1) that structural constraints do not completely determine the actions individuals take; and (2) that within the feasible set of actions compatible with the constraints, and possessed with a given 'preference structure', an individual will choose those that he or she believes will bring the best results. Analysis of such rational choices involves game theory, particularly because of the necessity to investigate the *interdependence of decisions* (1982a: 464). Elster argues that game theory has a particular contribution to make to Marxist social science,

> because classes crystallize into collective actors that confront each other over the distribution of income and power, as well as over the nature of property relations; and as there are also strategic relations between the members of a given class, game theory is needed to explain these complex interdependencies.
>
> (Elster 1982a: 464)

We will not here summarise Elster's presentation of game theory but only note some differences with Olson..

As we have seen Olson assumed that there was an invariable preference structure in which individuals would always value the 'free-rider' solution, à la the prisoner's dilemma, to one of universal cooperation. However, Elster argues in *Logic and Society*, following his analysis of various kinds of social contradiction, that appropriate collective action is likely to develop and to be more successful: (1) the more that actors *perceive* that there is some kind of contradiction characterising the society within which they are implicated; (2) the lower the 'communicational distance' between the members; (3) the less the rate of *turnover* in group membership; and (4) the greater the degree to which contradictions are reversible (1978: 134–50). More specifically, Elster argues that through continued interaction, workers in particular become both concerned and informed about each other (see 1979, 1982a). Concern for others changes the ranking of preferences and information about the others enables the actors to realise the solution of the ensuing game. This is termed the 'assurance game' as developed by Sen (1967) who suggested that under 'socialism' individuals would choose 'universal cooperation' over the 'free-rider' outcome. However, this solution rests upon perfect information – where the information is poor, workers will prefer 'universal egoism' (a free-rider outcome) rather than one in which they may all be 'suckers'. Leadership of political groups or trade unions is important in communicating such information and making possible the 'conditional altruism' of the 'assurance game' (Elster 1982a: 469–70).

Elster's response to criticism levelled by Charles Taylor lays bare some of the assumptions of his action theory (1980b). Taylor argues that Elster's

52

analysis in *Logic and Society* is perhaps only relevant to societies with 'atomistic forms of life' (1980: 139, 144). He notes that Elster is unaware of the necessity of community, of the norms of a *Sittlichkeit*, the 'common meanings' which make society possible. On a more doctrinal plane he questions the practicality and desirability of the highly individualistic brand of socialism which is linked with Elster's formulations. Elster's (1980b: 218) response is partly misguided since it conflates 'common meanings' with merely 'shared preferences'. More important, however, is the periodisation of the rationality of social action which Elster elucidates. In *Logic and Society* Elster had analysed two types of contradictions in social action, 'counter-finality' and 'suboptimality' (1978: Ch. 5). In the reply to Taylor he argues that in pre-modern societies, the main contradiction is 'counterfinality', which 'occurs because every actor assumes that he is working within a thing-like environment which in reality is made up of (or the result of the actions of) other intentional actors' (1980b: 216). This means that action will have unanticipated, often 'tragic', consequences (1980b: 281). In *Logic and Society* he mentions an intermediate stage in which agents see that others respond to their environment and adapt their action to take advantage of this perception. In a third stage the agent comes to realise that others are reasoning about the reasoning of others as well as about his/her reasoning. This is the beginning of game-theoretic or strategic action; now the 'dominant form of social contradiction' is 'suboptimality' (1980b: 218), which is best illustrated in the unhappy unanticipated consequences which occur in the prisoner's dilemma game. A fourth stage of the development of rational action would also be game-theoretic and is characterised by overcoming the contradiction of 'suboptimality'. In it the shared knowledge of the shared preferences of others would lead individuals to the assurance game's preference of universal cooperation over the free-rider solution and universal egoism.

It is thus important to note that for Elster game theory is an ontology of social process and is not merely a heuristic or instrumental device for generating predictions about the social world. His work (of which we have only discussed a fragment here) represents the most distinctive contribution to the new collective action framework. There are however some substantial deficiencies. First, Elster defines class consciousness operationally as the capacity of a class to overcome the 'free-rider' problem. This would empirically translate into the proposition that the Swedish and Austrian working classes are the most class conscious in the West and the French the least class conscious. Such a contention would seem an obvious absurdity or at least a Scandinavian idiosyncrasy. What Elster ignores are the diverse ideological conditions that cannot be simply reduced to whether the members of different classes are or are not in close interaction with one another. This is clear in the briefest cross-national consideration. In the USA, for example, the widespread existence of individualistic ideologies would appear to lower union membership and to maximise prisoner's dilemma preference structures by comparison with the UK or Italy. Second, although Elster elaborates the importance of the interdependence between classes (and presumably other social forces) he views them purely as comprised of individuals who may or may not engage in collective action. What is missing from his analysis is any examination of classes as comprising sets of 'resources, capacities, and powers' which may be realised within specific conjunctures. It is these resources, capacities and powers which are crucially relevant to the consideration of whether a particular class can be collectively organised and to the variable consequences of such organisation both on the class in question and upon other social forces within that society.

Offe, Wiesenthal and the Weak Thesis

Offe and Wiesenthal are concerned with the *different* organisational forms which characterise different social classes, and with how these relate to the different structuring of class relations (1980). They thus largely break with the methodological individualism of Roemer and Elster, as well as with conventional political science. The latter is taken to task for failing to analyse the distinctive differences between the associations of 'labour' and 'capital'.

First then, according to Offe and Wiesenthal, the crucial feature of labour is its *individuality*, it is atomised and divided by competition; moreover, labourers cannot merge, merely associate. Also, because of the indissoluble links between labourers and their labour-power, associations of labour must organise a wide spectrum of the needs of labour. Capital by contrast, is united and is merely organised to maximise profits, this being a matter which can generally be left to decisions by technical experts. At the same time, labour has to concern itself far more systematically with the well-being of capital, than does capital have to concern itself with the conditions of labour. Offe and Wiesenthal thus demonstrate that the associations of labour are defensive, they are responses *to* the collective organisation of capital. Capital may organise further in response to the associations of labour, either in informal cooperation between firms, and the employers' association – labour by contrast has merely one form of association. In any conflict between capital and labour, capital would seem certain to win since its collective action involves far fewer individuals, they are more united, and they possess clearer goals and greater resources.

Offe and Wiesenthal thus maintain that for the associations of labour to be viable an alternative organisational form has to develop, what they term the 'dialogical'. This involves, not merely aggregating the individual resources of the association members to meet the common interests of that membership, but also and more distinctly, defining a *collective identity*. Labour can only transform existing relationships by overcoming the relatively greater costs of engaging in collective action, as compared with capital. This can only be achieved by deflating the standards by which such costs are assessed within their collectivity. The establishment of this collective identity is essential since it is the only means by which the subjective deflation of the costs of organisation can be effected. Moreover, it is only labour that may develop this non-utilitarian form of collective action, a form in which it is held that the costs of membership of the organisation are not to be assessed instrumentally. The interests of labour thus can only really be met through their redefinition in terms of sustaining a collective identity.

This point relates to another crucial distinction. The organisations of labour rest upon the 'willingness to act', those of capital on the 'willingness to pay'. For the latter then there is no problem involved in maximising size – for the former this generates profound dilemmas. This is partly because an increase in size will probably produce a greater degree of bureaucratisation, and if this is so it will undermine that organisation's ability to mobilise its power to act; and it is also because an increase in size will increase the heterogeneity of members' occupations and interests, and hence will make it more difficult to establish the collective identity necessary for common action. The larger the organisation the more heterogeneous are the interests that have to be reconciled – not merely those of maximising members' wages, but also of ensuring security of employment, some control over the work process, and of pleasant working and living conditions (see Offe and Wiesenthal 1980: 82). Unlike organisations of capital, which can create and maintain the integration of their membership in a one-dimensional 'monological' manner, organisations of labour are involved in a complex and contradictory process of expressing/forming/sustaining a common identity – an identity which cannot be assessed in purely instrumental terms. The power of capital exists without organisation, the power of labour *only* exists with organisation, but it is an organisation which is precariously established. The organisation in part has to function 'dialogically', whereby the activity and views of the membership have to be represented and embodied so as to sustain the necessary collective identity. Thus Offe and Wiesenthal argue that if the organisations of capital are 'monological', those of labour have to be *both* 'monological' and·'dialogical'. Moreover, compared with labour the interests of capital are less ambiguous, controversial or likely to be misperceived. They do not require dialogical organisations in order to identify such interests.

Offe and Wiesenthal also argue that the greater the institutionalisation of liberal political forms and modes of political theorising, then the greater the difficulties that are created for labour to overcome these distortions of interest. Liberalism opposes those forms of 'dialogical' organisation which are, Offe and Wiesenthal note, essential for the realisation of the interests of labour. Liberalism thus favours the interests of capital because they are individualistic or 'monological'. Class conflict then is not just about the ends of politics, but it is also a conflict about the *forms*, about what means are necessary in order to articulate the undistorted interests of subordinate classes (and we might add, of other social groupings). Offe and Wiesenthal point out that there are imperatives within labour which tend to generate 'monological' or 'opportunistic' political forms by which they mean: (a) the inversion of the means/end relationship, with the institutionalisation of the former (the dialogical mode depends upon priority for the latter); (b) the primacy of immediate, short-term accomplishments; and (c) the emphasis upon quantitative criteria for recruitment and mobilisation. Offe and Wiesenthal argue that in recent decades the monological has increasingly come to replace the dialogical as the predominant form of labour organisation. The 'free-rider' issue is secondary; after a certain organisational size is reached, it is not increased membership, but the consequential creation of dialogical forms, which is the main problem.

This argument is tremendously instructive but there are two empirical problems worth noting. First, the distinction between the monological and the dialogical does not reproduce or help to explain differences between industrial and political radicalism that are elaborated in detail in Lash (1984: Ch. 7). Second, it is difficult – on Offe and Wiesenthal's account, which emphasises organisational imperatives – to explain the situation in the USA, where we find a combination of low union density with overwhelmingly monological organisations. Abercrombie and Urry argue that it is necessary to assess the relative causal powers of different social classes (1983: Chs 6 and 8). In particular, in the USA there was the early development of an especially strong 'service class' whose partially realised causal powers can be seen in the movement for 'scientific management', the enormous expansion of college education and the development of a status system based on educational credentials – all these severely weakened the American working class and produced the shift towards monological forms at lower levels of organisational membership (see Ch. 6).

NOTES TOWARDS A CRITIQUE

Although there are major problems in such theories, there are also a number of positive aspects which could provide the basis for a progressive research programme: (1) they are relatively rigorous containing elegant and sophisticated proofs of a sort rare in sociology (see Giddens 1982); (2) they problematise the relationship between interests and actions showing that the former only contingently generate the latter (see Crouch 1982, on the theory as an explanation of strikes); (3) they direct attention to certain *conditions*, rather than mental states, under which collective action may materialise (see Przeworski 1982); (4) they proceed from the assumption that social life consists of interdependencies and unintended consequences; (5) they draw out important game-theoretic implications of class alliances of both an offensive and a defensive sort (see Rule and Tilly 1975); and (6) they do not treat classes (and potentially other social forces) either in terms of a dependent

56

consciousness, or as simply structurally determined (see Brenner 1976; Roemer 1982a).

We will now consider some more general problems and issues involved in the theory. First, Berger and Offe argue: 'the game starts only after the actors have been constituted, and their order of preferences has been formed as a result of processes that cannot themselves be considered as part of the game' (1982: 325). The issue then is to identify the *determinants* of preference structures of individual actors and of the comparative capabilities of classes as agents. To identify such determinants is not however to resort, through slippage, to a naïve form of structural determination. We would rather, still in the framework of action theory, speak of classes as wielding 'resources'. Offe and Wiesenthal suggest that classes possess organisational and, apparently following Habermas (1976), 'motivational' resources (1980). However we would argue against the term 'motivational' on the grounds that this would seem to refer to the function of such resources. By contrast we would distinguish organisational and cultural resources, the latter being primarily 'symbolic' and hence of course crucially involved, in forms of 'motivation'. Language, ideologies and scientific and social scientific discourses can all serve as cultural resources of collective agents. The main organisational resources for labour are the trade union and the political party; and for capital, the enterprise itself, informal cooperation between enterprises and formal employers' associations.

If we consider individual workers within a given society then their 'preference structures' will be largely determined *by* the cultural and organisational resources that the working class in that society possesses, such as the cultural resources of 'norms of solidarity' or the organisational resources of a union able to enforce the closed shop. Where such resources are found then universal solidarity is likely to be preferred over universal egoism. Moreover, these resources are spatially and historically variable, so that we can talk of a set of repertoires for collective action (see Tilly and Tilly 1981). For example, the one-day widespread, politically oriented strike is an organisational resource which can be drawn on in France but not in Britain. Structural conditions permit the availability of Marxism as a cultural resource in Italy but not in contemporary West Germany. These resources and structures, which are crucial for explanation, can only be conceived of as at least partly external to rational choice theory itself.

Second, the new theory of collective action generally proceeds from the assumption of 'instrumental rationality'. In other words, the main issue addressed is explaining the choice of *means* which are appropriate given the ends of action. Where any consideration is paid to the analysis of ends then these are assumed to be material. This literature thus follows the conventional Anglo-American philosophy of action which has consistently refused to consider seriously the notion that some ends may be more rational than others.

There are a number of difficulties with such instrumentally rational notions. First, the new collective action theory fails to take account of the various criticisms that have been made of the concept of 'instrumental rationality'. In particular, a long tradition in continental philosophy and social theory (not least in Marxism) has systematically denounced such a concentration upon the rationality of means and indeed argues that such notions have had generally negative consequences upon Western civilisation. Second, it is extremely doubtful if large numbers of individuals do in fact exhibit this kind of rationality; or rather when we are trying to explain *collective* action then it is necessary to understand the rationality of *ends* that is often involved, a rationality focused upon notions of justice, fairness, equality and so on (see the discussion of this in Lash 1984). Third, there are important properties of languages, communities and social systems which cannot anyway be expressed as qualities or descriptions of the conduct of either individual or collective agents (the rules of syntax, for example; see Giddens 1982: 332). As Giddens argues, these properties should not be viewed as simply 'constraining', as though action consists of what is left after 'structure' has been delimited. Structure is rather both constraining *and* enabling – it is both the medium of *and* the outcome of actions which are typically not a matter of deliberated decision-making but rather of a routine 'monitoring' of the grounds of conduct in the everyday enacting of social life (1982; see discussion in Urry 1982).

This last point and especially the properties of *language* are increasingly the focus for empirical work on collective action. In this context Michelle Perrot has spoken of the 'discourse of the strike' (1974: 607–44). Here in the analysis of a mass of data she is able to point to a transition whereby the primacy of the written word gradually took the place of that of the spoken word. She, further, identifies three types of strikers' discourse: of the unorganised *parole sauvage*, of the trade union militant, and of the (in France) normally more political mass meeting. In each case it is insufficient to speak of language as only a constraint on workers; language primarily – and in each case in a different sense – plays the role of a cultural resource, a tool in the hands of striking workers.

Sewell (1980: 1–39) in a work subtitled *The Language of Labour from the Old Regime to 1848* has in a similar vein shown how discourse drawn from guild structures was intermeshed with the language of republicanism to produce the revolutionary artisan class of 1789. Lash in an interview-based study of French and American manual workers analysed the language used in the description of social imagery (1984). Here it was found that French workers tend to speak in an elaborated code ('bourgeoisie', 'capitalist', *'ouvrier'*, *'patron'*, *'cadre'*) which stresses oppositional relations of productive functions; while the Americans use a restricted language which is focused on the sphere of consumption. It is just as plausible to argue that differential language codes condition class consciousness as it is that codes follow from consciousness. Moreover, as relevant to collective action, classes can mobilise language as a cultural resource in connection with class consciousness. (Lash 1984: Ch. 5; also see Allheit 1982).

Thus, an adequate collective action theory must take language into account, and language is not a quality of actors. This however does not mean that collective (and individual) actors cannot use language as a *resource*. What this discussion points to is, transparently, the necessity for sociology and the theory of collective action to take pragmatics seriously, as Habermas has for some time and Anglo-American linguistics has recently come to do.

There are a number of analytical elements of a satisfactory causal explanation which remain obscure or unexplicated by the new theory of collective action:

1 An analysis of the *limits* to collective action (see Taylor 1980: 142), in particular, the existence of other social entities which mean that whatever the collective agents intend, these cannot be necessarily realised and must produce some *transmutation* of the explicit objectives (see Urry 1982).

2 An analysis of the related notion of 'unintentional causal agency', namely, that there are substantially unintended and unrecognised consequences on the collective action of a particular social grouping, which stem from the presence and partial realisation of the powers of *other* social entities. These consequences are neither intended nor explicable in 'functional' terms but may nevertheless be very important stemming as they do from the interdependence of such entities. Moreover, these unintended effects do not simply derive from the causal powers of 'dominant' groups – we intend to establish elsewhere that the most important determinant of social change within modern capitalist societies is in fact the changing capacities of the subordinate groupings, in particular the organisational and cultural resources of the working class (Lash and Urry 1987). We would argue, for instance, that the growth of neo-corporatism in many Western European societies in the 1960s was a consequence of the growing 'disorganisation' of contemporary capitalism, and in particular of the fragmentation of the working class through their decline in absolute numbers, the break up of working class communities, the homogenising consequences of the mass media, the bureaucratisation of trade unions and the conversion of class parties into *Volksparteien*.

3 The necessity to investigate the 'causal powers' of social entities and the degree to which these powers are in fact realised (see Bhaskar 1975; Keat and Urry 1982: Postscript). It is a contingent matter whether or not these powers require collective organisation. Abercrombie and Urry (1983), for example, maintain that there has been a profoundly significant realisation of the causal powers of the 'service class' in the USA since the First World War, but that this has not come about through class organisation as such. Although important organisations have indeed developed (especially the

59

professions, universities and bureaucracies) these should be seen rather as providing crucial organisational and cultural resources *for* the realisation of these class powers. But the class itself has not developed as a collective agent.

4 The analysis of the range of possible outcomes that may *follow* from collective action. These include (see Boudon 1981: 116): reproduction – of the structured properties of a society; innovation – such as the major expansion of welfare legislation; increased repression – because of the threat to law and order posed by the struggles; heightened contradiction – where, for example, the achievement of factory law legislation heightens the exploitation of workers through the growth of relative surplus-value production; institutionalisation – where struggles have the effect of producing complex and elaborate means of stabilising and regularising social conflict; heightened struggle – where the achievement of gains provides resources permitting further collective action.

5 The analysis of different organisational forms both over time and between different social groupings. Offe and Wiesenthal's exemplary analysis of the monological and dialogical forms closely follows Habermas who speaks of the monological in close conjunction with purposive rationality and the dialogical as an analogue of communicative action (1979: 118 ff.). However, while Offe and Wiesenthal see the shift towards the monological amongst labour as organisationally and conjuncturally dependent, Habermas views it as a secular development – that it is alternative agents, the 'social movements', which are now likely to develop dialogical forms of organisation (1979: Ch. 3 *passim*). This means that it is necessary to consider, not only the struggles around organisational form *within* (which of course depends in part on available resources), but also the struggles *between*, collective agents to establish and sustain particular forms of organisation. In modern capitalism, it is necessary to investigate, for example, whether and to what degree the growth of collective agents focused around gender, age, ethnicity and religion (what elsewhere is termed the horizontal elaboration of civil society; see Urry 1983a) undermines potential forms of class organisation. Collective action cannot therefore be understood separately from the overall structuring of civil society and of the changing effectiveness of different social groupings.

6 The analysis of the spatial-temporal structuring of social groupings is highly relevant to the development of collective action. Hence we would reinterpret Elster's theses on the emergence of collective action by maintaining that the working class (or any other social grouping) is more likely to engage in collective action, given a particular level of organisational and cultural resources, the more that:

i the spatially separated experiences of groups of workers can be viewed as representing the experiences of a whole class. This depends both upon 'local civil societies' being structured by class rather than by, say, the dichotomy between the state and the people and upon the structuring being the product of class relations rather than of other social forces (see Urry 1981a: Ch. 7, on changes within contemporary capitalism which render this condition more difficult to meet).

ii there are a number of spatially specific but overlapping and class-based 'collectivities-in-struggle' organised at least in part, on a 'dialogical' rather than a 'monological' basis (see Stark 1980: 119).

iii other collectivities within civil society are organised in ways which either reinforce class or at least are neutral with respect to it. In other words, working class collective action is more probable if civil society is not organised on an overwhelmingly horizontal basis in which there are a large number of social groupings and other social practices which are non-class specific (see Abercrombie and Urry 1983: 141).

iv other kinds of gains and benefits which could be attained through non-class actions (such as higher incomes, lower prices, increased opportunities, better conditions of work, etc.) are perceived to be and are unavailable. This condition will be more likely to hold where social inequalities are produced by the nationally based system of class relations.

v a substantial proportion of workers within diverse spatial locations conclude that class actions *can* be successful and are therefore worth pursuing even if they are not immediately successful. However, at the same time important resistances must be sustained to prevent organisations evolving into predominantly monological form.

CONCLUSION

In this paper we have argued that there is a new theoretical paradigm in sociology, that of game-theoretic Marxism. We have elucidated at some length the broad parameters of this paradigm and suggested that this theory is an integral feature of a more general shift from a focus on structure to an increased emphasis upon agency in Western sociology. We have identified a number of fundamental problems in the theory, but most importantly we have adumbrated the beginnings of a positive critique, of a revised version which preserves certain basic tenets of the original. These include the focus on collective and individual agency, the primacy of causation, and a rather more circumscribed use of game-theoretic notions to understand struggles. Our revised version stands, however, in strong relief to Elster's main thesis; and it draws importantly on the work of Offe and Wiesenthal and the analysis of systematically structured differences in organisational forms.

The central elements of this more adequate framework for the understanding of collective action are: (i) that class and other collective actors are possessed with resources; (ii) that 'class capacity' (or conversely the capacities of other collective agents) be defined as the strength of the organisational and cultural resources which the grouping can mobilise, especially over time and across space; (iii) that social change in civil society and the state in capitalism can be well understood through the consideration not simply of the dominant class, but through the analysis of the capacities of *subordinate* class (and other collective) agents; (iv) that instrumental reason and other forms of consciousness must not be understood as unconditioned but as constituted, in particular via the medium of language – language at the same time, however, is to be conceived as an important cultural resource for collective agents; (v) that the notion of causality in collective action theory be extended not only to account for the varied unintended consequences of intentional action, but for causal powers of entities whereby the mere presence, the 'inaction' so to speak, of collectivities is capable of producing social change; and (vi) that it is crucial to analyse the various *limits* upon the consequences of collective action, consequences that demand investigation of the unintended and changing anatomy of different societies and of the changing, overlapping, and interdependent effects of different patterns of collective action.

4

SOCIETY, SPACE AND LOCALITY*

INTRODUCTION

The explanation of the social patterning in particular places would appear to be fairly straightforward. It seems reasonably easy to account for the social relations which characterise a given locality. Reference would need to be made to two sets of factors: those *external* to the locality, including, particularly, processes of international and national change and central government directives; and those *internal* to the locality, which would appear to relate causally to the aspects requiring explanation.

However, in this chapter I shall suggest that such explanations are in fact by no means straightforward. Indeed the very term 'locality' or the 'local' is itself highly ambiguous and requires much more examination. This is because it refers to two interconnected sets of processes, the social and the spatial, which happen to produce particular combinations of social relations with a given geographically delimited area. In order then to explain such local social relations, attention has to be paid to a number of complex considerations: first, the relationship between the 'social' and space (and time); second, the very nature of social relations themselves, and of the ways in which they are spatially/temporally constituted; and third, the different senses of 'locality' which relate in a variety of ways to the analyses of society and space. These issues will be discussed in the rest of this chapter, the subsequent sections dealing with each issue in turn.

SPACE AND SOCIETY

Two deficiencies of much social scientific analysis lie in the inadequate specification of the relationship of the 'social' to both the 'temporal' and the 'spatial'. In terms of the first there has been a tendency to associate the temporal with social change, as though societies exhibit temporality only when they are experiencing change. If they are not so changing, then they are

* This first appeared in *Society and Space*, 1987, vol. 5: 435–44. Reprinted with permission of Pion Ltd, London.

taken to be a-temporal. With respect to the spatial, sociology (apart from its urban specialism) has tended to pay insufficient and ineffective attention to the fact that social practices are spatially patterned, and that these patterns substantially affect these very social practices. Moreover, this particular deficiency is now more significant because of the major changes that are occurring within contemporary capitalist relations, changes which are undermining the coherence, unity and wholeness of individual 'societies'. A crucial theoretical problem has been how to develop ways of understanding, not just how societies, as in some sense well-defined wholes, come into external relationships with each other, but the nature of such processes as internationalised money and industrial capital, culture and state structures, which transcend and 'disorganise' what are generally known as 'societies' (for discussion, see Lash and Urry 1987).

An initial point to make is that most, if not all, theories in the social sciences contain implications about the patterning of human activity within time-space, as such activity necessarily involves passing through time and space. Changes in the temporal order of social interactions generally involve changes in the spatial patterning. Even the repetitions of everyday life involve both temporary and spatial regularities. However, most scientific theories of such activities do not draw out the temporal and spatial implications. These implications tend to remain at an implicit level and in many cases if they were fully specified they would be found to contradict other aspects of the theory in question. To illustrate this, consider Marx's discussion of the growth of revolutionary consciousness and organisation amongst the working class (see Marx 1973: 238–9). I will take this for discussion because he, unlike many other social and political scientists, is well aware of the importance of certain spatial aspects of social relations (see Harvey 1982). It is a major element in his account that as capitalism develops there is an increasing concentration of workers within the progressively larger capitalist workplaces and cities. Hence, the growth in the productive forces produces increases in the size, organisation and effectiveness of the working class, a class which at least on some accounts is historically destined to revolt and overthrow capitalist relations of production. According to Marx, a necessary condition for this is the growth of the spatial proximity of workers within capitalist workplaces and cities. However, this account is not fully adequate, and there are two important spatial aspects which run counter to this argument and which seriously weaken it. On the one hand, although *each* capitalist enterprise grows in size, this does not mean that workers within each separate workplace are placed in even closer proximity to each other.

Marx fails to demonstrate how class organisation and consciousness can overcome this necessary 'friction of distance' between workers within spatially and often socially distinct capitalist enterprises. On the other hand, Marx does not sufficiently explore other important spatial foci within capitalist societies, namely the foci of the neighbourhood, town, region, and nation-state. Although these spatial foci are intimately related to the patterns of accumulation within the economy, they are not simply to be reduced to such patterns, nor are their political effects to be seen as simply subordinate to those within the economy. Thus capitalism dichotomises home and work for wage-labourers; yet the spatial location of one's home, in a particular spatial form, cannot be viewed as politically irrelevant. Marx fails to show that these spatial foci will become *less* politically salient as capitalism develops and more and more workers are thrust into capitalist workplaces, towns and cities. To the extent to which such spatial organisations are not reducible to the relations of production, a quite separate analysis is called for. In certain cases these non-economic spatial patterns may generate class divisions (see Cooke 1985 on 'radical regions'), but there is nothing *necessary* about this, nothing entailed by the logic of capitalist accumulation (see for further discussion the papers in Gregory and Urry 1985; Hoggart and Kofman 1986).

This brief discussion suggests that the spatial aspects of social life are of some importance. I will now make a few brief general points about the connections between social and spatial relations.

First of all, space should not be viewed as an absolute entity somehow separate from the material objects located 'within' it. But it is also the case that space cannot be merely reduced to such objects. In rejecting the thesis of space as an absolute, it is essential that we do not eliminate all spatial effects by concentrating upon the mere distribution of objects. It remains appropriate to use terms such as 'distance', 'continuity', 'betweenness', 'containment', etc. to characterise the different spatial relations taken by such objects.

This emphasis upon the spatial as consisting of the relations between social objects means that it is illegitimate to talk as though there were an interdependence between spaces *per se*. Spatial patterns cannot be said to interact, only the social objects present within one or more such spaces interact. It may therefore be incorrect to talk of one area exploiting another area; to suggest that a region is exploiting another region, or that the centre is exploiting the periphery, is to fetishise the spatial.

Another kind of fetishisation should be avoided – where the spatial structure is seen as *determining* the patterns of social organisation. This view was in part held by the human ecology school in urban sociology. It has since then been effectively criticised, although one reason why spatial notions have been so neglected until recently here has been to avoid accusations of 'ecological determinism'. It is also necessary to avoid the suggestion that spatial characteristics should be merely seen as providing the environment *within* which social activity happens to take place. Such a view leads to an easy academic division of labour between geography which studies the spatial structuring of the environment (physical and human) and the social sciences which study the manifold variety of social activities within such environments. This separation is in part erroneous because it neglects the manner in which most aspects of the spatial environment are themselves humanly produced and humanly changeable. They thus convey meaning, that they are part of the meaningful structures which flow from and which reproduce on-going social activity (see Tuan 1977). Thus, different areas, towns, agricultural zones, new trading estates, shopping centres, arterial roads, etc. are not merely elements of a given spatial structure and determinative of human activity from outside. Rather they are themselves social, socially produced, and socially reproducing. They cannot therefore be separated from the significant social objects present within a given society, and from the characteristic forms in which such objects are interconnected.

This suggests that it is impossible and incorrect to develop a general science of the spatial. The latter cannot be separated from the social in such a manner that a general set of distinct laws can be devised. This is because space *per se* has no *general* effects. The significance of spatial relations depends upon the particular character of the social objects in question. So the spatial relationship cannot be limited to some general effect – it only has effect because the social objects in question possess particular characteristics or powers. There is no simple 'space', only different kinds of spaces, spatial relations or spatialisations.

However, this in turn raises the question as to just how we should conceptualise social objects in any social scientific investigation once we acknowledge their spatial and temporal constitution. In the following section I shall address this issue through the analysis of some of the debates within the British literature on theoretical realism.

SOCIAL OBJECTS AND SPACE

Two distinctions drawn from the theoretical or transcendental realist literature are relevant here (see Harré 1970; Bhaskar 1975; Harré and Madden 1975; Benton 1977; Keat and Urry 1982; Sayer 1992). These are: first, the distinction between 'events' and 'structure', and second, the distinction between 'contingent' and 'necessary' relations. I shall consider them in that order.

First, it is necessary to consider what are the components, the building blocks, of physical and social reality. One influential conception derived from Hume is that the physical (and social) world is comprised of a myriad of individual events or phenomena which happen to be distributed in various temporal and spatial patterns. There are no relations of natural necessity, only contingent connections between one event and another. The major problem with this conception, of this event-ontology, is raised by the very concept of an event. This is because the term 'event' here has to be viewed as a phenomenon confined in both time and space; it is happening at a moment in time and at a point in space. As Harré and Madden put it: 'the Humean event

. . . is . . . instantaneous in nature, punctiform and elementary, and from this characterisation follows its atomicity, its lack of internal connections with anything else' (1975: 108).

This atomicity of events further means that there is a sequential independence of properties so that if a particular object displays the same property at a different temporal or spatial location, then in terms of this ontology it is impossible to refer to the 'nature' of the object in order to explain why that property is displayed across time or space. As events have to be conceived of as instantaneous time-space slices of the object, it is impossible to explain either the given property or the patterning of such properties. Given an event-ontology, no sense can be given to the notion that entities persist and demonstrate material continuity and identity. Moreover, the event-ontology is associated with a conception of time and space in which such events are seen as points distributed in terms of the absolute properties of the three dimensions of space and the dimension of time.

However, in a realist thing-ontology or structure-ontology, it would be maintained that there are entities which possess material continuity and identity and their persistence is explained by the causal powers which they possess across time and space. Empirical events are the product of at least the partial realisation of the powers of such entities. Nevertheless, such sets of empirical events are not to be explained in terms of a single entity. No entity will possess of itself the causal power to generate a whole class of empirical events. It is necessary instead to investigate the interplay between diverse social and natural entities whose combined powers will be such as to produce the range of empirical events under examination. Indeed there is a crucially significant interdependence between entities so that the causal powers of some constitute the conditions necessary for the realisation of the powers of other entities. Hence, the empirical events generated, such as the spatial distribution of the population of a country by region, are the product of highly complex interdependent processes, processes which are not simply to be aggregated, but in which there is in effect a synthesis of the respective causal powers of the entities in question. Marx considered it was this 'synthesis' that constituted the concrete, it was 'a synthesis of many definitions, thus representing the unity of diverse aspects' (1973: 101).

The implication of this for time and space is that their investigation must intrude at three different levels in any social analysis; there are in this sense three different 'spaces' or 'spatialisations'. First, empirical events are distributed *in* time-space. This is true both of the relatively routine features of everyday life and of more distinct and unique social events. Second, any particular social entity (relations of production, the state, civil society, classes, etc.) is built around a particular temporal and spatial structuring. For example, the modern state is highly centralised and contains spatially and temporally transformed means of surveillance over its subject-citizens.

67

Capitalist relations, to take another example, have become dramatically more extended. The need for spatial proximity, which derived from the need to minimise the time taken to convey information, decisions and control, has been transformed by the development of electronically transmitted information. This has enabled capitalist relations to be spatially transformed, with a functional separation of offices from workplaces, and of different workplaces from each other, in terms of different labour-forces and labour processes that are employed (as various papers in Scott and Storper 1986 show in detail). Third, social entities are temporally and spatially interrelated with each other, interrelationships which change over time and across space. A crucial example here concerns the changing profile of capitalist relations of production. There is an increased distance between capitalist production *per se* and civil society, within areas of contemporary capitalist societies. In other words, capitalist production is progressively deepened, particularly within so-called 'global cities' and yet is simultaneously spatially concentrated away from certain areas and sectors.

So time-space in a realist programme occupies complex and variable relations in an appropriate analysis: first, 'empirical events' are distributed in time-space; second, social entities with causal powers are structured in terms of time-space; and third, the relationships *between* such entities are structured temporally-spatially. In short, the social world comprises a number of temporally and spatially interdependent, mutually modifying, four-dimensional time-space entities, which constitute a particular complex 'open system', separate in part at least from physical time-space.

Thus far, I have not distinguished between the 'temporal' and the 'spatial', and in this I have loosely followed post-relativity physics. However, within the analysis of the 'time-space' constitution of social systems, it is important to consider the *relative* significance of time and of space. Marx argued that the development of capitalist relations had the effect of overcoming all spatial barriers; hence to 'annihilate space with time' (1973: 539). Although this is a fundamental *objective* of capitalist production, what Marx (and some other Marxists) ignored is the fact that this annihilation can be achieved only through the production of new, fixed and relatively immobile spatial configurations. As Harvey has most clearly demonstrated 'spatial organisation is necessary to overcome space' (1985: 145). Now some of these new spatial configurations are exceptionally significant and result in the constant revolutionising of the spatial constraints upon production, or more generally, upon social life and even upon the distribution of 'knowledge' (Thrift 1985).

In relationship to capital, new spatial configurations follow the contradictory tendencies of 'differentiation' and 'equalisation'. There are three interconnected processes: (a) the tendency for capital to see-saw from place to place seeking locational advantage – it being like a plague of locusts, settling on one place, devouring it, moving on to a new place while the old restores itself for another attack (see Smith 1984: 152); (b) the tendency for capital progressively to become spatially *indifferent*, by reducing its dependence upon particular raw materials, markets, sources of energy, areas of the city, supplies of skilled labour and so forth (see Urry 1981b); and (c) the tendency for certain characteristics of labour-power (skills, cost, supply, organisation, reliability) to become of heightened importance because it, unlike the physical means of production, cannot be produced capitalistically and hence is not subject to the same process of geographical levelling or *homogenisation* (Walker and Storper 1981).

The interconnections between these three processes do not reduce the importance of space and place for a number of reasons. Relations within space are always highly constrained since, although an infinity of objects may occupy a 'point' in time, no two objects can occupy the same point in space. Although the objective of capitalist production is to annihilate space with time it cannot literally be done because new sets of social relations have to be physically extended across space and cannot simply be concentrated within a single point in space. Those new spatial configurations will in turn structure and channel emergent patterns of social life. Moreover, the effect of heightened spatial indifference has profound effects upon particular places and upon the forms of life that can be sustained within them. Also, although labour is far less mobile than capital, it is clear that certain of the forms of managerial control rest upon there being fairly long-established patterns of social life sedimented within particular places and that people's commitment to those particular spaces are part of the conditions under which the forms of control by capital are sustained.

I have so far made out a fairly general case for the importance of the analysis of space. It is necessary to examine the interconnections between the social and the spatial more carefully, and I will do so by considering very briefly two kinds of relations between social phenomena: on the one hand, those relations which are external to one another and which are therefore '*contingent*'; and on the other hand, those relations which are *necessary* and hence internal to the phenomenon being considered (Sayer 1982). The former consist of those relations where the objects in question do not stand in any necessary relationship with each other, when they can exist independent of each other and of the relationships between them. The latter, by contrast, consist of those relations which are necessary for the very objects to exist; such objects cannot exist without such relations. An example of the former would be the relations between a firm and one particular town from which it employs its workers; an example of the latter would be the relations between landlord and tenant, neither 'object' being able to exist without those connecting relations. What then of 'space'? How does space relate to this distinction between necessary and contingent relations?

I shall consider this issue by taking one set of social relations, namely the capitalist relations of production, and showing the mixture of necessary and contingent relations which comprise this particular set ('time' will be omitted from the consideration here):

1 There are the *necessary* capitalist relations of production of capital and wage-labour.
2 There are particular agents who happen *contingently* to bear one function or the other (capital or wage-labour).
3 Given that particular agents will function as wage-labour or as capital, then it is *necessary* for at least some of these agents to be spatially proximate.
4 No necessary spatial division of labour will develop as industrial and commercial capital appropriates space in different ways; which develops is partly *contingent* on location of raw materials, physical constraints, relative transport costs, changes in labour supply, skill, and organisational levels, etc. and on the changing importance of these different factors.
5 There are *necessary* laws of the capitalist economy which constrain the possible form taken by the spatial division of labour; but the recent development of these necessary laws means that it is a relatively *contingent* matter as to where capitalist relations will be found and hence which particular labourers in which particular localities will be employed by which particular capitals.
6 As it is *necessarily* the case that individual sellers of labour-power act as subjects possessing a consciousness or a will, there have to be social practices within which those subjectivities are developed and sustained.
7 It is *necessarily* the case that the social practices mentioned above are structured by the commodity relations generated from the overarching capitalist relations; but the form taken by those practices depends upon various *contingencies* (such as the degree to which pre-capitalist associations and structures persist, the location and nature of the housing stock, the struggles by individuals and groups to extend or protect those practices, the relations of gender domination and of racial oppression, etc.) although these in turn may depend upon necessities implied by other structures, for example, patriarchy (see Walby 1986).

In order to account for a given social structure, it is necessary to decipher the interconnections between these various necessary and contingent relations within various causally powerful entities, a project of which there are at present no extant examples. Nevertheless a starting point for the analysis of the social structures of at least local areas is given by Massey when she argues that 'the social and economic structure of any given *local* area will be a complex result of the combination of that area's succession of roles within the series of wider, national and international, spatial divisions of labour' (1978: 116; and see Massey 1984). In the next section I shall examine directly how the interaction between social processes and their necessary and contingent relations can be used to analyse a wide variety of different kinds of local effects.

LOCALITIES

It is clear that many localities in contemporary societies are being transformed by diverse forms of extremely rapid economic restructuring. How
though are we to analyse those processes? What is the relationship between
changes in such causally powerful entities and sets of empirical events in
particular places? Although it is clear that many places are substantially
affected by economic changes in particular, it does not follow that everything
about such localities after restructuring simply reflects those very processes.
Indeed it may not even be the case that the most important aspects (either of
continuity or change) of a locality are determined by or reflect such processes
of restructuring, even though such processes do obviously have important
effects. However, in order to address this issue further it is necessary to
'unpack' what is meant by 'locality' or the 'local'.

It must be noted first of all that these terms do not mean simply the concrete
or the empirical, the real or actual, or agency. Locality is as much a theoretical
term as any other in the social scientific lexicon (see Savage *et al.* 1987, for
further analysis). Moreover, like other terms it is used in quite diverse ways
by different writers, it plays a variety of functions in different social scientific
discourses. The same term therefore denotes a wide variety of concepts. That
this is so has not been properly recognised because it is often assumed that
the word local is merely shorthand for the real or empirical. Once we
acknowledge that this is not so, then it becomes necessary to separate out the
different ways in which the term locality or local has been used. There seem
to be at least ten different forms in which use is made of the 'local', 'local
effects' or 'locality' in a realist-based social scientific discourse. I will now
set these out.

1 Some particular national or international processes (such as economic
   restructuring through 'rationalisation'; see Massey and Meegan 1982)
   take a particular form in a certain locality, although this may be the same
   as the form which it takes in one or more other localities. As all social
   processes are contextualised in particular places, the identification of the
   form taken by such a process in a given place is a useful research project.
2 A given social variable is differentially distributed between different
   localities and this may provide some index of underlying structural
   differences between those localities. An example would be the differential
   distribution of a given occupation between local areas and this may tell
   us a certain amount about the comparative social structure of different
   places (see discussion of various kinds of 'comparisons' between localities in Warde 1985). Another example would be the variation in
   expenditure on certain policies by different local authorities, such as that
   on 'economic development and promotion' (see Urry 1987a).
3 A particular social process which is intended to apply generally is not in
   fact found to be present to the same degree in a given locality and this is

because of the existence of some relatively powerful local grouping. For example, the current attempt to restructure the National Health Service in the United Kingdom is strongly resisted in certain localities, both by the workforce and by the local management.

4 The distribution between localities of one nationally distributed social phenomenon accounts for the variation by locality of some *other* nationally distributed phenomenon. For example, in the 1950s and 1960s the distribution of manual and non-manual voters in different constituencies in the United Kingdom largely 'explained' the variation in voting for Conservative and Labour in those constituencies (see Warde 1986).

5 The way in which a particular complex of wider or more general national or international processes impinges upon a local area produces a specific locally unique *combination* of such general processes. As a consequence, there are resulting unique social processes in that given locality, although the processes which produce that result are very general (see many of the chapters in Cooke 1986 which show this with respect to various local labour and housing markets).

6 There are systematic processes which occur at the local level, and these modify or transform the effect that the wider national or international processes have locally. For example, because of the actions of certain local employers, wage levels have been kept 'artificially' low and this has the consequence that new investment is attracted to that locality rather than to others. However, this effect occurs only because certain national and international processes are in part contingent, that is, they determine, for example, that there *should* be spatial relocation but not *where* it should occur.

7 One set of local variations are the product of certain other locally specific social processes. For example, voting patterns in different UK constituencies are partly determined by the proportion of employers and managers in each constituency through a so-called 'contagion effect'. The voting preferences, especially of workers, are distorted away from that which their 'occupation' would suggest (again, see Warde 1986).

8 New national and international processes are developing which are heightening the importance of contingency in industrial location. Because of the reduced significance of fixed raw materials and energy sources, and because of the importance of vertical disintegration, there is an increased importance of local variation (see Scott 1985 on vertical disintegration). Relatively small differences in what different local areas can offer to prospective employers may well have sizeable effects on the distribution of industry and employment.

9 It can be shown that social processes are such that it is localities rather than regions or provinces which have become more important forms of social organisation at the level below that of the nation-state. This may be seen as resulting from the ability of global corporations to subdivide

their internal division of labour and to take advantage of local variations; or from the decline in regionally specific industrial economies; or from the Conservative Party in Britain trying to tie together local taxes and local services; or from the development of new forms of political organisation which are much more locally decentralised (such as the so-called 'new social movements'; see Lash and Urry 1987; Dickens 1987).

10 It is part of the culture of those living in a given geographical area that there is a distinction drawn between those who are local, 'people like us', and those who are non-local, 'outsiders', 'offcomers', etc. This binary opposition may be set up and reproduced in a variety of ways, relating to people's very sense of belonging to a given 'community'. A general feature of the culture of a given region or nation may be that strong distinctions are drawn between the local and the non-local. The recent development of local vernacular architecture may well indicate that this is of heightened importance within contemporary Britain.

I have thus set out ten different ways in which recent social science has tried to analyse the local or locality. I would thus maintain that 'locality effects' are much wider in scope than Savage et al. would appear to admit; for them such an effect seems to occur only where 'the connections of different locally derived social entities are likely to be highly specific to each place' (1987: 32). For them therefore localities only properly exist if they are 'communities' with a distinctive and unique local culture. In this chapter by contrast I have argued that there are a wide variety of local effects. Thus what seems a relatively simple notion, the 'local', is in fact really complex and involves analysis of a mixture of social and spatial processes. In order to decipher those connections it is necessary to engage with the range of topics that I have considered here, and especially with the appropriate character of a reconstituted realist social science in which space (and time) are viewed as constitutive of social entities and of their respective causal powers.

Part II

RESTRUCTURING AND SERVICES

5

RESTRUCTURING THE RURAL*

In this chapter I shall reconsider some of the literature on rural social relations in the light of contemporary debates on the process of capitalist restructuring. In particular, it will be argued that:

1 The most important developments within contemporary capitalism are not those which generate ever-increasing concentrations of capital, state power and labour-power within urban rather than rural areas, and in which social relations in the latter are increasingly dominated by social relations in the former.
2 Nevertheless there are highly significant changes occurring within the time-space structuring of contemporary capitalist societies but their effects cannot be summarised in terms either of the dichotomy between rural and urban areas, or of apparently identifiable regions.
3 The most important of these changes involve the *spatial* restructuring of capitalist production *and* of civil society, and these patterns of spatial restructuring have had the effect of heightening the socio-political salience of local systems of social stratification.
4 In rural areas these local systems cannot be simply characterised in terms of the relations of a new 'middle class' to the existing rural class structure.
5 The stratification structure of any locality (whether formally urban or rural) is the interdependent effect of mutually modifying forms of structural determination, especially of the complex overlap between diverse spatial divisions of labour.
6 A most important process of contemporary change is what one might loosely describe as the ruralisation of industrial/urban relations. This process reinforces others which serve to fragment and decompose the industrial classes of contemporary capitalism, and to usher in a pro-gressively de-industrialised economy and attendant social relations.

---

* This first appeared in T. Bradley and P. Lowe (1984) (eds) *Rurality and Locality*, Norwich: Geo-Books. Certain sections have been shortened. It was originally entitled 'Capitalist restructuring, recomposition and the regions'.

I will begin by identifying a number of difficulties within rural sociology and shall then consider one important analysis of recent economic change which makes much of urban/rural differences. I shall then analyse changing patterns by which capital and labour-power are currently being reorganised. Finally, I shall consider the consequences for the generation of diverse local systems of social stratification.

PROBLEMS IN RURAL SOCIOLOGY

In recent years rural sociology seems rather to have lost its way in contrast with urban sociology which has been transformed both by the neo-Marxist debates introduced by Castells, Harvey, Lojkine and Lefebvre, and more recently in the UK by the post-Marxist writings of Dunleavy (1980) and Saunders (1982). In effect, British rural sociology involves the following claims, which constitute its main features:

1 Property rather than occupation is the defining principle of rural societies and, hence, it is the organisation of property relationships, rather than the division of labour, which shapes the rural class structure (Stinchcombe 1961; Banaji 1976; Newby 1978: 6–15).
2 In British agriculture there has been a substantial shift away from the landlord–tenant property system towards that of owner occupation, as well as a large increase in the ownership of land by finance-capital (Newby 1978: 12–15; Newby *et al.* 1978).
3 There is a profound and irreversible rationalisation of the agricultural industry, away from farming as a 'way of life' towards its organisation 'as a business'. In particular, there is the growth of so-called agri-business, although this is not to argue that small farms will necessarily disappear (Gasson 1966; Newby 1978: 19–20; Newby 1979).
4 In contrast with industry, the growth of mechanisation has reduced the division of labour amongst agricultural workers. This is because there has been a fairly massive reduction in the labour force employed on each farm although little reduction in the tasks to be performed which are sequentially rather than concurrently organised (see Newby 1977: Ch. 5; Gasson 1980, on the effects of the sexual division of labour in farming).
5 This outflow of labour from agricultural employment has both undermined whatever solidarities previously existed within rural areas when labour was far more plentiful (Newby 1977: Ch. 5; Newby 1978: 21) and *reduced* bureaucratisation on farms and, hence, the distance between farmers and their workers (Newby 1977: Ch. 6, 1978: 21–2).
6 There has been a marked expansion of an ex-urban middle class within rural areas and this has produced an 'encapsulated' rural community, particularly focused on the 'farm' and defined partly by opposition to the 'newcomers' (Pahl 1965; Newby 1977, 1980b).

7 A major determinant of social relations within the countryside since the Second World War has been the state. The policy of agricultural protection has particularly benefited large-scale capitalist farmers and landlords (Josling 1974; Newby 1980a: 54–66), and that of countryside protection has restricted economic growth and the development of competition for local labour (Newby 1980a: 267). Moreover, urban newcomers have reinforced this by seeking to preserve, in Pahl's felicitous phrase, their village in the mind (1965).

8 The analysis of rural social relations will only be successful if a more 'holistic' approach is adopted (Newby 1980a: section 5, 1982: 157–9).

Clearly, some very important insights have been developed, especially with regard to the social organisation of agriculture which has certain features derived from land as a distinctive means of production. However, Newby, amongst others, is well aware of some significant deficiencies and he commends the development of a more holistic approach on two grounds: first, that this would render problematic the categories 'rural' and 'urban' by identifying social processes *common* to both; and second, that this would explicitly relate the social structure to the 'spatial structure of regional development and underdevelopment' (1980a: 92). There are, however, serious difficulties associated with this programme, particularly if it is being claimed that new 'holistic', 'regional', 'theoretical' analyses could be unproblematically added to the existing research. Partly this is because notions of 'centre-periphery' and 'internal colonialism' have themselves been severely criticised for their relatively ahistorical, static and functionalist character (see Cooke 1983).

There are also problems highlighted by the recent elaboration of a realist philosophy of science which suggests that we should make very clear the distinction between the causal powers of designated entities and the actual empirical events to which these entities contingently give rise (Bhaskar 1979; Keat and Urry 1982: Postscript; Sayer 1982). Empirical events are the product of the complex interrelations between those entities whose causal powers are in part being realised. Within this account the category of the 'rural' seems to constitute neither an entity with specifiable causal powers, nor a range of empirical phenomena which stands in a coherent relationship to particular causally powerful social entities. It should be regarded, therefore, as a 'chaotic conception'. Inadequate theory will result if we try to generalise from such chaotically produced empirical phenomena. Rather it is necessary to abstract from empirical phenomena in order to arrive at theoretically informed analyses of the causal powers of social entities, powers which only contingently generate empirical events. A non-chaotic conception of the 'rural' could be based on one of the following:

1 The 'rural' refers to all those areas in which agricultural production dominates the local economy, either because there is no manufacturing and

service production, or because any that is present is dominated by the social relations of agricultural production, relations which stem in particular from land as the centrally significant means of production.

2 The 'rural' refers to a particular structuring of local civil societies in which the patterns of social reproduction and social struggle are structured by the class relations engendered by ownership and control of the agricultural means of production.

3 The 'rural' refers to those areas in which the density of the population is so low (whether or not because agriculture is the predominant industry) that the means of 'collective consumption' cannot be provided economically within that area and have rather to be located in non-rural, urban areas instead.

Finally, it should be noted that the legacy of the rural–urban continuum can be seen in the tendency to analyse the degree to which agricultural production is like or is becoming like industrial production (see Newby 1978: 25). Such an approach has two deficiencies: first, since industrial or manufacturing production only accounts for a quarter of the presently employed population in the UK, it is more important to consider any similarities with service production and employment; and second, since a growing proportion of labour is being carried out either within households (the self-service economy – see Gershuny 1978), or outside the formal economy, or within part-time employment (Pahl 1980; Urry 1983a), then it is agricultural production, especially in its simple commodity form, towards which at least some forms of urban-based labour are moving. When Karl Kautsky talks of 'a suppression of the separation of industry and agriculture' (Banaji 1976: 47) it may have less to do with agricultural production becoming like industrial production and more to do with major changes in the entire organisation of work in a de-industrialising society (see Urry 1983a).

British rural sociology, though, has failed to examine the changing economic and spatial structuring of manufacturing and service industry. This failure is especially striking since Fothergill and Gudgin (1982) have employed the distinction between urban and rural areas as a major explanation of the spatial restructuring of industry. They maintain that recent patterns of employment change cannot be analysed simply in terms of north versus south, or in terms of distinctive regions. They say: 'industrial structure has become more or less irrelevant as an explanation of disparities in regional growth' (1982: 59). Instead, they note that all the areas that experienced major employment loss between 1959 and 1975 contain a major conurbation, whereas many of the areas that gained employment in the same period are 'rural' (1982: 14). This contrast is particularly marked for manufacturing employment.

Moreover, if we break down the regions into various sub-regions then we find that there is a general relationship between the size of settlement and manufacturing growth – small cities grew faster than large cities; small towns grew faster than larger towns. Fothergill and Gudgin conclude that 'the shift from urban to rural areas is the major trend in industrial location in Britain' (1982: 24). The larger the settlement size the faster the decline in employment, especially of manufacturing. This is because the larger the city, the higher the rates of plant closure, the greater the losses through plant contraction, and the lower the rates of expansion of surviving firms (1982: 81). They maintain, somewhat implausibly, that the shift of manufacturing employment out of large cities is mainly because of the great difficulty that firms in the larger urban areas have in physically expanding their plant compared with those in smaller settlements and in rural areas. The relative lack of physical limitations on spatial expansion in the less urban and the more rural locations is seen by Fothergill and Gudgin as the crucial factor in explaining variations in employment change.

In order to provide the rudiments of what I consider to be a more precise and satisfactory explanation of changes to the civil society of 'rural' areas I shall, in the next section, use Fothergill and Gudgin's analysis as an example of the misapplication of conceptions of 'urban' and 'rural' space.

CAPITAL, LABOUR POWER AND THE 'RURAL'

There are two particular difficulties in Fothergill and Gudgin's analysis. First, as we have seen, identifying a locality in terms of its rural/urban characteristics is too simplistic. Second, they presume that the way to analyse industrial change is through identifying certain general processes which are then, to varying degrees, developed within any particular local economy (Murgatroyd and Urry 1983; Sayer 1982). Neither of these positions can be justified. In particular, any local economy should be viewed as the particular product of the overlap, in time and space, of the forms of capitalist and state restructuring within the pertinent sectors of extractive, manufacturing and service industry. As Massey argues: 'the social and economic structure of any given local area will be a complex result of the combination of that area's succession of roles within the wider, national and international, spatial divisions of labour' (1978: 116). Thus, relevant analysis does not consist of identifying certain general tendencies which are more or less developed in different localities, depending upon whether that locality happens to be more rural or more urban.

Broadly speaking the 'restructuring' analysis, which I am arguing for here involves the following claims:

1 There are a number of different patterns of economic restructuring, of different spatial divisions of labour.
2 These restructurings stem from changing patterns of capitalist accumulation and especially from the internationalisation and fractionalisation of capital.

3 In particular, changes in economic location cannot be explained in terms of 'economic' or 'political' factors, but, rather, in terms of the complex forms of restructuring necessary for sustained accumulation.

4 These restructurings both result from changes in class struggles and, in turn, transform the conditions under which social relations within particular areas are reproduced.

5 Any area can only be understood as the product of its location within a number of overlapping spatial divisions of labour.

6 The resulting patterns of uneven development cannot be analysed simply in terms of regions and regional decline.

What, then, are the main forms of the spatial division of labour which may characterise any sector? The following are six important forms (derived from Massey 1981; Walker and Storper 1981; Massey and Meegan 1982):

i   *regional specialisation* – until the inter-war period many sectors were characterised by a high degree of specialisation within particular regions (for example cotton textiles and textile machinery within Lancashire, mining and shipbuilding within the north-east, arable farming in East Anglia);

ii *regional dispersal* – other sectors are characterised by a high degree of dispersal, including most consumer services, some producer services, certain manufacturing industries (such as food processing and shoe production) and mixed farming. Labour reductions in this case will take the form of intensification – that is relatively uniform cutbacks spread throughout the different regions;

iii *functional separation* between management and research and development in the 'centre', skilled labour in old manufacturing centres, and unskilled labour in the 'periphery';

iv *functional separation* between management and research and development in the 'centre', and semi- and unskilled labour in the 'periphery';

v   *functional separation* between management and research development and skilled labour in a 'central' economy, and unskilled labour in a peripheral economy;

vi *division* between one or more areas, which are characterised by investment, technical change and expansion, and other areas where unchanged and progressively less competitive production continue with resulting job loss. The former may involve the development of new products as well as new means of producing existing products.

As we noted above we should not analyse a given area as purely the product of a single form of the spatial division of labour. To do so is, as Sayer points out, to 'collapse all the historical results of several intersecting "spatial divisions of labour" into a rather misleading term which suggests some simple unitary empirical trend' (1982: 80). Rather any such area is, economically and socially, the overlapping and interdependent product of a number of these spatial divisions of labour and attendant forms of restructuring.

An important consequence of these processes is that uneven development does not simply take the form of *regional* inequality. This can be seen, firstly, by noting the following observations about the north-west which, according to Fothergill and Gudgin, was one of only two UK regions to possess a 'regional' industrial structure. Even here, though, there were the following assorted variations in a number of indicators of economic structure: in the percentage change in male employment between 1960 and 1977, from − 27.7 per cent (Liverpool) to + 15.6 per cent (Crewe); in female employment, from − 33.5 per cent (Rossendale) to + 58.7 per cent (Northwich); and in the 1980 ratio of female to male employees, from 0.534 per cent (Warrington) to 1.165 per cent (Southport). Indeed, from their own study Fothergill and Gudgin conclude that, with the decline in distinctively regional patterns of inequality, there are enormous, significantly local variations, and 'much greater contrasts within any region than between the regions themselves' (1979: 157).

The importance of these intra-regional variations is also supported by the analysis of recent migration patterns where it was found that 'intra-regional shifts of population have been shown to overwhelm inter-regional contrasts' (Kennett 1982: 40). Such intra-regional variations, moreover, have stemmed from the trend towards decentralisation within, and deconcentration between, urban labour markets. Kennett suggests that the long-standing drift to the south from peripheral regions is now less important than the centrifugal movement from cities which has spilled across arbitrary, regional boundaries (1982: 41). Considering just those local authorities enjoying special development-ment area status in 1982, highly diverse population shifts were experienced between 1971 and 1981, ranging from population losses of 10 to 16 per cent (Knowsley, Liverpool) to population gains of 10 to 12 per cent (Kerrier, Anglesey). Hence, as Kennett says: 'to make any meaningful interpretation of labour migration, local labour markets should be used' as the relevant unit of analysis (1982: 41).

Before elaborating some further reasons for the importance of local labour markets, three other points about recent population movements should be noted. First, there is an extraordinarily high rate of residence change; about five million people in Britain change where they live each year and this has obvious implications for class composition and recomposition (Kennett 1982: 47). Second, the nature of such composition and recomposition is also related to the patterns of migration flow into and out of any particular local economy and it is wholly inappropriate simply to consider *net* migration. Interestingly, contrary to neo-classical migration models, which postulate rapid in-migration in the prosperous labour markets and rapid out-migration in the least prosperous areas, there is in fact a strong positive relationship between in-migration and out-migration in different areas (see the scattergram in

Kennett 1982: 42). Third, the general shift of population from 'urban' areas and especially from the conurbations to less 'urban', more 'rural' areas has not simply resulted from changes in relative labour demand due to economic restructuring. It has also stemmed from an increased privatisation of civil society – or a rejection of certain, urban-based socialised forms of reproducing labour-power – tendencies made possible by the widespread growth of private transport.

Thus, Fothergill and Gudgin's research on shifts in manufacturing and service industry, alongside other studies on the restructuring of regional and local economies and analyses of recent trends in population growth and migration, all suggest that sub-regional *local* economies, are of particular significance within the contemporary British economy. These forms of restructuring produce new and significant local variations in class structures, an increasing significance of spatial deprivations based on the 'inferiority' of one's own class structure *vis à vis* other class structures and the increasing importance of struggles centred around defending or recapitalising the locality *vis à vis* other local/regional/international structures (see Urry 1981b; Harris 1983; Urry 1983b; on the second point, see Donnison and Soto 1980).

The following points summarise the reasons why patterns of spatial unevenness should not be viewed as taking a regional form:

1 The concept of 'region' is conceptually arbitrary and problematic (Grigg 1969; Urry 1981b).
2 Pre-existing patterns of regional specialisation have become overlaid by new forms of the spatial division of labour (Walker and Storper 1981; Massey and Meegan 1982).
3 The development of national and international branch circuits of capital led to a marked decrease in the degree to which productive systems are focused upon a particular region (Lipietz 1980).
4 The 'periphery–centre' pattern of new employment in the period from the mid-1960s to the 1970s produced a considerable reduction in regionally based variations of unemployment and economic activity rates (Keeble 1976: 71–85; Dunford *et al*. 1980: 12–13).
5 The major divisions in contemporary England no longer appear to be regionally based but are rather based on a three-fold division: between the south-east; what Donnison and Soto call 'middle England', i.e. Luton, Swindon, Coventry, Peterborough, etc.; and the old industrial north (1980: 140–2).
6 Internationalised capital is now so constituted that it is both relatively spatially indifferent as to location, and can distribute different parts of its global operations into different labour markets, so taking advantage of variations in the price, availability, skills and organisation of the local labour force. There is no reason why it will be regionally distributed (Westaway 1974; Massey 1981; Walker and Storper 1981; Urry 1981b).

7 There is increasing politicisation of economic change, that is, the allocation of economic activity (whether public or private) is significantly a matter of political organisation, although there are, as yet, no effective regionally based organisations in the UK.

Walker and Storper have neatly summarised the significance of some of these points within the USA:

> the past concentration of industry has created areas with the most experienced, skilled, well organised, high cost, and militant labour force; as a result many industries, not only those which are labour intensive, have found it advantageous to seek out greener pastures in the suburbs, small towns, the south and beyond.
>
> (Walker and Storper 1981: 496)

So far, however, I have considered these changes from the viewpoint of capital and the effects which it must necessarily bring about – and indeed this is something of a deficiency of much of the 'restructuring' literature. Nevertheless, it is crucially important to consider as well some aspects and effects which follow from the processes of production of wage-labour. The most important aspect of this is that, unlike other commodities, labour-power is not itself produced under capitalist relations of production (Lebowitz 1980; Urry 1981a). It is of course produced, but partly within domestic relations (within 'civil society'). Production involves not simply consuming commodities produced within the sphere of capitalist production, but rather through human labour systematically converting the use-values available for consumption into refreshed and energetic labour-power. Three aspects of this process are particularly noteworthy.

First, the fact that other inputs into the production of commodities, apart from land and unprocessed raw materials, are themselves capitalistically produced means that they are subject to a process of geographical levelling or homogenisation. This occurs as the spheres of production and circulation are developed and generalised, first within national economies, and then across national boundaries. This means both that industrial plants have greatly heightened locational freedom and are much less tied to particular spaces, and that competitive advantage in location can primarily be gained by exploiting differences in labour supply. The latter includes not simply the quantity and costs of labour-power within a given labour market, as neo-classical theory would propose, but also its skill level, the conditions under which its reproduction is effected and its reliability and susceptibility to control (Walker and Storper 1981: 497–500).

Second, the organisation of civil society is not something which simply mirrors the wider capitalist economy. Various forms of social struggle and practice should be viewed in part as attempts to maximise the distance between such an economy and civil society. For example Humphries argues

85

that the nineteenth century working class family can be so viewed, as providing insulation from the anarchy and exploitative relations of the dramatically expanding capitalist economy (1977).

Third, recent changes in the organisation of capital and of the state have changed the parameters within which such relations can be established and sustained. In particular, the growth of multi-plant enterprises and of national and international circuits of capital (rather than local/regional circuits) have reduced each individual centre of population to the status of a *labour pool*. The important linkages within a town or city are those which pass through the household, through civil society, and not through the private or public enterprises located within that area. The other linkages, involving the sale and purchase of commodities between enterprises, occur *across* the urban boundary. Cities are, thus, increasingly significant sites for the production of wage-labour. They are sites within which pools of labour-power are systematically created and reproduced. The urban area is a system of *production*, a relatively closed system comprised of a large number of interdependent, relatively privatised households wherein wage-labour is produced under conditions of systematically structured gender inequality (Broadbent 1977). Cities are not so much an interlocking economy of producing and consuming enterprises but a *community of subjects* who produce and who consume in order to produce. Moreover, this production is necessarily local, it is principally produced for the *local* market and, as such, is subject to the constraints of time imposed by the particular relations between households and workplaces. Cities are viewed as relatively independent labour pools, each comprised of a large number of separately producing households, linked with each other and competing for urban space. A substantial shift in the structuring of each urban locality has, therefore, taken place. Previously such localities were integrated within the production and reproduction of capital. However, as each urban locality is reduced to the status of a labour pool it ceases to be integrated within the production process of capital but, instead, becomes the sphere for the production of wage-labour, within the civil society.

These points help to explain why it is that 'rural' areas have become important locations for capital investment in recent years. International capital has been transformed, first, through an increasing spatial indifference, and second, by the fractionalising of its different global operations. Potential plants are often relatively small (even if part of massive multinationals) and capital will be relatively indifferent as to where they are located. Hence, labour-power assumes a particular importance as to location – and this includes differences in cost, skill, control and reproduction. Provided there is or could be sufficient labour in a 'rural' area then expansion may well take place in that (green field) site rather than in alternative urban areas. Cities have become relatively less distinctive entities, by-passed by various circuits of capital and of labour-power. Civil society is thus extended and, as a result of private transport, typical spatial constraints upon local civil societies are transcended. Individual subjects can increasingly choose where their labour-power is to be reproduced, in cities, or towns or 'rural' areas; and yet, at the same time, the organisation of the resulting local civil societies assumes a particular importance in the response of individual localities to economic restructuring and change.

LOCAL STRATIFICATION STRUCTURES

Four distinct local class structures that could be found in urban areas in the UK (ignoring ethnic differences) are:

i   large nationals or multinationals as dominant employers – smallish inter-mediate classes; large working class, either male or female, depending on supposed skill level;
ii state as dominant employer – largish intermediate classes; declining working class; high employment of women;
iii traditional small capitals as dominant employers – large petty bourgeois sector; largish male working class; lowish female employment;
iv private service-sector capitals as dominant employers – largish inter-mediate classes with high female component; smallish working class.

Certain points of clarification should be added. First, local *social* structures should be analysed as local civil societies and not merely as local *class* structures. A crucial, yet relatively unexplored, determinant of the con-sequences of such structures is that of the recruitment into, and expulsion from, distinct places within the social division of labour. These processes of the formation and reformation of social groupings involve analysing the changing structure of *local* markets, one important feature of which is geographical mobility within and between such markets. The social structures of rural areas will be exceptionally diverse because of both the variety of ways any such area may be located within agricultural divisions of labour and because of the complex patterns of inter-relationship between such an agricultural spatial division of labour and that area's location within other spatial divisions of labour. Finally, the competition between localities seeking, in Massey's phrase, to be 'struck by the lightning' of outside capital becomes an important focus of socio-political organisation within any locality, as well as ensuring that some such localities become constituted as a spatial reserve army through what Walker terms the 'lumpen-geography of capital' (1978: 32).

These points raise important issues related to the changing patterns of labour market segmentation. Kreckel (1980) has usefully distinguished a number of different processes of segmentation: namely, demarcation (craft unionists versus all other workers); exclusion (regularly employed adult white males versus those not so 'blessed'); solidarism (of workers employed in an enterprise, occupation or industry); inclusion (protecting and encircling

a skilled sub-market through corporation or occupation-specific qualifications); and exposure (of non-organised groups to easy replacement by
unemployed or marginal workers). However, this categorisation of strategies
ignores potential changes in the labour process which may effect some
homogenisation of labour market conditions; and transformations within the
capitalist economy which ensure that some of these strategies of segmentation
are spatially differentiated, particularly within different rural social relations.

First, the consequences of such developments may well produce social
polarisation within 'rural' areas. As Davies says:

> the introduction of industry allows particular sections of the local
> society to jump on the bandwagon represented by the industry, notably,
> sectors of the working class such as skilled workers, especially those
> near the area, and those sectors of the petty bourgeoisie whose capital
> is invested in retail consumption. A large percentage of the population
> will not participate, will have their relative life chances reduced . . . as
> they move further down the queue for the scarce social infrastructure
> which exists in the area.
>
> (1978: 96)

Second, when it is asserted that there are substantial increases in the
number of managerial and professional workers in rural areas, it should be
specified what kinds of labour market qualifications they possess – whether
these are 'inclusive' or 'general'. It should also be determined how these
workers are related to the functional division of labour characterising the
sectors involved, identifying in particular whether they function as a 'service
class' for capital, or as part of the state, or as relatively 'deskilled white-collar
workers'; and how they are related to the pertinent *spatial* divisions of labour,
and attendant forms of labour market segmentation, especially whether they
function within central, semi-peripheral or peripheral plants.

Third, in order to unravel the socio-political consequences of these
processes it is important to have some understanding of political struggles
prior to the recent period of restructuring and economic decline. Broadly
speaking, the most significant form of oppositional struggle within the
industrial period of British capitalism was economic militancy, combined
with support for separate political struggle within the Labour Party. This
pattern was found in the major urban-based industries – coal, steel, docks,
railways, engineering, automobiles, etc. In each case there were a number of
distinctive features: large numbers at each workplace, a high proportion of
male workers, some development of an occupational community and the
centrality of that industry to the national economy. Yet, at the same time,
many areas both urban and rural were not economically militant. It is now
necessary to consider not only what are the forms of politics typical of an
economy experiencing profound restructuring and decline but also what
effects this pattern will have on *existing* forms of political organisation.

88

CONCLUSION

In this chapter, I have attempted to demonstrate that various critical notions – of different, overlapping spatial divisions of labour, of all localities as sites for the reproduction of labour-power, of variations in local social structures, etc. – render problematic the notion that there are distinct 'rural' localities. The 'new international division of labour' involves not just the export of industrial employment to rural localities in the Third World – but also, to some extent, to such locations in the First World. This is highly variable, though, and will not ensure that there is a distinct rural social structure. However, although the effects may even heighten class relations within certain rural areas, the overall consequence must be to undermine important social bases for class actions.

Changes in the structuring of certain contemporary capitalist societies are such that new concepts are necessary in order to make sense of what I term 'former industrial countries', of which the UK is the leading example. Undoubtedly the changing relations between formerly urban-industrial and rural-agricultural areas are one aspect of this restructuring and the recomposition of the industrial classes of such countries. In this context, it is not only rural sociology which is losing its distinctive focus but also the categories and concepts applicable to theorising the 'urban' and the 'industrial'.

6

CAPITALIST PRODUCTION, SCIENTIFIC MANAGEMENT AND THE SERVICE CLASS*

INTRODUCTION

Changes in the organisation of production in capitalist societies have been understood in recent years as resulting from either the needs of capital accumulation, or from the dialectic of capital *and* the resistance of labour. In this chapter I do not wish to dispense with the insights that such formulations have generated. However, both such formulations ignore one particular set of developments which concern what has been discussed in the USA under the term 'professional-managerial class' thesis (see Walker 1979); or in Britain, the thesis of the 'service class' (see Goldthorpe 1982; Abercrombie and Urry 1983). In the next section I shall argue that changes in the organisation of capitalist production in the USA in the first third of this century partly resulted because 'management' was able to wrest control away from 'capital'. I shall consider what it was that made this possible. What was it that enabled new forms of management to develop, particularly the one known as scientific management? Why were there fewer constraints upon the development of management in the USA compared with countries in Western Europe, and in particular Britain?

Furthermore, the initial growth of scientific management, and of more complex managerial hierarchies generally, had a number of important consequences: to increase the size and powers of social groupings intermediate between capital and labour; to expand the number and influence of occupational professions; and to enlarge the systems of higher education and more generally of credentialism. In short, I shall suggest that the initial development of scientific management was a catalyst that provoked a major restructuring of capitalist America in which an extremely powerful professional-managerial or service class transformed the basic structuring of class relations. The USA, which is often taken to be the paradigmatic capitalist society, is paradoxically that society in which a profoundly significant third force (or 'class') gradually came in a sense to make itself, to realise some of its causal powers and thus

* This first appeared in A. Scott and M. Storper (eds) (1986) *Production, Work, Territory*, Hemel Hempstead, Herts: George Allen & Unwin.

to develop organisational and cultural resources separate in part from capital and labour. The particular features of the capital–labour relationship in the USA provided the context in which the 'service class' gradually came to make itself.

In the final section I shall consider the British experience over the same period. I shall show that management was not able to wrest control away from capital, that scientific management was implemented much less quickly and in a less thorough-going form, that its general effects were much more limited, and that there was nothing like the same growth of a 'service class' before the Second World War. Class structures are thus to be viewed as geographically specific. Variations in such class structures have, moreover, profoundly significant cumulative consequences. The contrast between Britain and the USA demonstrates that changes in technology and production cannot be separated from wider social structures and that these vary considerably.

MANAGEMENT, THE SERVICE CLASS AND AMERICAN SOCIETY

It is now commonplace to note that the growth of the factory had a profound effect in changing people's work habits and experiences. There was some shift from an orientation to task towards an orientation to time (see Thompson 1967). However, it is also clear that the growth of the factory did not result in a direct increase in the social control that capital exercised over labour. What Marx called the 'real subsumption' – of the labourer – was not simply brought about by the factory system. There is widespread evidence that before the development of 'scientific management' in its various forms the labourer was not generally placed under conditions of real subsumption by *capital*. There were three alternative bases of control: first, that exercised by skilled craft workers – as Nelson says, 'the factory of 1880 [in the USA] remained a congeries of craftsmen's shops rather than an integrated plant' (1975: 4; and see Braverman 1974; Montgomery 1979: Ch. 1 on union rules and mutual support); second, that effected by 'foremen,' especially through 'driving' the workers via authoritarian rule and physical compulsion (see Nelson 1975: Ch. 3 on the 'foreman's empire'); and third, that produced through 'internal contracting' by which contractors hired and fired their own employees, set their wages, disciplined them and determined the production methods to be used (see Littler 1978, 1982b: Ch. 11; Larson 1980: Ch. 3; Stark 1980).

There was of course great variation between different industries and areas as to which of these different forms of control were found; and indeed there was often a combination of such forms within a single enterprise. Littler suggests that internal contracting was important in the period up to 1914 in the following industries: iron and steel, foundries, coal, engineering, armaments, arsenals, potteries, glass, newspaper printing and clothing (1982b: Table 11.3; see also Clawson 1980: 74–9). Internal contracting was more common in the traditional industrial areas on the east coast, and was often structured along lines of ethnic division as waves of immigrants settled in the USA beginning in the east (Buttrick 1952; Soffer 1960; Littler 1982b: 165–71). It was also in certain cases, such as clothing, structured along lines of gender division (see Benenson 1982: 70). Thus, as Clawson points out, inside contracting was an importantly non-bureaucratic form of control since the contractor 'did production work as well as supervision, there were no set qualifications, no levels of authority, essentially no written documents or files were kept, and there were no codified rules (or very few rules)'(1980: 73). For the growth of 'management' and hence of managerial bureaucracies, this power of the inside contractor had to be substantially broken (see Stone 1974; Montgomery 1979, on how this constituted a form of 'workers' control'; see also Clawson 1980: Ch. 3).

It was a basic premise of all such systems of control in nineteenth century America that workers knew more than anyone else about how to do the detailed work and that they possessed the knowledge relating to the relevant labour process. Capitalist control was effected but only indirectly. It rested upon the power of skilled workers, foremen, or inside contractors, who exercised dictatorial control over labour, often of a patriarchal or racist form. Control was overwhelmingly 'personalistic' rather than bureaucratic. In general, as Hobsbawm argues, nineteenth-century capitalism operated 'not so much by directly subordinating large bodies of workers to employers, but by subcontracting exploitation and management' (Hobsbawm 1964: 297). Within about 30 years, however, much of this was to change in the USA. In the following discussion of the emergence of scientific management, I shall consider what it was that transformed the American social structure. In the mid-nineteenth century there were no middle managers in the USA; while the number of 'administrative employees' within American industry increased four and half times between 1899 and 1929, from 7.7 per cent to 18.0 per cent of total employment (Bendix 1956: 214; Chandler 1980: 11). The growth of 'management' and what I elsewhere term the 'socialisation of un-productive labour' (Abercrombie and Urry 1983: Ch. 6) occurred in the USA because of a struggle waged in part against both labour and capital. It is necessary to explain how and why this struggle was successful. Why was it that in, at least, parts of the USA labour lost its monopoly on the knowledge of the day-to-day organisation of work, and why did the form of capitalist control which had persisted during the nineteenth century collapse? Part of my approach here will be to try to examine the issue posed by Stark when he says of the growth of management that

the occupants of the new positions did not simply 'fill in' a set of 'empty places' created by forces completely divorced from their own activity,

92

but actually participated, within a constellation of struggling classes, in the creation of these positions themselves.

(1980: 101)

In particular, the development of a large-scale management involved overcoming two particular forms of resistance: on the one hand, from the workforce itself, especially from the skilled craftsmen; and on the other hand, from the owners and existing managers who believed that 'scientific' management was an unnecessary and dangerous expense (on the details of scientific management, see Taylor 1947; Littler 1982b). Montgomery argues that the basic principles of scientific management had been very widely accepted in the 1920s. These principles included the centralised planning and integrating of the successive stages of production; the systematic analysis of each distinct operation; detailed instruction and supervision of each worker in the performance of each discrete task; and the designing of wage payments to induce workers to do what they were told (1979: Ch. 5; Littler 1982b: 179–83).

The main conditions which facilitated this growth of scientific management in the USA, a development which had profound effects on the structure of American society, were: (a) technological changes which outstripped the capacity of craftsmen trained in traditional techniques to organise production in the way they had in the past (see Chandler 1980: 16–23); (b) growth in the size of enterprises and plants after 1865 (see Chandler 1980: 23–6, Herrmann 1981: 188, 388); (c) declining rate of profit and merger boom especially around the turn of the century (see Nelson 1959; Littler 1982b: Ch. 2); (d) dramatic growth of immigration, especially from 1897, which segregated and fragmented the labour force (see Foner 1955; Montgomery 1979: Ch. 2); (e) the growing strength of organised labour, especially between 1894 and 1919, and the perceived need by capital to deal with this (see Foner 1955; Montgomery 1979; Brech 1982; Dubofsky 1983); (f) the impact of the First World War and the growth of standardised product lines and corporatist state strategies (see Bendix 1956: 284–5; Stark 1980; Dubofsky 1983); (g) the growth in the numbers and influence of industrial engineers and their increasingly symbiotic relationship with corporate capital (see Noble 1979); and (h) the growth of progressivism between 1890 and 1920, which particularly involved the movement for 'improved efficiency' (see Kolko 1963; Palmer 1975; and on all of these points Urry 1986).

These conditions should be viewed as constituting an appropriate context within which 'management' began to challenge existing capital. The movement for scientific management not only emerged out of these conditions but also began to change them, as it provided the basis for the appearance of a fully fledged service class in the USA in the inter-war period. The term 'service class' here refers to all those places in the social division of labour which are involved in the management and supervision of the functions of capital (of control, reproduction and reconceptualisation), to the extent to which these are separated from capitalist ownership (see Renner 1978; Abercrombie and Urry 1983: Ch. 7; Goldthorpe 1982). The service class thus 'serves' capital as ownership and control become divorced; but as its own forms of intra-class organisation develop (universities and colleges, bureaucracies and careers, professions and credentials), it gradually comes to make itself a separate class, a class-in-struggle, opposed in part to both capital and labour.

The 'causal powers' of the service class are considerable. They are to restructure capitalist societies so as to maximise the divorce between conception and execution and to ensure the elaboration of highly differentiated and specific structures within which knowledge and science can be maximally developed. They are thus to deskill productive labourers and to maximise the educational requirements of places within the social division of labour. This implies the minimising of non-educational, non-achievement criteria for recruitment to such places; and the maximising of the income and resources devoted to education and science, and more generally to the sphere of 'reproduction'. The service class will thus possess powers to enlarge the structures, whether private or public, by which they can organise and 'service' private capitalist enterprises.

I shall try to show below that certain of these powers were realised in the USA in the inter-war period. They were in a sense set in motion by the early growth of scientific management, which led to the elaboration of the intra-class organisation central to the 'service class'. It is also important to note that the very movement for scientific management was well organised. The viewpoint was represented particularly strongly in the *Engineering Magazine* and the *Transactions of the American Society of Mechanical Engineers* and various organisations were formed such as the Efficiency Society, the Taylor Society and the Society for the Promotion of Scientific Management (see Copley 1923: vols I and II; Palmer 1975: 34–5). Crucial meetings were held, especially the 1903 meeting when Taylor read his paper on 'shop management' to the American Society of Mechanical Engineers. And although the 'movement' was characterised by considerable discussion (for example, over the importance of 'motion' studies), by 1912 and the hearings before the House of Representatives Special Committee there was widespread public awareness, and some acceptance, of the broad objectives of the new scientific managers (Nadworny 1955: Ch. 4). I shall now consider some aspects of their emergence, in particular that they were located in struggle with both labour *and* capital, and that to succeed they had to undermine resistance from both the work-force and from capitalists and existing foremen and managers who generally believed that a growth in 'scientific' management was an unnecessary expense that would undermine their own prerogatives (see Nelson 1975: 101). I will consider the first resistance of labour to the growth of scientific management.

The first struggle can be examined initially by reference to Braverman's

Labour and Monopoly Capital (1974). In this he argues that the development of scientific management involves the separation of conception and execution, the former coming to reside with capital, the latter with labour. However, as Burawoy argues, this is strictly speaking not correct: 'Rather than a separation of conception and execution, we find a separation of workers' conception and management's conception of workers' knowledge and management's knowledge' (1978: 277). Partly as a result, he argues, workers showed great ingenuity in opposing, outwitting, and defeating the agents of scientific management before, during and after the 'appropriation of knowledge'. However, up to about 1910 there was in fact relatively little union opposition to 'scientific management', partly because it had not been introduced into strongly unionised plants; while for the next ten years or so there was widespread opposition. This came initially through the American Federation of Labour (AFL) which was particularly important in attempting to protect the 'secrets of the craft' (Nadworny 1955: Ch. 4). Sam Gompers well realised how scientific management would 'reduce the number of skilled workers to the barest minimum' (cited in Nadworny 1955: 53), and the costs for labour were strongly emphasised in Professor Hoxie's report on scientific management prepared for the US Commission on Industrial Relations (see Nadworny 1955: Ch. 6). Apart from the opposition at the Watertown Arsenal (Aitken 1960), perhaps the most impressive opposition of labour to new forms of management was to be seen in the strike of the railroad carmen on the Illinois Central and Harriman lines, which lasted for nearly four years and involved about 30,000 workers (see Palmer 1975: 42). The carmen maintained an extraordinarily determined opposition to the transformation of their skilled trades which resulted from the attempt to introduce piece work and bonus systems, speed-ups, and time and motion studies. In the course of the strike, 533 strikers were jailed, 91 per cent of strikers were forced to move to cheaper housing, and sixteen men committed suicide (Palmer 1975: 42).

However, for all the sustained and militant opposition of some groups of craft workers to scientific management, such workers were generally unwilling to develop broad-based industrial alliances with semi-skilled and unskilled workers, especially immigrants, blacks or women workers. Benenson suggests that the very earliest industrial unions were established in industries where skilled workers were not threatened by displacement from the less skilled – as in coal and garment-making (Benenson 1982: 73, and generally on the organisation of different industries). The organisation of labour during this period was not simply the result of craft workers responding to the degradation of skill (as in Braverman's analysis), but was much more varied, geographically, industrially and historically, and involved differing and complex alliances of workers, not only struggling against specific 'deskilling' but much more generally over the forms of control, both within the workplace and the community (see Foner 1955; Palmer 1975).

By 1919–20 the opposition of labour to scientific management had partly subsided, although as Palmer points out this was much more true of the official union leadership than of all groups of works (1975: 41f). This reduced opposition resulted from a number of conditions. First, there were various semi-corporatist arrangements established in wartime, which ensured, as Person put it, 'labour's interest in good management and increased productivity' (1920: 20). Second, there was the more conciliatory and accommodating attitude of the engineers themselves. Thus, in 1917, C. B. Thompson argued that 'scientific managers have been freely advised to recognise more fully the necessity of cooperation with the unions' (1917: 269). Third, labour was decimated during the period 1919–20 when up to 20 per cent of the American labour force went on strike. One and a half million members were lost by the AFL (American Federation of Labour), and the union advocated a new doctrine of labour-management cooperation (see Brody 1980: 44–6).

I will now consider scientific management's other struggle, with capital and existing management. The starting point here is to recognise Burawoy's claim that 'one cannot *assume* the existence of a cohesive managerial and capitalist class that automatically recognises its true interests' (1978: 284). Indeed, the very growth of 'scientific management' in the USA in a sense reflects not so much the strength of capital and its ability to deskill labour but rather its relative weakness in the early years of this century, in particular to prevent the appropriation of effective economic possession by a new class of 'managers'.

This opposition from existing capital and management was well recognised at the time. C.B. Thompson described scientific management as a 'veritable storm-centre' (1917: 211), while H. Person talked of the general reluctance of most existing managements to undertake theoretically 'revolutionary improvements' rather than continue existing opportunistic practices which were, according to Litterer, 'increasingly chaotic, confused and wasteful' (Person 1920: 1–12; see also Litterer 1963: 370). Taylor himself stated in his testimony in 1912 to the Special House Committee to Investigate the Taylor and Other Systems of Shop Management that:

> nine-tenths of our trouble has been to 'bring' those on the management's side to do their fair share of the work and only one-tenth of our trouble has come on the workman's side. Invariably we find very great opposition on the part of those on the management's side to do their new duties.
>
> (Taylor 1947:43)

This was confirmed in Nelson's survey of 29 Taylorised plants where he found that opposition came both from foremen and supervisors, and more generally from existing management. Nelson concludes that 'the experts encountered more opposition from managers than workers' (1975: 75). For example:

96

Gantt encountered serious opposition from the management at the Sayles Bleachery and Joseph Bancroft & Sons, and less formidable problems at the Canadian Pacific shops; Barth antagonised his employers at the S. L. Moore Company and lost the confidence of the Yale & Towne officers; Gilbreth alienated the managers of the Herrmann, Aukam Company; SCAB. Thompson complained bitterly of the opposition he encountered from the supervisors at the Eaton, Crane & Pike Company; Cooke reported a similar experience at Forbes Lithograph; Sanford Thompson noted the suspicions of the managers at Eastern Manufacturing; Evans faced substantial opposition from certain superiors and many foremen; and the experts who worked at the Pimpton Press and Lewis Manufacturing Company found Kendall, Taylor's friend and admirer, a highly critical observer of their work.

(Noble 1979: 75)

One reason for the opposition of existing management was that Taylor attempted, as he put it, to substitute 'exact scientific investigation and knowledge for the old individual judgement or opinion, either of the workman or the boss' (1947: 31). This involved giving considerable autonomy to the industrial engineer. Layton argues that the effect was that 'Taylor has opened the possibility of an independent role for engineers in an area in which their position had been that of bureaucratic subordinates' (1971: 139).

The first and most obvious effect of the development of scientific management, or of complex managerial hierarchies more generally, was to produce a substantial change in the American occupational structure. Thus the ratio of administrative to production employees in manufacturing industry increased from 7.7 per cent to 17.9 per cent in the first third of this century (Bendix 1956: 218). Furthermore, over the same period the proportion of American workers in the tertiary or service sector increased from one-third to almost one-half (Sabolo 1975: 9). These changes were particularly important within the chemical and electrical industries which formed the vanguard of modern technology in the USA. The development of new innovations in these industries fostered the gradual 'electrification' and 'chemicalisation' of older, craft-based industries which thus rapidly acquired 'scientistic' features, partly through the recruitment of chemical and electrical engineers (Noble 1979: 18–19). This led to the growth of technical education, which was well summarised by Professor J. B. Turner's call to replace the 'laborious thinkers' produced by the classical colleges by the 'thinking labourers' necessary for industry (Noble 1979: 21). The emergent, technically trained, electrical and chemical engineers were predominantly employed within large corporations and promotion mainly consisted of movement within the corporation into management (see Layton 1974). Professional advancement consisted of promotion *within* the corporate hierarchies of the science-based industries. These professional engineers were

97

particularly significant in effecting major changes in the USA over the period 1860–1930: developing science-based industrial corporations, large industrial research laboratories with a heightened division of labour, integrating industrial and university-based research, ensuring an appropriate industry-based curriculum within the dramatically expanding university system, and encouraging the general development of modern management and related techniques (see Noble 1979: Part 2).

Thus, the development of engineers/managers helped to weld science and technology into the growing corporate structure, and this had the effect of further separating engineers/managers from the directly productive workers (see Noble 1979; Stark 1980; Abercrombie and Urry 1983: 149). This was in part because their growth served to generate an 'ideology of technical expertise' which then served other occupations as they systematised cognitive categories and developed new organisational forms in, as Stark puts it, 'their attempts to define and maintain their privileged position over and against the working class and [they] struggled to increase their autonomy from the capitalist class in the schools, the universities, and the state' (1980: 118; see also Burrage 1972; Larson 1977, on why they did not develop a full professional identity). The engineers thus provided a model of how education and industry were to be integrated over the course of the twentieth century as one occupation after another sought to strengthen its market-power by connecting together the production of knowledge with the production of the producers via the modern university. Schools of business administration had already been established, the first (the Wharton School of Finance and Commerce) in 1881, with others at Berkeley and Chicago following in 1898, at Dartmouth and New York University in 1900 and at Harvard as early as 1908 (Touraine 1974: 29). There was a structural linkage effected between two sets of elements, specific bodies of theoretical knowledge on the one hand, and markets for skilled services or labour on the other hand (see Larson 1980: 141–2, and 1977 more generally). Thus higher education became the means for bringing about professionalisation and for the substantial transformation of the restructuring of social inequality. As Noble puts it, 'the integration of formal education into the industrial structure weakened the traditional link between work experience and advancement, driving a wedge between managers and managed and separating the two by the college campus' (1979: 168, and see Chs 7 and 8 on the changing engineering curriculum). He goes on to note that in emphasising the role of formal education as a vital aspect of their professional identity, engineers at the same time laid the foundations for the educationally based system of occupational stratification that characterises the USA (1979: 168; see also Abercrombie and Urry 1983). Thus the very process of professionalisation contributed to the restructuring of the patterning of social inequality, to a system based on the salience of occupation, to legitimation via achievement of socially recognised expertise and to a heightened concentration on education and the possession of credentials (see Wiebe 1967: 121; Disco 1979: 179; Abercrombie and Urry 1983: Ch. 6).

This set of developments led to an extraordinary expansion of higher education in the half century after 1880. By 1930 the USA possessed more institutions of higher education than France possessed academic personnel and its university and college population was ten times larger than the secondary school population in France, while the population in the USA was only three times that of France in 1930 (see Debray 1981: 43–4; Mulhern 1981: 49). It would also seem plausible to suggest that this especially large increase in both the size of the middle classes and of the mobility into them in the USA – their proportion increased from 12 per cent to 22 per cent between 1900 and 1930 (see Kocka 1980: 19) – was one factor which prevented the development of strong work, market and political divisions between such employees and the working class in this period. Kocka talks of the 'indistinctness and relative insignificance of the collar line in industry' (1980: 117 and *passim*), although it should be noted that he attributes this to the lack of bureaucratic and corporate structures in pre-industrial America (compared particularly with Germany up to 1933).

One important reason for the development of a large number of occupations all pursuing a programme of professionalisation through colleges and universities was that the development of industrial engineering had raised but left unanswered a whole series of questions and issues concerned with the nature of work and the worker. Bendix summarises:

When Taylor and his followers proposed that the selection and training of workers be put on a scientific basis, they opened the way not to the promotion of industrial harmony on the basis of scientific findings, but to the involvement of industrialists in intellectual debates for which their training and interests had not prepared them.

(1956: 288)

Especially during the 1920s and 1930s a large-scale debate developed as to what workers were really like and how they could be appropriately motivated. A resulting battery of tests and testers emerged to investigate their typical attitudes and aptitudes (Bendix 1956: 289). This was associated with the more general bureaucratisation of industry and the realisation by management that the exercise of control would ideally involve the elaboration of rules, the delegation of authority, the specialisation of administrative functions and the development of complex systems of personnel investigation and management (Bendix 1956: 298; Baritz 1960: Ch. 4). Each of these developments presupposed new occupations, especially various branches of organisational psychology and sociology, which literally became in Baritz's term 'servants of power' and which copied the professionalisation strategy employed by the industrial engineers (see Baritz 1960; Church 1974, on the development of 'economists as experts'; Nelson 1975: Ch. 10). And this was part of a general movement which Wiebe summarises:

the specialised needs of an urban-industrial system came as a godsend to a middle stratum in the cities. Identification by way of their skills gave them the deference of their neighbours while opening natural avenues into the nation at large. Increasingly formal entry requirements into their occupations protected their prestige through exclusiveness.

(1967: 113)

He also points out that each of these groups, making up a 'service class', appeared first in the older, larger and more industrially developed cities in the north east. Wiebe talks of the development of 'an aggressive, optimistic, new middle class' sweeping all before it from about 1900 onward (1967: 166). This was then reflected in a further development of the 'helping professions', a process which should not be seen as simply one which involved responding to certain clearly defined 'social needs' (see Wiebe 1967; Bledstein 1976). But such professions should not be seen as purely autonomous since as Lasch argues we should not ignore 'the connection between the rise of modern professionalisn and the rise of professional management'; or more critically 'American professionalism has been corrupted by the managerial capitalism with which it is so closely allied' (1977: 17). Lasch points out the considerable similarities between the appropriation of knowledge, centralisation and deskilling in the industrial and in the non-industrial spheres of social activity, especially within the American health service (see Brown 1980). Hence, a powerful and wide-ranging 'service class' developed in the USA and its emergence weakened labour not merely in the sphere of work, but within most areas of social and political life.

BRITAIN AND THE 'SCIENTIFIC MANAGEMENT' MOVEMENT

In this section I shall explore some implications of what Littler illuminatingly terms the 'Ambrit' fallacy (1978: 187; 1982a: 145). By this he means the continual tendency to conflate the history and culture of two very different societies, namely the USA and Britain, and the attempt to draw significant sociological conclusions on the basis of this conflation between the two. Littler maintains that it is necessary to investigate the precise conditions and circumstances under which scientific management was introduced in each society, rather than to presume that there is almost a natural history of 'the deskilling of the capitalist labour process' (as is argued, for example, in Braverman 1974; and in rather different terms in Bendix 1956). In particular, Littler argues that scientific management was introduced into parts of American industry before the First World War during a period of economic expansion; in Britain by contrast scientific management, where it was introduced, occurred later – in the 1920s and 1930s during a period of profound economic depression (1982a: 145). Furthermore, the 'rationalisation' of work was not something which affected all industries to anything like the same degree. In the USA we have already seen that the transformations of the metal-working, electrical and chemical industries were particularly important (see Noble 1979). In Britain, the movement to scientific management primarily affected the food, drink, tobacco, chemical and textile industries (Littler 1982a: 145, 1982b: 114).

In the following section I shall, first, show that the 'Ambrit' fallacy is indeed a fallacy, since British developments did lag far behind the Americans. I shall also show that they also lagged considerably behind developments in certain other countries in Europe. In this I shall follow what has now been fairly clearly established in much of the literature, both by commentators at the time, like Cadbury, Devinat and Urwick, and by contemporary historians of economic and social change, such as Levine, Maier, and Wiener. My main purpose here will be to establish just why British industry failed to adopt new forms of managerial control and hierarchy and I shall argue that existing explanations are unsatisfactory. In particular, it is necessary to examine the balance of social forces. Far from scientific management being something that would be introduced unless resisted, it is rather the case that such innovations would *not* be introduced unless they are very specifically struggled for *and* unless undoubtedly widespread opposition can be effectively neutralised. Hence, although such developments are broadly 'functional' for capital, it does *not* follow that such functions explain either the growth of, or the persistence of, scientific management as a form by which capital controls labour. In particular, it is necessary to investigate the industrial and spatial variations involved in order to explain how and why struggles to 'scientise' management were only variably successful and in general were less successful in Britain than in the USA, Germany and Japan. Hence, in order to explain just why managerial change was particularly developed in the USA, it is necessary to show why the existing social forces there were not able to prevent change, whereas in the UK they were.

First, however, I shall briefly detail the restricted uptake of scientific management in the UK. Although, as Littler shows, some changes did occur in the period up to 1914 – development of piece work and other bonus systems, the gradual and variable replacement of internal contractors with a directly employed supervision system, and revived forms of paternalism (see Littler 1982b: Ch. 7; Burgess 1980: Ch. 4) – systematic schemes of scientific management aroused little or no interest amongst engineers and managers in this period and were very rarely implemented. Maier summarises:

Not merely did this reflect an industrial leadership set in its ways; an underlying satisfaction with decentralised production, with the premises of a liberal regime in a country where the middle classes felt little anxiety about the social order, postponed real interest until the economic difficulties of the 1920s and 1930s.

(1970: 37)

In 1911 the journal, *Engineer*, objected to American notions of scientific management with the comments that 'there are fair and unfair ways of diminishing labour costs . . . We do not hesitate to say that Taylorism is inhuman' (cited in Wiener 1981: 143; see also Urwick and Brech 1946: Ch. 7). Urwick summarised the reaction of capital by claiming that only a few employers here and there had given serious attention to Taylor's work and this was because the industrial *milieu* presented an infertile soil because of scepticism and apathy. There was an incapacity to understand that anything other than technology was of any consequence (1929: 58). He goes on to suggest that where employers did take up aspects of Taylor's work (even during and after the First World War) they tended to over-emphasise one particular aspect (such as 'welfare and psychology on costing or technical research') and as a result their 'business suffered the usual penalties of lack of balance' – because they then revised scientific methods, when what they needed was more science (Urwick 1929: 70).

Other contemporary commentators reinforced this interpretation. A. Shadwell, for example, the author of the monumental *Industrial Efficiency* (1906), maintained in 1916 that in British industry:

Very often there is no planning at all; it is left to the operative and rule of thumb. Generally there is planning of a rough and ready kind, but some of the most famous workplaces in the country are in such a state of chaos that the stuff seems to be turned out by accident.

(1916: 375–6)

Similarly critical comments were developed by J. A. Hobson in *Incentives in the New Industrial Order* (1922, but see 1913), and Sidney Webb in *The Works Manager Today* (1918), while Edward Cadbury pointed to the potential dehumanising consequences of the implementation of scientific management (1914a, although see 1914b). Levine details the specific lack of attention devoted to Taylor's seminal papers in the British engineering journals – for example, his 'Shop Management' was ignored by all four of the major British engineering journals (Levine 1967: 61). Levine classifies the reactions to scientific management into three types: the humanitarian, as in the quote from the *Engineer* above; the economic, as in the claim that scientific management was unnecessary in Britain because labour costs were lower; and the anti-scientistic, as in another leader from the *Engineer* in which it is claimed that 'too much science . . . is likely to lead to a decrease of efficiency rather than an increase' (25 April 1913: 443), or in E. T. Elbourne's view that 'golden rules' or organisation *per se* 'can never be a substitute for good men' (1914: 169).

Finally, we might note that in C. B. Thompson's survey conducted in 1917, he claimed to have found 201 factories where Taylorist schemes of management had been introduced – yet only four of these were in Britain (1917: 39; see also Levine 1967: 67). Likewise Levine, in his survey of the related development in mass production, maintains that there were very few traces in Britain in the period up to the First World War, particularly because of the failure to develop the characteristics of specialisation, standardisation and interchangeability (Levine 1967: 52–4).

There is some controversy as to when any widespread implementation of scientific management actually did occur in Britain. Certain commentators see the period of the First World War as marking some kind of watershed. Burgess, following Pollard, maintains that it 'was one of the major long-term effects of the War that it marked the widespread implementation in Britain of the methods of "scientific management"' (1980: 166; see also Pollard 1969: 53–6, 81–2). However, he cites no contemporary evidence for this and it seems more plausible to suggest that while the war did produce a number of significant effects, such as increased standardisation, advances in mass production techniques in government arsenals, and some erosion of skill differentials, the most important innovations in Britain did not take place until considerably later (see Littler 1982b: 99–100). Littler has drawn attention to the importance of the Bedaux system for the understanding of changes in management in Britain in the inter-war years (see Bedaux 1917; Livingstone 1969; Layton 1974; as well as Littler 1982a: 139–43, 1982b: Chs 8 and 9).

The Bedaux consultancy firm was begun in 1918 in Cleveland, Ohio, and within a few years Bedaux was the owner of two networks of consultants, one American, one international. His extraordinarily rapid financial success was particularly due to his salesmanship. As Littler points out, while Taylor was keen to justify his system intellectually, Bedaux simply set out to sell himself and his system to engineers and managers (1982b: 107). Moreover, while Taylor's system took a long time and was difficult to install (see Layton 1974), Bedaux's was quick and easy and involved relatively little change to the existing management structure. Indeed, the main innovation of Bedaux was to appear to have solved the problem the solution to which had eluded Taylor, namely the nature of the relationship between work and fatigue (see Layton 1974: 382). Bedaux claimed to be able to determine the exact proportions of the two necessary for the fulfilment of any task. Moreover, it was then possible to compare all the different tasks within the factory; they would all be based on particular combinations of work and rest. They could all be reduced to the same measuring grid and hence subject to a systematic control and monitoring system. At the same time, Bedaux built a fairly crude reward system into his proposals which is summarised by Livingstone:

If a man earned £3 a week for producing 40 articles, Bedaux offered him £4 a week if he produced 80. Put in these terms, the confidence trick is too obvious, but the logic was confused by jargon. . . . For instance, Bedaux always started from the premise that the man should have been producing 60 articles for his £3, and thus if he produced a third more – 80 – he got a third more pay – £4. What could be fairer?

(1969: 50)

An investigation of the Bedaux system by the AFL concluded that beneath its pseudo-scientific jargon it was basically a means of speeding up the work done with little consideration being paid to other aspects of good and efficient management (see Brown 1935). In other words, it enhanced the existing power of management at the expense of the workers and it gave managers an illusory sense of being able to understand and control efficiency (see Layton 1974: 382). Bedaux was in fact frequently criticised for not doing enough to improve methods of working and indeed for thrusting all the burden of increasing output on to the workers (see Littler 1982b: 112). Indeed the Taylor Society itself, fearful of the charge that they were concerned merely to 'speed up', struggled to dissociate itself from the Bedaux system (see Nadworny 1955: 134).

This system was widely adopted in Britain. In 1937, of the 1100 or so firms using it, 500 were American, over 200 British and 150 French (Littler 1982b: 113). The firms involved in Britain included many of the new and expanding firms of the 1930s – food processing (Huntley & Palmers), light engineering (GEC (Coventry)), motor components (British Goodrich Rubber Co. Ltd), chemicals (Boots Pure Drug Co.), and services (Vernons Ltd.), as well as certain older industries, particularly textiles (Wolsey Ltd) (see Littler 1982b: 114, and 1980: Appendix A). There are two important aspects of the implementation of the Bedaux system in the UK. First, in very few cases did its introduction involve the destruction of some long-established craft skill. Most of the industries in which it was introduced depended on semi-skilled or unskilled labour, not on craft labour. Even where there was some craft deskilling involved this seems to have occurred *before* the implementation of the Bedaux system (Littler 1982b: 128–30). Second, the introduction of this system activated considerable opposition and antagonism in the work-force. This was both because it brought about increases in unemployment during periods of already very high national and local unemployment, and because of the obvious resentments about being spied upon, and speed-ups at work. However, much of the opposition was unsuccessful so that strike action quickly evaporated (Littler 1982b: Ch. 9). Nevertheless, the effect of such resistance was that the unions often became *active* participants in creating and sustaining effort norms, a process reflected in the generally accommodatory response of the national unions and the TUC to Bedaux by the 1930s (as reflected, for example, in the TUC Report 1933: 16).

These developments during the 1930s did not involve the simple pattern of craft deskilling as suggested by Braverman. As Littler argues, the pattern of craft deskilling mainly occurred in a 'non-confrontational' manner through changes in occupational/industrial structure, that is, the growth of new industries, the emergence of new firms with different technologies, the development of new production processes and the spatial relocation of industries, firms and plants both within the UK and abroad (see Littler 1982b: 141). The introduction of Bedaux mainly occurred within these new industries and firms, where there were not well-established craft skills waiting to be 'deskilled'. Changes were nevertheless brought about in the 'confrontational' manner but these did not involve the simple destruction of craft skills – indeed the main effects of Bedaux were to 'legitimise' the speeding of work and of the introduction of new forms of control and payment, but not to 'restructure' management and its relationship with labour in anything like the fashion effected in the USA (through more thoroughgoing Taylorist systems). There was considerable worker resistance to the introduction of such schemes in the UK (also from foremen and supervisors; see Littler 1982b: 142–3) but this was not generally successful in preventing their implementation, only in modifying it.

So far, then, we have seen that management was restructured in the UK both later and in a far less thoroughgoing fashion than in the USA. Before analysing why this was the case I shall briefly consider what happened in the rest of Europe during this period (on related developments in Japan, see Wood and Kelly 1982: 80; also Littler 1982b: Ch. 10; in the USSR, see Wood and Kelly 1982: 81; for a contemporary account see Devinat 1927; for a general survey see Maier 1970).

The country which most rapidly copied American innovations in this area was Germany. According to Kocka, 'scientific management' first appeared in the workshops of large enterprises at the turn of the century (1978: 574; see Devinat 1927: 80–3). This partly stemmed from the fact that German entrepreneurs and managers took study trips to the USA in order to investigate the 'Taylor' system at first hand. But it also derived from pre-existing features of German society, namely the bureaucratic tradition which led to written instructions, precision and formalisation within organisational structures. Kocka maintains that from fairly early on a clear division was established within large engineering workshops between the preparations for and control of production on the one hand, and the execution of production on the other. There was also the widespread growth of offices including paperwork and card index systems, some standardisation of production, and reduction in the power of foremen, the growth of organisational specialists, and an increased devotion to science, technology and technical training (see also Levine 1967: 46, 75, 147). Such developments were moreover given a heightened impetus during the First World War (see Pichierri 1978).

Considerable interest in scientific management was also found in France before the First World War. In the eighteenth and nineteenth centuries French engineers had been in the vanguard of technological change and so they were among the first to study and attempt to implement Taylorist systems of management. Particularly important were Henry le Chatelier and Henri Fayol (see Devinat 1927: 30–2; Maier 1970: 37–8; Layton 1974: 379–80). The main industry where such theories were applied was the rapidly growing one of automobile production, especially at Renault and Packard (Layton 1974: 380). Fayol was important in developing the idea that parallel with already recognised functions of management there was also something he terms the 'administrative function' which covered forecasting, organisation, direction, coordination and supervision (Devinat 1927: 31). Generally it would seem that the *overall* impact of scientific management was less marked than in Germany, although it is interesting to note that in 1918 Clemenceau was suggesting that it was necessary to establish Taylorite planning departments (Copley 1923, vol. I: xxi).

There was no substantial international exchange of scientific management ideas until after the First World War. The first international congress was held in Prague in 1924 and attended by delegates from six European countries and from the USA. Further congresses were held in 1925 and 1927 when 1400 delegates heard over 170 papers (for details, see Urwick 1929: 75). In 1927 the ILO established at Geneva the International Management Institute to collate, classify and disseminate all known schemes of scientific management.

So far, then, I have shown that scientific management was established considerably later and in a weaker form in the UK compared particularly with the USA and partly with Germany and France (and, incidentally, Japan). There are a number of causes for this which I will discuss below. However, these causes should be viewed in a rather different light from the customary one. That is to say, their importance lies in the fact that they prevented the realisation of the 'causal powers' of the service class in Britain to anything like the degree to which they have been realised elsewhere, especially in the USA. These causal powers were not realised in the UK because there were other entities sufficiently strong and organised which were able to prevent the 'service class' emerging in the UK to restructure the society, particularly strong capitalist and working classes. Moreover, in Britain there was not the same development of appropriate 'collectivities-in-struggle' specific to the service class. Stark summarises the contrasting situation in the USA:

> In attempting to defend their claims to technical expertise or to maintain the currency value of their certified degrees, the members of these new occupations stand not with one foot in the working class and one foot in the capitalist class but with one foot in a professional association and one foot in a bureaucratic (corporate or state) organisation. The constellation of relations of conflict and alliance between these associ-

ations and other organisations arising from work, community, and political life must be the object of study in the analysis of class relations in the current period.
(Stark 1980: 119; see also Abercrombie and Urry 1983: 132–3)

I shall now try to summarise just why the service class in the UK was never able to realise its powers in a fashion remotely similar to that achieved in the USA in the first third of this century, a process under the leadership, as we have seen, of the industrial engineers. Four important features of the economic structure should initially be noted: first, family firms remained of much greater significance in Britain than elsewhere and there was little tendency for ownership and control to become divorced (Chandler 1976: 40); second, there was relatively little increase in the overall level of industrial concentration until after the First World War when the 1920s merger booms brought about substantial increases (Hannah 1976: 105); third, even in these industries where increases in industrial concentration did take place the owners did not try to construct an integrated and centralised administrative system (see Littler 1982b: 103, on the Calico Printers Association founded in 1899 which possessed 128 directors and eight managing directors!); and fourth, there was an extraordinarily high rate of capital export in the years up to 1914, so much so that in that year British investments accounted for over one-half of the world's total (see Burgess 1980: 113; see also Rubinstein 1977; Wiener 1981: 128–9, more generally). The consequence of these features was that industry remained relatively unchanged and subject to continuing forms of familial control. Alfred Marshall wrote in 1903 that '[Many] of the sons of manufacturers [were] content to follow mechanically the lead given by their fathers. They worked shorter hours, and they exerted themselves less to obtain new practical ideas than their fathers had done' (Marshall 1938: 21). At the same time there was an expanding and increasingly profitable development of finance-capital. The latter, as opposed to industrial-capital, 'was decidedly richer, more powerful, and possessed of a more distinguished historical pedigree . . . the City, with its centuries-old traditions, its location near the heart of upper-class England, and its gradually woven, closely knit ties to the aristocracy and gentry, enjoyed a social cachet that evaded industry' (Wiener 1981: 128). As a consequence, the financial institutions within the City of London did not greatly contribute to the financing of British industry, especially the new industries of electrical engineering and automobile production which in the USA were particularly significant sites for the implementation of Taylorism and Fordism (Wiener 1981: 129). Moreover, the enormous rewards from such overseas investment and the secure imperial markets both cushioned the British economy so that the pressures to restructure management were less intense (see Wood and Kelly 1982: 42; more generally, see Ingham 1982).

The effects of this were moreover particularly important because of the fact that Britain had been the first to industrialise and that broadly speaking its capital stock was of an older vintage compared with other economies (see Levine 1967: 122–3, on differences with the USA). New schemes of management would have been more likely to be introduced either where the latest technology was to be found, or where new capital investment was about to be implemented. Two examples where this restriction seems to have been an important factor preventing the development of new management structures in the UK were, first, in the high levels of existing investment in steam and gas in Britain which militated against the widespread development of electrification and hence of electrical engineering; and second, existing investments in iron and steel were so enormous that this fact in itself constituted a formidable barrier to change (see Levine 1967: 123–4). This problem was further exacerbated because of the essentially 'interconnected' nature of industrial organisation so that it was impossible to introduce any particular innovation without in effect restructuring the whole industry (see Frankel 1955). This was a particular problem in Britain for two reasons: first, because of the highly fragmented pattern of ownership in most of the leading industries; and second, because unlike the USA Britain was a national social and political entity which meant that it was much more difficult for new investments to be developed hundreds of miles away from those already established (see Littler 1982b: 183–5).

It is also widely claimed that wage levels were not high enough in Britain for them to provide a major incentive to introduce new management schemes. The share of wages in the national income, for example, fell steadily from the peak in 1893 so that by 1913 they constituted a smaller share than in 1907 (Pollard 1965: 101). Moreover, both money and real wages rose more slowly in Britain that in the other advanced economies after 1890 and indeed real wages fell in Britain from 1895–1913 (Brown and Browne 1968: 67). The coal mining industry was a good example of where employers were able to recruit labour at very low wage-rates before the First World War (see Levine 1967: 77). However, Levine convincingly shows that this is by no means a sufficient explanation (Levine 1967: 76–8). We have to consider both why managers and engineers could not force through appropriate changes and why workers, even if low paid, were able to resist. One reason for this is that according to Burgess 'there is substantial evidence to support the argument for increasing working-class "solidification" since the late 1870s, both at the workplace and in the community' (1980: 97). This is related to the growth in trade union membership from one million in 1889 to four million in 1913. Particularly if labour resisted it was much more difficult to invest elsewhere. Moreover, employers in Britain were unwilling to encourage their workers to share in the productivity gains that would result from a transformed managerial structure (see Littler 1982b: 95). British capital simply sought to keep wages as low as possible rather than to develop a high wages, high productivity economy. As a result it is hardly surprising that the rapidly unionising, community-organised labour movement was able to mount fairly effective and sustained opposition to any attempts to effect substantial managerial restructuring.

This was also true for another reason. As J. A. Hobson put it, the country's 'great business men' appear to have carved out their niche in the world without science or 'trained brains in others' (1922: 62; see also Levine 1967: 70). He points to their 'contemptuous scepticism of science and all that science stands for' (1922: 81). Alfred Marshall likewise maintained that England could not 'maintain her position in the world, unless she calls science to her aid in a much more thorough way than hitherto' (quoted in Levine 1967: 70). Particular deficiencies were noted with regard to the failure to apply the fruits of scientific knowledge and to develop the field of chemical engineering: Wedgwood's in 1994 claimed, for example, not to employ any chemists (Wiener 1981: 201). These problems moreover were effected in the general failure to develop anything like the same 'progressive' ideology which characterised the USA in the early years of this century. As Maier argues: 'Rationalisation in Europe, therefore, was only a stunted offspring of the American productive vision as originally conceived' (1970: 59). Indeed, the USA provided a very distinctive negative example, especially during the later years of the nineteenth century and the early years of the twentieth. Disparagement of the American way of life – one centred on idolising technology and wealth – became commonplace. Indeed Wiener suggests that the industrial revolution itself became redefined as a characteristically un-English event (1981: 88–90).

This in turn was related to the development of two preferred agents of management within British industry, agents that do not have the same significance in the USA. These two agents were the educated amateur, the 'gentleman' on the one hand, and the 'practical man', on the other (Wiener 1981: 138–9). The latter was in effect the defensive ideal of those who were excluded from functioning as the former, especially through the absence of an elite education. For them training on the job was central and they disparaged the value of education or formal training for their work. The twin cults of the two models, the educated amateur and the practical man, mutually reinforced opposition within management and industry to science, technology and to formal education. Coleman summarises: 'Economics, management techniques, industrial psychology: all were frequently looked upon with grave suspicion, for they represented attempts to professionalise an activity long carried on jointly by "practical men" and gentlemanly amateurs' (1973: 113). Management was typically not regarded as something to be pursued simply for itself but rather more as the *means* to something else, to politics, land-ownership, culture, or a position in the City (see Shanks 1963: 62). Management did not develop in Britain as a relatively autonomous set of interrelated professions, able to force through further widespread educational, technical and organisational reforms.

I have so far sought to establish that (a) the service class is a potentially powerful social entity within twentieth century capitalist societies; (b) the service class has substantially realised its powers within the USA – a process activated by, but not reducible to, the early and wide-ranging scientisation of management; and (c) for a number of reasons the service class did not realise its powers to anything like the same degree in the UK, where scientific management was introduced somewhat later and in a less far-reaching form, and where this class did not develop anything like the same institutional and organisational structures. I shall now mention certain of the consequences for British society which follow from point (c). Incidentally, these are not consequences which follow simply from the absence of a 'service class consciousness' because that was substantially absent in the USA. Rather, the service class in Britain before the Second World War did not possess sufficient organisational and cultural resources to produce a substantial restructuring of British society (on the importance of analysing a class's organisational and cultural resources, see Chapter 3). Although Goldthorpe (1982) most interestingly investigated this service class concept he does not examine two points being emphasised here: namely, that the service class is of variable significance in different periods in different capitalist societies, and that a class (especially this one) can exert powers whether or not that class develops a distinctive 'socio-cultural identity' (Goldthorpe 1982: 172).

Briefly, then, the consequences for British society of a weak 'service class' were as follows. First, the rapid development of the professions occurred before the growth of scientific management and thus much more under the sway of the landed-aristocratic class – the gentry model of 'status professionalism' rather than the bourgeois one of 'occupational professionalism' (see Elliott 1972; Larson 1977: 103; Wiener 1981: 15). Rubinstein summarises, particularly noting the spatial significance of London for this process of status professionalisation:

> The process of incorporation, acquisition of an expensive and palatial headquarters in central London, establishment of an apprenticeship system, limitations on entries, and scheduling of fees, are all manifestly designed to 'gentrify' the profession and make it acceptable to society. This aspect of professionalisation is profoundly anti-capitalist, and hence at odds with much of the rest of nineteenth-century British society.
> (Rubinstein 1977: 122; for further details, see Perkin 1961–2: 128–9)

Second, neither industrial engineers in particular nor managers in general became professionalised over this period in Britain. This is well demonstrated by the survey conducted by Nichols in the early 1960s – he concluded that the managers he interviewed

110

cannot be regarded as professionals. They lack professional management qualifications and were seldom members of professional bodies. They have a low level of participation in such bodies. And, most important, they deny the legitimacy of such bodies and very rarely accept even the *existence* of a body of management theory.

(1969: 88–9)

Moreover, of those few managers identifying themselves as professionals, none of them considered that they were professional *managers*.

Third, there was a much slower and less marked development of non-productive workers in British industry (compared with the USA or Germany). Thus in 1930 while the ratio of non-productive to productive workers was 17.9 per cent in American manufacturing industry, it was only 11.3 per cent in Britain (see Sargant Florence 1948: 143; although see also Burgess 1980: 203–4).

Fourth, educational qualifications continued to play a relatively less important role in British industry. In particular, Nichols maintained that there was only a 'limited and late development of institutions concerned with higher management education' (1969: 90). By contrast Kocka suggests that in Germany even by 1930 formal education was especially important for the recruitment of salaried entrepreneurs (1978: 583).

Fifth, the labour movement was not weakened in Britain in the way in which it was in the USA through the early deskilling effected through scientific management. At the same time there was a slower development of a successful industrial economy in Britain which could generate the high wages necessary to convert the trade unions into the kind of business unionism characteristic of the USA.

Sixth, formal educational qualifications played a less significant role in the UK as compared with the USA. Education in Britain remained far more tied to the pre-existing elite structures and was characterised by 'sponsored' rather than the 'contest' pattern as found in the USA (see Turner 1961).

Finally, there was much less development of the range of social sciences associated with assessing the output and characteristics of industrial workers. These were not seen as aspects which could be assessed scientifically; and as a consequence the social sciences did not develop to the same degree as in the USA or in such close harmony with the processes of occupational professionalisation as found in American universities.

7

IS BRITAIN THE FIRST
'POST-INDUSTRIAL SOCIETY'?*

David Shepherd, the Bishop of Liverpool, has said:

> Liverpool is sometimes dismissed as a maverick council and city . . .
> When we look back in 20 years' time, I believe that we shall see that
> it was the first, or one of the first, of many post-industrial cities.
>
> (cited in Halsall 1987)

In this chapter I want to assess this idea, that at least in parts of Britain
there is a sea change taking place in the dominant economic, social and
political structures. Once upon a time these could have been described as
'industrial' but they have now been transformed. It is argued that there has
been a qualitative change so that some parts of Britain are now to be described
as no longer industrial but as 'post-industrial'. I shall be concerned to analyse
what is meant by the idea of a society whose structures and typical modes of
experience are no longer based on manufacturing industry as providing the
central motor, its inner dynamism.

I hope to *demonstrate* through example the virtues of what C. Wright Mills
(1959) called a 'sociological imagination'. And I shall suggest that sociology
must be concerned with these big questions of social and cultural change and
that in doing so it cannot be based upon a narrow view of the social which
is separated off from the historical, economic, geographic, and political
dimensions of social life. Sociology must therefore concern itself with many
of its neighbouring social sciences. And indeed my view is that it provides a
particularly favourable intellectual and social space in which the findings,
arguments and theories from these various subjects can be brought together,
compared, juxtaposed and on occasions synthesised. Auguste Comte, the
early nineteenth century writer who 'invented' the term 'sociology', maintained that it should be the 'Queen' of the sciences. By contrast I would prefer
the more democratic and prosaic metaphor of sociology as the 'crossroads'
of the social sciences. It is the site where the arguments, findings and theories

* This was first given as an Inaugural Lecture delivered at Lancaster University on 18
March 1987.

relating to the fundamental sociality of human life can be brought together. Sociology is thus a centrally important social science in part because of the space it offers for drawing together the more 'social' aspects thrown up by, but not fully investigated by, its neighbours amongst the social sciences.

First, I shall summarise the thesis of the post-industrial (PI) society and refer to some of the evidence which supports the kind of argument that David Shepherd was advancing. Second, I shall show that although modern Western societies are indeed changing in quite spectacular ways, the specific PI society is insufficiently precise and glosses over some exceptionally important aspects of recent change. In particular, it will be shown that the thesis is overly 'economistic', it reduces social and political life to changes in the structure of the economy and fails to address complex transformations in the ways in which people *experience* such changes. Third, I shall consider the question of people's experiences more directly by analysing briefly how this had been transformed by the development of nineteenth century industrial and urban life, with the growth of the modern personality or of modernity. It will be suggested that such developments resulted in part from some extraordinary changes in the very way in which time and especially space were organised and structured in the emerging industrial world.

Finally, I shall return to the future, so to speak, and consider whether there may be developing some current changes of time and space which are setting the ground for supposedly postmodern experiences. Overall I shall argue that what has in fact been developing in Britain is not really the growth of some new form of *society*, that is post-industrial or postmodern or indeed as other writers have argued, post-capitalist. But rather that there has been the systematic breakdown in the existing structuring of society which I shall describe as 'organised'. There has been an extraordinary complex of changes which have begun to undermine, disrupt and disorganise the existing structures of social life – disruptions of economy, politics and culture which the notion of post-industrialism does not begin to grasp adequately. Britain is not then the first post-industrial society but it is one of the first 'former industrial countries' (what economists might I suppose call FICs) characterised by marked levels of *dis*-organisation.

First, then, I shall consider the PI society thesis in an absurdly truncated fashion (see Bell 1974). There are a number of points. First, there is taking place a major shift in the structure of employment in modern societies. Both primary and secondary production require decreasing labour inputs because of the exceptional possibilities for technological change and innovation. Especially in manufacturing industry there is a dramatic decline in the labour required per unit of output. Tertiary industry (services) by contrast is more labour-intensive and there are fewer chances of implementing labour-saving innovations. There has been as a result a major shift in the employment structure of modern economies with dramatically increasing numbers employed in the provision of services.

113

Second, there is a simultaneously marked increase in the demand for services. People's basic needs, especially for food, clothing, housing, do not rise as fast as real incomes rise; and out of such rising income there is increasing expenditure on services rather than on material goods.

Third, much labour in all forms of employment becomes increasingly based on 'theoretical knowledge' and its codification into abstract systems. The production, distribution and control of knowledge is the central characteristic of a PI society. Establishments concerned with education, research and information-handling assume a heightened importance.

Fourth, the individual firm becomes subject to increased government regulation as the whole society comes to be much more socially planned. There is a shift from the 'economising' mode of behaviour to what Daniel Bell terms a 'sociologising' mode, to take into account values, needs and human purposes, the 'public interest', that is not necessarily well-reflected in the market.

Fifth, there is a growing technocracy as those engaged in the planning and control of knowledge will gain increased power. Birth, property and family background become less important bases of social stratification than skill and education, or what Dore calls the 'diploma disease' (1976).

Sixth, there is the development of new social classes and social groups and the reduced importance of what Alain Touraine terms the 'old social classes' which were based on the ownership and the non-ownership of property. Overlaying those forms of social conflict are the new forms structured by divisions between those possessing and those not possessing certain forms of knowledge, between those employed in large bureaucracies and those excluded, and between those who are powerful technocrats and those who are not. Manufacturing industry no longer generates the social class divisions which structure the whole of society (Touraine 1974).

There is moreover plenty of empirical evidence to support elements of this thesis in modern Britain. Thus the proportion of the employed population working in manufacturing industry has fallen from 36 per cent in 1971 to 24 per cent in 1986; while the proportion of people working in service industry has risen from 52 per cent in 1971 to 67 per cent in 1986. Or to put it another way, in 1971 there was 1 manufacturing worker to 1.4 service workers; in 1986 the ratio was 1:2.7, almost double (*Employment Gazette*, January 1987). There has been a marked increase in those people working in non-manual occupations, from 1 in 7 in 1911 to nearly 1 in 3 in 1981; the proportion of the employed population in professional and managerial positions has risen from 1 in 7 in 1911 to over 1 in 4 in 1981 (OPCS 1991; Routh 1980: 5). The fastest growing areas of employment between 1971 and 1986 have been in hotels and catering, banking, finance insurance, and other services, such as government, education, leisure, research, etc., which have overall increased by over 60 per cent. Social conflicts as reflected in strike rates in different industries are at a markedly lower level in the service industries where only

114

9 per cent of such establishments recorded a strike/lockout in the previous year, compared with 27 per cent in manufacturing industry (calculated from Daniel and Milward 1983: table IX.II). There has also been the growth in the last twenty or so years of an amazing array of pressure and interest groups aiming in part to moderate the influence of the market and to ensure that 'social' criteria are partly brought to bear on matters of public policy. Of the groups listed in the *Guardian Directory of Pressure Groups and Representative Associations*, over half had been formed in the 1960s and 1970s (Lash and Urry 1987: 462).

To return briefly to Merseyside, David Shepherd made his comment about Liverpool as the first post-industrial city in the light of some recent developments: the reduction in the number of manufacturing workers from 240,000 in 1971 to 150,000 in 1981; the decline in the shipbuilding workforce from 20,000 to 3,500 in the past few years; the extraordinary success of the Garden Festival with 3.3 million visitors in 1984; the expected 5 million visitors a year to the transformed Albert Docks complex; the bewildering array of other tourist/service industries including the Tate Gallery of the North, and so on (Halsall 1987).

Thus far then I have summarised some of the main tenets of the PI thesis and briefly considered some of the empirical evidence which lends support to it. I shall now turn to consider some deficiencies of this argument. A first point to consider is that the thesis is a little dated. Thus Miller wrote of the American formulations in the 1960s that: 'the post-industrial society was a period of two or three years when GNP, social policy programme, and social research and universities were flourishing. Things have certainly changed' (1975: 25). There are two very obvious ways in which things have changed. First, there has been the growth of unemployment and of underemployment, now 20 per cent in Liverpool (*Employment Gazette*, March 1987). It is obviously much more sensible to talk of Liverpool and indeed many towns and cities as simply 'deindustrialised'. Second, it has clearly been part of Conservative Party policy to try fairly systematically to reverse certain aspects of the PI society. Although it has done more to encourage service industries through changes in its regional policy, it has by contrast attempted to undermine employment, funding and supposed power of the knowledge-based elite (as most of us are only too painfully aware!), and to re-emphasise the central role of the market, of 'economising' rather than 'sociologising'! As Riddell says of Thatcherism; it is an attempt to construct a society which is 'a cross between nineteenth century Birmingham and contemporary Hong Kong, located in Esher' (1983: 165).

Government policy is not the end of the matter though. One undoubted difficulty in the PI thesis is that there is considerable ambiguity in the very idea of a service itself. Two criteria are normally proposed; that the item can only be consumed at the point of production (such as a lecture, a haircut, a restaurant meal); and that the item takes a non-material form (such as consultation with a GP, live theatre, a seminar). The trouble is that not all services meet both criteria, and some, for example take-out meals from McDonald's, do not really meet either criterion.

Indeed some services really consist in part at least of material commodities and the more that this is the case then such industries may contain forms of scientifically managed and relatively less skilled labour similar to much of manufacturing industry. Indeed it may be more correct to think of modern societies as dualistic, with considerable differences maintained over time between those people who have relatively well-paid, skilled, secure jobs protected by unions or professional bodies and those who have less well-paid, relatively unskilled, part-time/temporary jobs which are not protected by either unions or professions. Jobs in the service industry consist of both of these, the division between the two often being drawn on gender, ethnic or age grounds (see discussion in Miles 1985). Three points should thus be noted about services at this point: most of us are service-producers, all of us are service-consumers, and services are an extremely heterogeneous category with few if any characteristics which unite them.

There is also only limited evidence that people do in fact increasingly wish to purchase services as such. Although there has been a dramatic increase in employment in service industry, there has been much less of an increase in spending on services *per se*. Thus while it is true that the higher a person's income, the greater the proportion of it that is spent on services, data over time show relatively little increase. Thus in Britain the proportion of the national income spent on services has risen from 9.5 per cent of total expenditure in 1954 to 12 per cent in 1985 (*Family Expenditure Survey*, 1986). The categories of expenditure to increase most over this period have been on housing and cars, whose proportions have both doubled. At the same time however there have been much faster increases in the prices of services as opposed to those of manufactured goods. This means that there has been a considerable increase in real expenditure on our homes, cars and consumer goods in the post-war period (see discussion of the 1954–74 period in Gershuny 1978: Ch. 5). There has thus been some growth of what Gershuny has described and analysed as the *self-service* society (Gershuny 1978; Gershuny and Miles 1983). Thus we entertain ourselves, drive ourselves, feed ourselves, do up our houses, using often highly sophisticated material goods produced within manufacturing industry. In a way then many of us are more skilled but that is the result of providing more services ourselves. At the same time, many of those working in services are in fact employed directly or indirectly in producing services *for manufacturing firms*, as accountants, lawyers, systems analysts, R. & D., etc. So while a very high proportion of the employed population are to be found in service employment, this does not at all mean that all those people are providing final services to the consumer. Perhaps up to half do not.

There are three other problems I want to discuss with the PI thesis. These might be described as the problems of history, geography and sociology. First, then, history. It is a commonplace to say that societies proceed through three economic stages, in which first primary industry, second secondary industry, and finally tertiary industry is the largest and most dynamic sector each in turn (normally called the Fisher-Clark thesis). At best however this thesis could apply to Western countries (and it does not work for Japan) but even in the case of Britain it is rather misleading. During the supposed heyday of Victorian manufacturing industry there was in fact a considerable growth of service industry, in both income and employment terms. By the beginning of the twentieth century only about 40 per cent of the national income stemmed from 'manufacture, mining, industry' and well over half was accounted for by a variety of services. *Employment* in services was also fairly high, accounting for 45 per cent of the labour force by 1911 and this was by no means all in domestic service (Deane and Coles 1962). Service employment was of course particularly important in the south east, as a result of the exceptional influence of the City of London, whose importance lay in the near monopolisation of the commercial activities necessary for the development of world, and not merely just of British, trade (see Ingham 1984).

The geographical problem is that there is considerable variation in the degree to which a post-industrial pattern is to be found. Indeed there are really marked variations within relatively limited areas. Consider the five urban areas identified in Liverpool in 1981. The proportion of higher professionals and managers varies by a factor of almost 7 between the area with the highest and lowest proportions; while the percentages of non-manual employees varies from 17 per cent to 38 per cent of the economically active population. Furthermore, the proportion of the workforce with higher education qualifications varies by a factor of 4 for men and by a factor of 5 for women. There was also twice as high a proportion of manufacturing employees in some areas than in others.

There is of course further geographical variation *between* cities both within a country and between countries. These variations reflect at least in part an international division of labour with certain service industries and occupations concentrated in particular cities, particularly those in which the headquarters of the major world corporations tend to be based. There has been the growth of what one can loosely term 'world cities' whose power and influence stem in part from providing the location of the headquarters of the major world manufacturing and services enterprises. They are thus substantially dependent upon the locational decisions of manufacturing firms and are not simply to be viewed as PI service cities. Liverpool most definitely is not a world city (except of course for two consumer services, namely music and football).

The sociological problem is perhaps the knottiest of all and concerns the degree to which these changes in the structure of the economy actually affect the ways in which people live their day-to-day lives. Is there some distinctive 'PI' way of thinking and feeling which somehow corresponds to these current economic changes? I shall approach this issue by briefly considering some of the ways in which it was thought that the growth of industrial society in the nineteenth century actually transformed people's day-to-day experiences, that it led to a modern consciousness or modernity. I shall suggest furthermore that central to these changes in the nature of modern life were amazing changes in how people's lives were organised through time and space.

I will begin here with one of the most perceptive early attempts to describe such changes in the nature of life in industrial Britain. This is to be found in *The Manifesto of the Communist Party*, where Marx and Engels wrote of the:

> Constant revolutionizing of production, uninterrupted disturbance of all social relations, everlasting uncertainty and agitation, distinguish the bourgeois epoch from all earlier times. All fixed, fast-frozen relationships . . . are swept away. . . . All that is solid melts into air, all that is holy is profaned.
>
> (Marx and Engels 1964: 53–4)

In other words, modern society is the first known society in which the dominant class has a vested interest in change, transformation, and in dissolving economic and social relations as fast as they come to be established. The bourgeois class thus moves within a profoundly tragic orbit. Marx and Engels wrote that:

> Modern bourgeois society, a society that has conjured up such gigantic means of production and exchange, is like the sorcerer who is no longer able to control the powers of the underworld that he has called up by his spells.
>
> (Marx and Engels 1964: 58)

There is thus a kind of permanent revolution involved. For modern society to flourish there has to be a continuous transformation in people's very personalities. They have to be much more fluid and open, they must strive for change and renewal, they must not long nostalgically for the fast-frozen relations of the real or fantasised past, and they should actively seek out new forms of activity and belief. Social life was thus transformed, particularly with the growth of large cities in which all sorts of people were thrown together, with the concentration of workers within uncharacteristically large workplaces, and with the transformed means of communication between these new industrial cities.

Two features of nineteenth century modern life are especially worth noting. First there was the modernisation of public urban space, the quintessential form being the Parisian boulevard, brilliantly designed by the irrepressible Baron von Haussmann, the Prefect of Paris, during the Second Empire (see Berman 1983). The boulevards were envisaged as arteries in a transformed system of urban circulation. Paris was developed as a unified physical and human space through which people could move at greatly enhanced speed. Distances were transformed and people came to accept as normal the multitude of casual, superficial contacts and experiences characteristic of normal urban life, the 'passing moment' as Baudelaire terms it (quoted Berman 1983: 133). The boulevards provided the context for new kinds of urban experience, particularly that of being privately close while under public gaze. This anonymity was particularly facilitated because of the growth of *traffic* which is the setting for Baudelaire's primal modern scene where he says (in translation): 'I was crossing the boulevard, in a great hurry, in the midst of a moving chaos, with death galloping at me from every side' (cited in Berman 1983: 159).

Second, in a way even more striking was the central importance of the growth of the railway in structuring the modern consciousness (see Schivelbusch 1980). What this development did was to bring machinery into the foreground of people's everyday experience outside the workplace. An incredibly powerful, moving mechanical apparatus became a relatively familiar feature of everyday life. Unfortunately for British Rail it was the second half of the *nineteenth* century that was the age of the train. This generated one of the most distinctive experiences of the modern world, restructuring the existing relations between nature, time and space. There were a number of amazing changes: the very building of the railways flattened and subdued nature; rail travellers were propelled through space as though they were mere parcels; the landscape came to be viewed as a swiftly passing series of framed panoramas; passengers were thrown together with large numbers of strangers in an enclosed space and new ways of maintaining social distance had to be learnt; the greatly faster speed of rail traffic meant that the existing patchwork of local times had to be replaced with a standardised time based on Greenwich; and the extraordinary mechanical power of the railway created its own space. A commentator wrote in 1839 that if railways were established all over England then the whole population:

> would . . . sit nearer to one another by two-thirds of the time which now respectively alienates them. . . . As distances were thus annihilated, the surface of our country would, as it were, shrivel in size until it became not much bigger than one immense city.
> (Cited in Schivelbusch 1986: 34; on other changes, see Kern 1983: 66–7 on the wireless, and 215–16 on the telephone)

I will now return from the nineteenth century to speculate a little more about the future. What are going to be the main changes in the structure of economic, social and political life as we approach the year 2000? What are the late twentieth century ways of experiencing the world corresponding to the boulevard and the railway? Are there some characteristic PI or 'postmodern' sites in which new kinds of personality are being constructed?

I will approach the final section of this chapter by suggesting that the problem about the distinction between industrial and PI societies is that too much emphasis is placed upon one aspect of economic change minimising other aspects of the social structure of Western countries. I want instead to argue that such societies are best thought of as having once been not simply 'industrial' but 'organised' during the first half to two-thirds of this century and that what is now happening in such societies is that a mutually reinforcing set of disruptions of those organised patterns has been established. There were a number of interconnected features of such organisation: increasing dominance of large national economic, social and political institutions over people's lives; increasing average size of workplaces; rising rate of capital concentration; banks, industry and the state working together; residence and plant locations becoming more and more urbanised; collective bargaining taking place more and more on a national scale; the industrial male working class reaching its greatest size; and politics and culture reflecting the confrontation of nationally organised social classes. British politics was very much structured by such divisions of social class. People largely lived in class homogeneous neighbourhoods, people voted significantly in terms of one class or another, other forms of politics took their patterning from divisions of social class. The considerable powers of the working class and the labour movement in Britain derived from the leading role of particular groups of workers – of mainly male workers living in certain major cities, mostly employed in large plants in manufacturing industry and mining. Relations within the workplace structured social conflict and political life. Furthermore, it seemed that these processes would continue to grow in importance – that is, that plants would get bigger and bigger, that Western economies would become increasingly monopolistic, that more and more people would live in large cities, that major manufacturing industries would increasingly dominate whole regions, that male-based trade unions would continue to grow in importance and so on.

That pattern has now shifted into reverse in many advanced Western societies and in the last decade or two they have begun to 'disorganise' as Scott Lash and I have argued at length elsewhere (see Lash and Urry 1987, 1994). Some Western societies such as the USA began this process at an early date; others, such as Sweden, rather recently. Britain began to disorganise somewhere in between. There are a number of interdependent processes involved.

The first point to note relates to the very term 'society' which I have been using quite often in this chapter. It is in some ways the central concept of sociology. It can be loosely defined as the complex of relations between the major social institutions within a given state-determined territory. Society corresponds to the nation-state. As such, relatively well-defined national societies are a fairly recent invention of human ingenuity. Moreover within a century or two of their invention they are already past their prime. A bewildering array of developments have recently occurred which have undermined the obvious coherence, wholeness and unity of individual societies. Such developments include the growth of multinational corporations whose annual turnover dwarfs the national income of some individual nation-states; the spectacular development of electronically transmitted information which enables geographically distant units to be organisationally unified; the fragile growth of means of mass communication which can simultaneously link 20–30 per cent of the world's population in a shared cultural experience; the possibility of technological disasters that know no national boundaries and the awesome realisation that human existence itself is dependent upon the relatively unpredictable decisions of the leaders of major powers. There has thus been a marked 'globalisation' of economic and social relationships and a greatly heightened awareness of the 'simultaneity' of events and experiences occurring in geographically distant locations.

Second, mass production of standardised products in manufacturing plants employing thousands of male workers will undoubtedly become a thing of the past. What manufacturing workers there are will increasingly produce more specialised products in plants employing considerably fewer workers with higher levels of capital equipment. There have been a number of interrelated changes in Britain: sizeable increases in the number of self-employed people; the growth in the size of the secondary labour force so that it is now calculated that one-third of the labour force consists of part-time, temporary and home workers; a considerable rise in the rate at which new firms have been formed and hence in the number of small firms in both manufacturing and service industry; a very large increase in the proportion of manufacturing employment to be found in small enterprises; a sizeable decline in the numbers of people employed in the average manufacturing plant even in very large multi-plant, multinational enterprises; a tendency for large firms to be broken up into smaller decentralised units, or to develop new forms of devolved ownership such as franchising or new sub-contracting arrangements which enable much more flexible responses to new products and markets (see Hakim 1987; Shutt and Whittington 1987; and Lash and Urry 1987).

Third, there have been enormous changes in the spatial organisation of production. Companies are now able to operate on a world scale, to move in and out of countries taking advantage of different wage and strike rates, to subdivide their operations in pursuit of a global strategy, to force workers to compete with each other to gain or keep new production. As the *New York Times* put it, firms had to 'automate, emigrate, or evaporate'. For example, the components that make up the Apple II E microcomputer are produced in a bewildering array of factories, in California and Texas in the USA, in Cork, Denmark and West Germany in Europe and in Japan, Taiwan, Singapore and various other countries in SE Asia (see Large 1983). The 42 chips that are put together in each Apple microcomputer have travelled in total at least a million miles before being combined together. The development of new forms of electronically transmitted information and of jet transport and travel have permitted extraordinary levels of vertical disintegration and spatial relocation. Even within the UK there has been a marked tendency for whatever new industry there is to be located outside the major cities and for there to be extremely high rates of depopulation from the major conurbations and a general growth of employment and population away from the industrial heartlands of Britain (see Lash and Urry 1987; also see Lash and Urry 1994, for analysis of more recent developments).

Furthermore, a fourth point is that employers appear to be much more mobile and innovative, the workforce seems to be increasingly reactionary – seeking to preserve or even to return to outmoded patterns of industry, technology and values. Employers increasingly appear as progressive, as being on the side of the new, as being not in favour of the *status quo* but in favour of change, breaking with tradition, and modernising for the future. Simultaneously, a number of developments have served to bring about a heightened identification of workers in the private sector with their firms. This has in turn encouraged a commitment to the career chances given by the firm's internal labour market, to becoming employee-shareholders, and to collective bargaining at the level of the individual enterprise.

Fifth, social life, culture and politics are no longer predominantly organised in terms of social class. This is partly because current inequalities of income, wealth and power do not produce homogeneous social classes which share common experiences of class deprivation, or even vote the same way at elections. It is also because a much wider variety of other social groups are now willing and able to organise. Such social movements struggle around issues of gender, the environment, nuclear weapons, urban inequalities, racial discrimination, social amenities, level of rates and so on. Such groups are generally organised on a relatively decentralised basis – in the case of urban riots no real organisation at all – and the focus of their hostility is particular to the 'state' and sometimes to the labour movement itself. Indeed we may well expect increasing amounts of social conflict simply because there are more bases now of opposition in contemporary Britain. In a paradoxical sense fewer and fewer groups have a strong vested interest in the *status quo*. But that in turn means that the labour movement no longer has a monopoly on principled opposition and struggle. Social conflict has become more pluralistic, structured by a much wider variety of interests, and involving very many different enemies including the state, bureaucracies, male trade unionists, white workers, and so on.

Finally, culture too has changed. Popular music, styles of dress, new developments in film, TV and theatre have been in part structured by a strong opposition to authority and especially to the authority of 'age'. It was an undoubted consequence of the political and cultural changes in the 1960s and

1970s that personal identity and individual self-assertion became highly valued goals of human experience in the West. But this emphasis not only challenges authority structures such as the family, the school, the monarchy, the police and courts and so on; it also questions the basis of joining and participating in collective organisations such as trade unions. As Raphael Samuel says: 'Collectivity . . . is seen rather as an instrument of coercion, promoting uniformity rather than diversity, intimidating the individual, and subordinating the minority to the unthinking mass' (Samuel 1985). There has thus grown up a suspicion of the centralised organisation, whether it is a trade union, a professional association, an educational institution, a political party or a pressure group. This kind of radical individualism has profoundly contradictory effects. It leads both to challenges to authority in many spheres of social life, *and* it makes it harder and harder to sustain collectivities and collective action. This set of developments has been generated by a number of significant processes: the growth of the electronic mass media, the disruption of class homogeneous neighbourhoods and the development of a relatively unattached middle class. It has been suggested that what results is a relatively depthless world in which people no longer pursue life-time projects or narratives and seek short-term advantage in a kind of 'calculating hedonism'. People's lives are not therefore viewed as the pursuit of ideals, or as part of a collective project. They are much more like those immortalised in the deeply cynical writings of Erving Goffman, of whose vision of human life Clifford Geertz has said: 'life is just a bowl of strategies' (1983: 25).

This is in turn connected with the growth of what postmodernist writers have described as the development of play, distance, spectacle, mobility and transgression. Some of the clearest examples of these can be found in contemporary architecture, one aspect of this being the development of some cities of consumption, as opposed to previously dominant industrial cities. To take just one example: it has been suggested that the shopping mall in West Edmonton in Canada represents the ultimate in this postmodern nirvana. The completed mall will be the ultimate temple of depthless consumerism, playfulness and hedonism. It is a mile long with over 800 shops, a 2.5-acre indoor lake with four deep-sea mini submarines, a reproduction Spanish galleon, dolphins, an eighteen-hole mini golf course, 40 restaurants, a 10-acre water park, a nineteenth century imitation Parisian boulevard (Haussmann will no doubt be turning in his grave), a New Orleans street with nightclubs, and a hotel offering a variety of theme rooms in such styles as Hollywood, Roman and Polynesian!

However, at the same time, there has been another interesting development in contemporary architecture – the development of vernacular or neo-vernacular design. Incidentally this can be seen locally in the Lancaster Plan where a distinctive Lancaster vernacular style has been identified and elaborated (Jencks 1991: 96–104; and see Bagguley *et al.* 1990). This development has become relatively widespread so that it would be fairly difficult these days to propose new shops, offices or houses in existing town centres which were not in part at least related to existing architectural style, building materials and the immediate context. As Jencks says, even large multinational developers these days adopt a form of local pastiche (1991). The main exceptions to this are to be found in residues of modernism such as Milton Keynes. While the modern movement viewed space as abstract, rational, homogeneous and the very essence of architecture, this post-modernist, neo-vernacular variant sees space as historically specific, rooted in conventions, particularistic, ambiguous and subordinate to context (see Edgar 1987, for a brief consideration of some political implications).

Such a shift is moreover part of a more general reaction against the modern and in a way against the future. It is part of a trend within post-industrial Britain – a kind of collective nostalgia not merely for the supposedly *Gemeinschaft* qualities of rural communities but for the skills, meanings and certainties of our immediate industrial past (see Turner 1987, on 'nostalgia'). As Britain becomes rapidly deindustrialised so a huge industry has grown up around the 'authentic' reconstruction of the workplaces, houses and streets of that industrial era. It is more than somewhat paradoxical that some of the least prepossessing sites of industrialisation have become transformed into some of the more successful tourist locations in contemporary Britain. Apart from the Albert Dock complex, other northern examples include Bradford, Wigan Pier, the Beamish Industrial Museum in the north-east, Black Country World in Dudley, Ironbridge Gorge and so on. It is as though once most people no longer work in industry so such industrial workplaces and streets become celebrated – they can be represented as part of our interesting past, part of our national heritage. As Patrick Wright asserts, there is something distinctive about 'living in an old country' (1985). Preservationism enables a kind of nationalisation of history but a nationalisation in which work, industry and indeed the working class become part of our national history. The PI thesis thus ignores how once industry has declined, so it can and will be celebrated and preserved. As Americans now say, all Britain is a museum. Nostalgia then for industrial times past is a widespread and permanent feature of PI Britain. It is believed that there has been a huge loss, that a plethora of skills, solidarities and meanings which were bound up with particular places, have been eroded for ever. The PI thesis is therefore far too modernist, it is based on the idea that history is future-oriented, and moves forward through time while the world of industry will be shunted to the sidings of history.

So to return to David Shepherd. We do live in a society which could be described as PI but that is not a very useful way of thinking about such developments. Culturally we live in a society where nostalgia, the vernacular and tradition mingle in a kind of pastiche with play, spectacle and transgression. Economically, the society is one in which the products of manufacturing industry are still absolutely central in providing us with goods that enable us to provide ourselves with services: but it is a national economy dislocated by both globalisation and fragmentation. Politically, Britain is a former industrial country and many of the certainties of politics derived from that period are dissolving before our eyes. At the same time that industrial past is endlessly available to us, to be mined and manufactured in political forms such as 'Victorian values' or the 'traditional working class'. That past will not as a consequence be evacuated from the centre stage of British culture for many decades to come.

Part III

CONSUMPTION, PLACE
AND IDENTITY

8

THE CONSUMPTION OF
TOURISM*

Tourists are vulgar, vulgar, vulgar.
(Henry James, cited Pearce and Moscardo 1986: 21)

INTRODUCTION

To the extent to which there can be said to be a sociology of consumption it has been mainly concerned with the differential purchase, use and symbolic significance of material objects. Such objects include not only housing but also clothes, cars, electrical goods, furniture and so on. In this chapter I shall suggest that this is an overly restricted focus and that there are a range of alternative items of consumption, of various services, which raise particular complex problems of interpretation and explanation. In particular I shall be concerned with those services related to tourism and holiday-making. It will be argued that interesting and complex issues arise with regard to the social relations surrounding such tourist-related services, in particular the nature of so-called 'positional goods'. A paradox will be detailed, namely, that, although within economics rather than sociology, some advance has been made in explaining the consumption patterns of tourist-related services, the conclusion of such work is that such consumption is indelibly social. Explaining the consumption of tourist services cannot be separated off from the social relations within which they are embedded.

Before turning directly to these issues, I shall outline a number of programmatic arguments. First, as already stated, the sociology of consumption must consider services as much as material objects. Indeed, given the importance of services in contemporary Western economies, one could well argue that the analysis of the social differentiations involved in services will now be of greater significance than is the case for material objects (see Urry 1988, for a review of such material).

Second, one particular kind of service that has been particularly under-examined by sociologists is that of travel. There is really no sociology of

* This first appeared in *Sociology*, 1990, vol. 24. I am very grateful for Alan Warde's comments.

travel. The two most useful kinds of analysis have been the work carried out by social historians, such as on the social impact of the railway in the nineteenth century, and the more recent cultural investigation, such as the social features of boulevard life which developed in the Paris of the Second Empire (see Perkin 1976; Berman 1983). One aspect that needs analysis is the democratisation of travel. Until the nineteenth century being able to travel, particularly for non-work reasons, was only available to a narrow elite and was itself a mark of status. This was true of all horse-drawn forms of transport. The mid- to late-nineteenth century development of the railway permitted mass travel for the first time. Status distinctions came to be drawn less between those who could and those who could not travel but between different classes of traveller. In the twentieth century further distinctions became drawn between different modes of transport (sea, air, rail) and between different forms that this took (scheduled/package air flights). But also as geographical movement became democratised so extensive distinctions of taste were established between different *places*. Where one travelled to became of considerable significance. In nineteenth century Britain this gave rise to a resort hierarchy with considerable differences of 'social tone' established between otherwise similar places (Perkin 1976; Urry 1987b).

Third, a further crucial feature of consumption is to be able to buy time, that is, the ability to avoid work and to replace it either with leisure or with other kinds of work. Veblen most famously investigated the social dynamics of a 'leisure class', that is the class that demonstrates esteem through leisure. He says that 'the characteristic feature of leisure-class life is a conspicuous exemption from all useful employment' (1912: 40). Now however in western societies, leisure patterns are immensely more complex than this. Everyone has at least some rights to leisure, to be conspicuously non-working for particular times in the week or the year. Being able to go on holiday, to be obviously not at work, is presumed to be a characteristic of modern citizenship which has become embodied into people's thinking about health and well-being. 'I need a holiday' is a particularly clear reflection of such a modern view of the need to consume time away from work. Sixty-three per cent of the UK population define as a 'necessity' at least one week's holiday a year without older relatives (Mack and Lansley 1985: 54).

Fourth, two further deficiencies of much writing about consumption are the presumption of an a-social individual and the supposition that consumption occurs without further work once an object has been purchased. These assumptions are not problematic for some relatively trivial kinds of consumption, where the purchase by an isolated individual of an object involves fairly direct consumption, such as a bar of chocolate. But most forms of consumption involve breaking with these two assumptions. This is first because much consumption is conducted by social groups, obviously by households, but also by large organisations (global corporations) and by informal social groups (buying a round in a bar). Forming a view as to the appropriate scale and nature of consumption is in all these cases irreducibly social and cannot be sensibly analysed by assuming utility-maximising isolated individuals (see Pahl 1984 on how 'consumption' involves household work strategies). The second assumption, that consumption equals purchase, is also often inappropriate since there is generally a considerable amount of work involved in transforming what is purchased (such as meat and vegetables) into an object of consumption (a hot meal). Much feminist literature on households, which demonstrates the fact that housework is *work*, brings this out very clearly. It means that there is here also a fundamentally *social* process and one often involving social relations of considerable inequality. Specifically, in relationship to tourism it is crucial to recognise how the consumption of tourist services is social. It normally involves a particular social grouping, a 'family' household, a 'couple', or a 'group'.

To a significant extent different kinds of holiday experience are devised with these different social groupings in mind. It is also clear that converting a range of tourist services into a satisfactory 'holiday' involves a great deal of 'work'. This work involves both the grouping itself determined to have a 'good time', and it involves those selling the services who, to varying degrees, try to guarantee a particular holiday experience (hoteliers, tour operators, restaurateurs, flight attendants, etc.). One problem however with tourist services is that there is a rather unclear relationship between the objects and services purchased (ice creams, flights to Majorca, etc.) and a good holiday experience. This is partly because many of these services involve the production and consumption of a particular *social* experience which cannot be reduced to, say, the details of a restaurant menu. This is an extremely difficult quality to ensure and to the extent that it is not provided (the surly waiter, the abrupt flight attendant, the careless amusement park attendant), so the customer will be dissatisfied although it may be difficult for management to identify just what is missing (Bagguley *et al.* 1990: Ch. 3). Moreover, at least part of the social experience involved in many tourist contexts is to be able to consume particular commodities in the company of others. Part of what people buy is in effect a particular social composition of other consumers, and this is difficult for the providers of the services to ensure. It is this which creates the 'ambience' of a particular cosmopolitan city, a stylish hotel, a lively nightclub and so on. The satisfaction is derived not from the individual act of consumption but from the fact that all sorts of other people are also consumers of the service and these people are deemed appropriate to the particular consumption in question.

Fifth, it is already clear that consumption in the case of many tourist services is a rather complex and inchoate process. This is because what is the minimal characteristic of tourist activity is the fact that we look at, or gaze upon, particular objects, such as piers, towers, old buildings, artistic objects, food, countryside and so on. The actual purchases in tourism (the hotel bed, the meal, the ticket, etc.) are often incidental to the gaze, which may be no more than a momentary view. Central to tourist consumption then is to look individually or collectively upon aspects of landscape or townscape which are distinctive, which signify an experience which contrasts with everyday experience. It is that gaze which gives a particular heightening to other elements of that experience, particularly to the sensual. In conclusion to this introductory section I shall summarise some key elements of the 'tourist gaze' which, as I have just suggested, is central to the consumption of tourist services (for much more detail see Urry 1990).

1 Tourism is a leisure activity which presupposes its opposite, namely regulated and organised work. It is one manifestation of how work and leisure are organised as separate and regulated spheres of social practice in 'modern' societies. Indeed being a tourist is one of the defining characteristics of being 'modern' and is bound up with major transformations of paid work. Work has come to be organised within particular places and to occur for regularised periods of time.

2 The tourist gaze arises from a movement of people to, and their stay in, various other destinations. This necessarily involves some movement through space, that is the journey, and a period of stay in a new place or places.

3 The journey and stay are to, and in, sites which are outside the normal places of residence and work. Periods of residence elsewhere are of a short-term and temporary nature. There is a clear intention to return 'home' within a relatively short period of time.

4 The places gazed upon are for purposes which are not directly connected with paid work and normally they offer some distinctive contrasts with work (both paid and unpaid).

5 A substantial proportion of the population of modern societies engages in such tourist practices, and new socialised forms of provision are developed in order to cope with the mass character of the 'tourist gaze' (as opposed to the individual character of 'travel').

6 Places are chosen to be gazed upon because there is an anticipation, especially through day-dreaming and fantasy, of intense pleasures, either on a different scale or involving different senses from those customarily encountered. Such anticipation is constructed and sustained through a variety of non-tourist practices, such as film, newspapers, TV, magazines, records and videos which construct that gaze. Such practices provide the signs in terms of which the holiday experiences are understood, so that what is then seen is interpreted in terms of these pre-given categories.

7 The gaze is directed to features of landscape and townscape which separate them off from everyday and routine experiences. Such aspects are viewed because they are taken to be in some sense out-of-the-ordinary. The viewing of such tourist sights often involves different forms of social

132

patterning, with a much greater sensitivity to visual elements of landscape or townscape than is normally found in everyday life. People linger over such a gaze which is then visually objectified or captured through photographs, postcards, films, models and so on. These enable the gaze to be endlessly reproduced and recaptured.

8 Moreover, the gaze is constructed through signs and tourism involves the collection of such signs. When for example tourists see two people kissing in Paris what they are gazing upon is 'timeless, romantic Paris'; when a small village in England is seen, tourists think they are gazing upon the 'real (merrie) England'. As Culler argues: 'the tourist is interested in everything as a sign of itself. . . . All over the world the unsung armies of semioticians, the tourists, are fanning out in search of the signs of Frenchness, typical Italian behaviour, exemplary Oriental scenes, typical American thruways, traditional English pubs' (1981: 127).

9 An array of tourist professionals develop who attempt to reproduce ever-new objects of the tourist gaze. These objects are located in a complex and changing hierarchy. This depends upon the interplay between, on the one hand, competition between different capitalist and state interests involved in the provision of such objects; and on the other hand, changing class, gender and generational distinctions of taste within the potential population of visitors.

In the following section I shall consider some of the contributions made by economists to understanding the complex processes of congestion and crowding which results from various social limits upon 'consuming' such objects of the tourist gaze. It will be shown that there are in fact two distinct forms of the gaze which have different implications both for visitors and for the objects gazed upon (such as 'lovers' in Paris, residents of quaint English villages, and so on).

THE SOCIAL LIMITS TO TOURISM

The economist Mishan presents one of the clearest accounts of the thesis that there are fundamental limits to the scale of contemporary tourism (1969). These limits derive from the immense costs of congestion and overcrowding. He perceptively writes of: 'the conflict of interest . . . between, on the one hand, the tourists, tourist agencies, traffic industries and ancillary services, to say nothing of governments anxious to augment their reserves of foreign currencies, and all those who care about preserving natural beauty on the other' (1969: 140). He quotes the example of Lake Tahoe, whose plant and animal life has been destroyed by sewage generated by the hotels built on its banks. A 1980s example would be the way in which the coral around tourist islands like Barbados is dying, both because of the pumping of raw sewage into the sea from the beachside hotels, and because locals remove both plants and fish from the coral to sell to tourists.

Mishan also notes that here is a conflict of interest between present and future generations which stems from the way in which travel and tourism are priced. The costs of the marginal tourist take no account of the additional congestion costs imposed by the extra tourist. These congestion costs include the generally undesirable effects of overcrowded beaches, a lack of peace and quiet and the destruction of the scenery. Moreover the environmentally sensitive tourist knows that there is nothing to be gained from delaying their visit to the place in question. Indeed if anything the incentive is the other way round. There is a strong pull to go as soon as possible – to enjoy the unspoiled view before the crowds get there! Mishan's perspective as someone appalled by the consequences of mass tourism can be seen from the following: 'the tourist trade, in a competitive scramble to uncover all places of once quiet repose, of wonder, beauty and historic interest to the money-flushed multitude, is in effect literally and irrevocably destroying them' (1969: 141). His middle-class, middle-aged elitism is never far from the surface. For example, he claims that it is the 'young and gullible' who are taken in by the fantasies dreamt up by the tourist industry.

However, Mishan's main criticism is that the spread of mass tourism does not in fact produce a democratisation of travel. It is an illusion which destroys the very places which are being visited. This is because geographical space is a strictly limited resource. Mishan says: 'what a few may enjoy in freedom the crowd necessarily destroys for itself' (1969: 142). Unless international agreement is reached (he suggested the immensely radical banning of all international air travel!), the next generation will inherit a world almost bereft of places of 'undisturbed natural beauty' (1969: 142). Therefore allowing the market to develop without regulation has the effect of destroying the very places which are the objects of the tourist gaze. Increasing numbers of such places come to suffer from the same pattern of destruction.

This pessimistic argument is criticised by Beckerman who makes two important points (1974: 50–2). First, concern for the effects of mass tourism is basically a 'middle class' anxiety (like much other environmental concern). This is because the really rich 'are quite safe from the masses in the very expensive resorts, or on their private yachts or private islands or secluded estates' (Beckerman 1974: 50–1). Second, most groups affected by mass tourism do in fact benefit from it, including even some of the pioneer visitors who return to find services available that were unobtainable when the number of visitors was small. Hence Beckerman talks of the 'narrow selfishness of the Mishan kind of complaint' (Beckerman 1974: 51).

This disagreement over the effects of mass tourism is given more theoretical weight in Hirsch's thesis on the social limits to growth (1978; see also Ellis and Dumar 1983). His starting point is similar to Mishan's when he notes that individual liberation through the exercise of consumer choice does not make those choices liberating for all individuals together (1978: 26). In particular he is concerned with the positional economy. This term refers to all aspects of goods, services, work, positions and other social relationships which are either scarce or subject to congestion or crowding. Competition is therefore zero-sum; as any one person consumes more of the goods in question, so someone else is forced to consume less. Supply cannot be increased, unlike the case of material goods where the processes of economic growth can usually ensure increased production. People's consumption of positional goods is relational. The satisfaction derived by each individual is not infinitely expandable but depends upon the position of one's own consumption to that of others. This can be termed coerced competition. Ellis and Heath define this as competition in which the status quo is not an option (1983: 16–19). It is normally assumed in economics that market exchanges are voluntary so that people freely choose whether or not to enter into the exchange relationship. However, in the case of coerced consumption people do not have such a choice. One has to participate even though at the end of the consumption process no one is necessarily better off. This can be summarised in the phrase: 'one has to run faster in order to stay still'. Hirsch cites the example of suburbanisation. People move to the suburbs to escape from the congestion in the city and to be nearer the quietness of the countryside. But as economic growth continues so the suburbs get more congested, they expand and so the original suburbanites are as far away from the countryside as they were originally. Hence they will seek new suburban housing closer to the countryside and so on. The individually rational actions of others make one worse off and each person cannot avoid participating in the leap-frogging process. No one is better off over time as a result of such coerced consumption.

Hirsch argues that much consumption has similar characteristics to the case of suburbanisation, namely that the satisfaction people derive from it depends upon the consumption choices of others. This can be seen most clearly in the case of certain goods which are scarce in an absolute sense. Examples cited here are 'old masters' or the 'natural landscape' where increased consumption by one leads directly to reduced consumption by another (although see Ellis and Heath 1978: 6–7). Hirsch also considers the cases where there is 'direct social scarcity', which are luxury or snob goods enjoyed because they are rare or expensive and possession of them indicates social status or good taste. Examples include jewellery, a residence in a particular part of London, or designer clothes. A further category Hirsch considers is that of 'incidental social scarcity', that is goods whose consumption yields satisfaction which is influenced by the relative extensiveness of use by others. Examples here include car purchase that doesn't lead to increased satisfaction because of the increased congestion as everyone else does the same; also the obtaining of educational qualifications but with no improved access to leadership positions because everyone else has been acquiring similar credentials (Ellis and Heath 1983: 10–11).

It is fairly easy to suggest examples of tourism which fit these various forms of scarcity. On the first, access to Windermere in the English Lake District is in a condition of absolute scarcity. One person's consumption is at the expense of someone else's. On the second, there are many holiday destinations which are consumed, not because they are intrinsically superior, but because they convey taste or superior status. For Europeans, the West Indies, West Africa and the Far East would be current examples, although these will change as mass tourism patterns themselves change. On the third, there are many tourist sites where people's satisfaction depends upon the degree of congestion, currently such as Greece. Hirsch quotes a middle-class professional who remarked that the development of cheap charter flights to a previously 'exotic' country means that 'now that I can afford to come here I know that it will be ruined' (1978: 167).

Although I have set out these different types of positional good identified by Hirsch, the distinctions between them are not consistently sustained and they merge into each other. Furthermore, there are a number of major difficulties in his argument. It is ambiguous just what is meant by consumption in the case of much tourism. Is it the ability to gaze at particular objects if necessary in the company of many others? Or is it to be able to gaze, without others being present? Or is it to be able to rent accommodation for a short period with a view of the object close at hand? Or finally, is it the ability to own property with a view of the object nearby? The problem arises,  as we have noted, because of the <u>importance of the gaze to touristic activity.</u> A gaze is after all <u>visual, it can literally take a split second, and the other services provided are in a sense peripheral to the fundamental process of consumption,</u> which is the capturing of the gaze. This means that the scarcities involved in tourism are more complex than Hirsch allows for. One strategy pursued by the tourist industry has been to initiate new developments which have permitted greatly increased numbers to gaze upon the same object. Examples include building huge hotel complexes away, say, from the coastline itself; the development of off-peak holidays so that the same view can be gazed upon throughout the year; devising holidays for different segments of the market so that a wider variety of potential visitors can see the same object; and the development of time-share accommodation so that the facilities can be used all of the year.

Moreover, the notion of scarcity is problematic for other reasons. I shall begin here by noting the distinction between the physical carrying capacity of a tourist site, and its perceptual capacity (Walter 1982). In the former sense it is clear when a mountain path literally cannot take any more walkers since it has been eroded and effectively has disappeared. Nevertheless, even here there are still thousands of *other* mountain paths that could be walked along and so the scarcity only applies to *this* path leading to *this* particular view, not to all paths along all mountains.

However, the notion of perceptual capacity further complicates the situation. Although the path may still be physically passable, it no longer signifies the pristine wilderness upon which the visitor had expected to gaze (Walter 1982: 296). Its perceptual carrying capacity would have been reached, but not its physical capacity. However, perceptual capacity is immensely variable and depends upon particular conceptions of nature and of the circumstances in which people expect to gaze upon it. Walter cites the example of an Alpine mountain. As a material good the mountain can be viewed for its grandeur, beauty and conformity to the idealised Alpine horn. There is almost no limit to this good. No matter how many people are looking at the mountain it still retains these qualities. However, the same mountain can be viewed as a positional good, as a kind of shrine to nature which individuals wish to enjoy in solitude. There is then a 'romantic' form of the tourist gaze, in which the emphasis is upon solitude, privacy and a personal, semi-spiritual relationship with the object of the gaze. Barthes characterises this viewpoint as found in the *Guide Bleu*: he talks of 'this bourgeois promoting of the mountains, this old Alpine myth . . . only mountains, gorges, defiles and torrents . . . seem to encourage a morality of effort and solitude' (1972: 74). For example, Stourhead Park in Wiltshire illustrates

> the romantic notion that the self is found not in society but in solitudinous contemplation of nature. Stourhead's garden is the perfect romantic landscape, with narrow paths winding among the trees and rhododendrons, grottoes, temples, a gothic cottage, all this around a much indented lake. . . . The garden is designed to be walked around in wonderment at Nature and the presence of other people immediately begins to impair this.
>
> (Walter 1982: 298)

When I discussed Mishan it was noted that he emphasised that 'undisturbed natural beauty' constituted the typical object of the tourist gaze. But this is only one kind of gaze, the 'romantic'. I shall now set out the characteristics of an alternative, which I shall call the 'collective' tourist gaze.

I will begin here by considering a different Wiltshire house and garden, Longleat, which is:

> a large stately home, set in a Capability Brown park; trees are deliberately thinned . . . so that you can see the park from the house, and the house from the park. Indeed the house is the focal point of the park . . . the brochure lists twenty-eight activities and facilities. . . . All this activity and the resulting crowds fit sympathetically into the tradition of the stately home; essentially the life of the aristocratic was public rather than private.
>
> (Walter 1982: 198)

137

In other words, such places are designed as public places. They would look strange if they were empty. It is in part other people who make such places. The collective gaze thus necessitates the presence of large numbers of other people, as are found for example in English seaside resorts. Other people give atmosphere to a place. They indicate that this is *the* place to be and that one should not be elsewhere. Indeed one of the problems for the contemporary English seaside resort is precisely that there are not enough other people to convey these sorts of messages. 'Brighton or Lyme Regis on a sunny summer's day with the beach to oneself would be an eerie experience' (Walter 1982: 298). It is the presence of other *tourists*, people just like oneself, that is actually necessary for the success of such places which depend upon the collective tourist gaze. This is particularly the case in major cities, whose uniqueness is their cosmopolitan character. The presence of people from all over the world (tourists in other words) gives capital cities their distinct excitement and glamour.

A further point here is that large numbers of other tourists do not simply generate congestion as the positional good argument would suggest. The presence of other tourists provides a market for the sorts of services that most tourists are in fact eager to purchase, such as accommodation, meals, drink, travel and entertainment. New Zealand is an interesting case here. Once one leaves the four major cities there are almost no such facilities because of the few visitors compared to the size of the country. The contrast with the Lake District in north-west England is most striking, given the scenic similarity.

Thus Hirsch's arguments about scarcity and positional competition mainly apply to those types of tourism characterised by the romantic gaze. Where the collective gaze is to be found then there is no problem about crowding and congestion. Indeed, Hirsch's argument rests on the notion that there are only a limited number of objects which can be viewed by the tourist. Yet in recent years there has been an enormous increase in the objects of the tourist gaze, far beyond those providing 'undisturbed natural beauty'. It was reported in a study conducted by the Cabinet Office in the UK that of all the tourist attractions open in 1983, half had been opened in the previous fifteen years (Cabinet Office 1985). Part of the reason for such an increase results from the fact that contemporary tourists are collectors of gazes. They are less interested in visiting the same place year after year. The initial gaze is what counts and people appear to have less and less interest in repeat visits (Blackpool being almost the exception that proves the rule).

There are two concluding points to note here. First, those who value solitude and a romantic tourist gaze do not see this as merely *one* way of regarding nature. They consider it as 'authentic', as real. And they attempt to make everyone else sacralise nature in the same sort of way. Romanticism has become widespread and generalised, spreading out from the upper and middle classes, although the notion of romantic nature is a fundamentally *catch 22*

invented pleasure. Yet the more that its adherents attempt to proselytise its virtues to others, the more the conditions of the romantic gaze are undermined: 'the romantic tourist is digging his [*sic*] own grave if he seeks to evangelise others to his own religion' (Walter 1982: 301). The romantic gaze is part of the mechanism by which tourism is spreading on a global scale and drawing almost every country into its ambit, thereby providing uniformity, minimising diversity, and encouraging the 'romantic' to seek ever new objects of the romantic gaze (see Turner and Ash 1975 on this extension of the 'pleasure periphery').

Second, the tourist gaze is increasingly signposted. There are markers which identify what things and places are worthy of our gaze. Such signposting identifies a relatively small number of tourist nodes. The result is that most tourists are concentrated within a very limited area. As Walter says, 'the sacred node provides a positional good that is destroyed by democratisation' (1982: 302). He in turn favours the view that there are 'gems to be found everywhere and in everything . . . there is no limit to what you will find' (Walter 1982: 302). We should get away from the tendency to construct the tourist gaze at a few selected sacred sites, and be much more catholic in the objects at which we may gaze. This has begun to occur in recent years, particularly with the development of industrial and heritage tourism. However, in part the signposts are designed to help people congregate and are in a sense an important element of the collective tourist gaze. Visitors come to learn that they can congregate in certain places and that is where the collective gaze will take place.

markers

I will conclude this section on the economic theory of tourism by noting the pervasiveness of the romantic as opposed to the collective gaze and the consequential problem of the positional good of many tourist sites:

★ class difference

> professional opinion-formers (brochure writers, teachers, Countryside Commission staff, etc.) are largely middle class and it is within the middle class that the romantic desire for positional goods is largely based. Romantic solitude thus has influential sponsors and gets good advertising. By contrast, the largely working class enjoyment of conviviality, sociability and being part of a crowd is often looked down upon by those concerned to conserve the environment. This is unfortunate, because it . . . exalts an activity that is available only to the privileged.
>
> (Walter 1982: 303)

CONCLUSION

I have tried to demonstrate here that the consumption of tourist services is important yet by no means easy to understand and explain. The importance derives from the centrality of tourist activities in modern societies. Indeed, elsewhere it will be argued that the way in which tourism has been historically separated from other activities, such as shopping, sport, culture, architecture and so on, is dissolving. The result of such a process is a universalising of the tourist gaze (see Ch. 9).

Sum.
✗

The difficulty of understanding tourist activities derives from the unclear character of just what is being consumed. I have suggested that it is crucial to recognise the visual character of tourism, that we gaze upon certain objects which in some ways stand out or speak to us. I have also shown there are two characteristic forms of such a gaze, the romantic and the collective, and that problems of congestion and positionality are very different in these two cases. More work needs to be undertaken on the impact of these different gazes on particular places, and how the providers of different services structure them in relationship to such different gazes. A particular issue is that of authenticity. It is argued especially by MacCannell that what tourists seek is the 'authentic', but that this is necessarily unsuccessful since those being gazed upon come to construct artificial sites which keep the inquisitive tourist away (MacCannell 1976, 1989). Tourist spaces are thus organised around what he calls 'staged authenticity'. Two points should be noted here. First, the lack of authenticity is much more of a problem for the 'romantic gaze' of the service class for whom naturalness and authenticity are essential components. It is less of a problem for those engaged in the collective tourist gaze where congregation is paramount. Second, it has recently been suggested that some tourists might best be described as 'post-tourists', people who almost delight in inauthenticity. The post-tourist finds pleasure in the multitude of games that can be played and knows that there is no authentic tourist experience. They know that the apparently authentic fishing village could not exist without the income from tourism or that the glossy brochure is a piece of pop culture. It is merely another game to be played at, another pastiched surface feature of postmodern experience.

9

TOURISM, TRAVEL AND THE MODERN SUBJECT*

INTRODUCTION

The modern subject is a subject on the move. Central to the idea of modernity is that of movement, that modern societies have brought about striking changes in the nature and experience of motion or travel. This has been explored by a number of seminal commentators who have discussed how modern cities have entailed new forms and experiences of travel, such as Baudelaire on the Haussmannisation of Paris, Simmel and Benjamin on the rush of life in a metropolis such as Berlin and Le Corbusier on the effects of the automobile on the urban experience (see Berman 1983; also Friedman and Lash 1992). There has been some analysis of the changing nature of transport between towns and cities, particularly following on the development of the railway (see MacKenzie and Richards 1986; Schivelbusch 1980). Also there is some general analysis of the impact of new technologies of transportation and communication, especially those of the late nineteenth and early twentieth centuries which dramatically increased 'time-space distanci- ation' (see Giddens 1981, 1984; also Kern 1983, and Harvey 1989 on 'time- space compression'). However, this literature does not connect together the changing forms of transportation *between* urban areas with the more general debates on the nature of the modern subject. Yet in many ways the modern world is inconceivable without these new forms of long-distance transporta- tion and travel. It is not the pedestrian *flâneur* who is emblematic of modernity but rather the train-passenger, car driver and jet plane passenger.

I shall examine some aspects of such travel and its implications for the modern subject in this chapter. In the next section, it will be argued that it is necessary to analyse the *social* organisation of travel and not to presume a technological determinism. Travel and tourism entail some striking changes in the nature of modern subjectivity. In the following section it will be shown that travel is intimately bound up with an increasing reflexivity about the physical and social world and that this is connected with the shift from legislation to interpretation. In the final substantive section analysis is

* This chapter first appeared in *Vrijetijd en Samemleving*, 1991, vol. 3/4.

provided of the nature of contemporary consumption. It is claimed that there has been a shift towards post-Fordist consumption and this entails the 'end of tourism' *per se*. There is a brief conclusion.

THE SOCIAL ORGANISATION OF TRAVEL

In much of the writing about various types of travel there is a technological determinism. Since each new system of transport appears in retrospect to be technologically superior to its predecessor, so it is argued that people quickly and readily found ways to travel which took full advantage of each latest technology. However, this is simply not the case. As important as new transportation technologies have been, it is organisational innovations which, in certain cases only, ensure that the new technologies have been economically successful and culturally emblematic of the modern world. Some examples of new technologies which illustrate the importance of organisational innovation include: the early railways where the railway companies did not at first realise the potential leisure and holiday possibilities of the new technology; the railways and steamships in the late nineteenth century which required the innovation of Thomas Cook's voucher system to develop their international market potential; the jet engine which required the innovation of the inclusive holiday organised by the tour operators to be fully successful; and Concorde which was a superior technology but where no corresponding innovation occurred within the travel industry. Transportation technologies therefore necessitate corresponding organisational transformations in order to be successful and to become dominant within a given historical period.

Another way of putting this is to emphasise the crucial significance of the *social* organisation of travel. This is after all a huge industry, and it is the industry which serves to organise the modern experience. None of the accounts of organised capitalism or Fordism take into account the changing ways in which travel is socially organised, a matter which as we have just seen is far more than merely a question of new transportation technologies. One interesting point to note is that the company which is conventionally taken to stand for twentieth century organised capitalism, namely Ford, actually made cars – that is, means of transportation. But the crucial question to ask is why people came to think, on the incredible scale that has occurred, that journeys by car were necessary, desirable and safe? How were those car journeys socially organised, involving as they did novel and potentially risky ways of transcending space? What has been the relationship between those journeys and those undertaken by other means of transport, or other forms of communication?

Some of these limitations of analysis are now coming to be evident, especially within the new 'urban studies' literature. The causes and consequences of mobility are increasingly seen as central determinants of the nature of urban life. This has been classically shown in the case of nineteenth century Paris and twentieth century Los Angeles (see Berman 1983 on the former; and Soja 1989 and Davis 1990 on the latter). But there are two aspects of the study of mobility that have not been much investigated. These are the social organisation of mobility *between* urban areas, and the effects of such movement on people's subjectivity in the modern world.

First then, certain organisational innovations have transformed the nature of travel in ways which have often been highly socialised. Some examples of this include Thomas Cook and Son who, beginning in the 1840s, were the first major travel agent and tour operator (see Brendon 1991); the growth of monumental city centre hotels in the late nineteenth century (see Mennell 1985); the inter-war development of holiday camps providing far superior facilities for mass tourists (see Ward and Hardy 1986); and the immense growth in the post-war period of package or inclusive holidays that made foreign travel available to the mass market in northern Europe (see Urry 1990).

The recent work on risk can begin to provide the explanation of why these innovations have been so significant. As Giddens says, one of the key features of modernity is that social relations are disembedded from local contexts of action (1991a: 209). Disembedding means the 'lifting out' of social relations from local involvements and their recombination across larger spans of time and space. Such disembedding depends upon trust, people must have faith in institutions or processes of which they possess only limited knowledge. Trust arises from the development of expert or professional knowledge which gives people faith in the forms of transport which convey them through time-space. Mobility depends upon the development of trust in professional experts who have developed systems of mass travel and transport which limit the risk involved.

Brendon (1991) has recently described the role of Thomas and John Cook in the middle to late nineteenth century who first constructed professional expertise in travel and tourism, expertise which made journeys relatively risk-free. Many of the early travellers with Thomas Cook eloquently describe his role in reducing risk and generating trust, even where the travel involved what now seem to be quite staggering feats of endurance, danger and uncertainty. Likewise Sontag wrote of how photography is a risk-reducing stratagem enabling people:

> to take possession of space in which they are insecure..... The very activity of taking pictures is soothing and assuages general feelings of disorientation. . . . Unsure of other responses, they take a picture.
>
> (Sontag 1979: 9–10)

Giddens makes some further comments about the growth of this kind of professional expertise. First, it involves a deskilling of day-to-day activity. In the case of travel people have lost that knowledge of local routes and environments which enabled often quite extraordinary distances to be travelled by foot (this is well shown in the diaries of the Lake District poets).

Second, there is no straightforward 'colonisation of the life-world' by such expert systems. There is always a tension between expert knowledge and that held by lay actors. In the case of travel the availability of an enormous written literature means that people are by no means only dependent upon travel industry professionals.

Third, it also does not follow that impersonal forms of knowledge simply dominate personal experience. Rather the very nature of the person or the personal is transformed in modernity. This can be seen in a number of ways: that trust is not something simply given but has to be worked at and continually negotiated and contested; that in modernity people have to learn to 'open' out to others who are often geographically very distant – to develop something of a cosmopolitan attitude; and that the self participates in the collective forms of reflexive knowledge that modern societies have about themselves. Giddens concludes: 'We can live "in" the world of modernity much more comprehensively than was ever possible before the advent of modern systems of representation, transportation and communication' (Giddens 1991a: 211).

Further, living 'in' the world of modernity is even more complex than this account suggests, since these modern systems generate quite novel forms of experience which cannot be reduced to, for example, Giddens' concept of time-space distanciation (see Urry 1991). Rapid forms of mobility have radical effects on how people actually *experience* the modern world, indeed on the very production of subjectivity. These effects include the way that landscapes and townscapes have come to be typically viewed as through a frame; that landscape consists of a series of swiftly passing panoramas; that nature can and should be subdued, or flattened or even by-passed; that new public areas should develop, such as railway stations, airports, hotels and so on, where novel norms of social life apply; that mobility has to be socially organised and involves forms of surveillance and regulation (especially true with car travel); that new forms of social distance have to be learnt within the confined contexts of mobility (generalisation of Simmel's blasé attitude); that social life has to be timetabled and hence the importance of clock-time, the telephone, diaries, secretaries, the filofax, answering machines, and so on; that people come to gaze at many different places which can be compared and juxtaposed with each other; and that multitudinous 'place-myths' develop which come to organise people's knowledge of themselves and of their social world (see Schivelbusch 1980; MacKenzie and Richards 1986; Ousby 1990; Shields 1991; Urry 1991).

Mobility is therefore responsible for altering how people appear to experience the modern world, changing both their forms of subjectivity and sociability and their aesthetic appreciation of nature, landscapes, townscapes and other societies. Such mobility according to MacCannell (1989) has the effect of legitimating modern society, of it appearing in a benign and accessible form. Many of the objects of the tourist gaze are functionally equivalent to the objects of religious pilgrimage in traditional society. When people travel (make a pilgrimage) to the great tourist sites of the modern world, MacCannell suggests that they are in effect worshipping their own society.

AESTHETIC REFLEXIVITY AND THE 'INTERPRETER'

However, there is one crucial aspect of modernity which MacCannell ignores, namely reflexivity. It is increasingly argued that a key aspect of modern societies is that people are able to monitor and evaluate their society and its place within the world, both historically and geographically. The more that societies modernise, the greater the ability of increasingly knowledgeable subjects to reflect upon their social conditions of existence. This can be characterised as 'reflexive modernisation' (see Lash 1991). Such reflexivity is normally viewed in the Habermasian tradition as being cognitive or normative (1981). However, reflexivity can also be aesthetic. This involves the proliferation of images and symbols operating at the level of feeling and consolidated around judgements of taste and distinction about different natures and different societies. Such distinctions presuppose the extra-ordinary growth of mobility, both within and between nation-states. This can be described as the development of an aesthetic 'cosmopolitanism' rather than a normative and cognitive 'emancipation' (see Lash 1991). Such a cosmopolitanism presupposes extensive patterns of mobility, a stance of openness to others, a willingness to take risks and an ability to reflect upon and judge aesthetically between different natures, places and societies, both now and in the past. Indeed the present fascination with history (the 'heritage industry') is not solely the product of the capitalist commodification of history but is an element of reflexive modernisation (see Chapter 11 for further discussion).

This argument thus consists of a number of steps: first, that in the 'west' over the course of the nineteenth and twentieth centuries a reflexivity about the value of different physical and social environments has been established (see Ousby 1990); second, that this reflexivity is partly based upon aesthetic judgements and stems from the proliferation of many forms of real and simulated mobility; third, that this mobility has served to authorise an increased stance of cosmopolitanism – an ability to experience, to discriminate and to risk different natures and societies, historically and geographically; and fourth, that the social organisation of travel and tourism has facilitated and structured such a cosmopolitanism. Mobility, especially that which is non-routine and non-work related, is thus not the trivial and peripheral activity which it has been presumed to be within the academy (as resulting from the dichotomies mentioned above). It is central to aesthetic reflexivity and becomes ever more important as 'culture', 'history' and the 'environment' are increasingly central elements of the culture of contemporary western societies.

modernity

This can in turn be connected to recent debates on postmodernity via Bauman's (1987) analysis of the changing role of knowledge and intellectuals. In modernity the emphases are upon an orderly totality, the search for control, and an increasing and irreversible knowledge of the natural order. Intellectual work is that of 'legislating', making authoritative statements which arbitrate. This authority to arbitrate is legitimised by superior knowledge. Various procedural rules ensure truth, moral judgement and artistic taste. Modernity produces intellectuals as 'legislators', experts who, as we saw above, minimise risk and generate trust for the mass of the population.

post-mod.

Postmodernity by contrast proclaims the end of certainty. There are an unlimited number of models of order, each of which makes sense in terms of the practices which validate it. Validation is particular to a given practice, including modernity's own criteria which can be seen to be historically specific. Systems of knowledge can only be evaluated from within, from inside a given, local, or specific framework (Bauman 1987). Intellectual work is no longer that of a legislator but an 'interpreter'. It consists of translating statements, facilitating communication, and preventing the distortion of meaning. What remains for intellectuals to do is to interpret meanings for those outside and to mediate communication between different provinces of meaning. Systems of meaning are moreover roughly equivalent to each other, not higher or lower in some hierarchy of truth, value or aesthetics (for further discussion, see Urry 1990: Ch. 5).

How does this shift relate to the previous discussion of modernity and mobility? First, there have been comparable changes in the forms of professional expertise supplied by the tourism and travel industry. There has been a shift away from the didactic legislator who instructed visitors where to look, what to look for, and when to look, the attitude as found in Baedeker's guides, Michelin's guides or the *Guide Bleu* (see Barthes 1972).

Instead visitors are encouraged to look with interest on an enormous diversity of artefacts, cultures and systems of meaning. None are presumed to be superior and the main role of the 'expert' is to interpret them for the visitor. Indeed whole new bodies of expertise have developed which are precisely concerned with 'interpretation' (see for example the journal *Heritage Interpretation*). At the same time it is presumed that certain kinds of people have the prior knowledge, values or aesthetic insight to benefit from mobility. Provided people can pay, everyone (in certain north Atlantic countries and Japan) is entitled to travel and to engage in, for example, the democratic and promiscuous practices of photography (see Sontag 1979). Likewise travellers can visit museums which these days may contain artefacts of almost every sort, from mundane household objects to instruments of torture, from representations of manual work to those of elite occupations (see Urry 1990: Ch. 6). In each case the professionals are concerned to interpret and not evaluate. Aesthetic reflexivity is at least in theory open at all.

Today

In the following section I will consider whether such postmodernity is also

146

reflected in changing travel and tourist practices. And does the social organisation of travel parallel shifts which appear to be taking place in other spheres of economic, social and cultural life?

POST-FORDIST CONSUMPTION AND THE 'END OF TOURISM'

In Lash and Urry (1987) we argued that capitalism moved through a series of historical states: liberal, organised and disorganised. Each of these appears to be associated with a particular dominant configuration of travel and tourism. These are set out below in Table 9.1, together with the pattern identifiable in pre-capitalist societies (and see Lash and Urry 1994: Ch. 10).

Table 9.1 Capitalism, tourism and travel

Form of society	Form of travel
pre-capitalism	organised exploration
liberal capitalism	individual travel by the rich
organised capitalism	organised mass tourism
disorganised capitalism	the 'end of tourism'

Paralleling these developments in travel have been some associated developments in the nature of 'hospitality'. Heal (1990: 389) suggests that open hospitality is practised in those societies characterised by a presumed naturalness of the host–guest relationship, a belief that the outsider is deserving of special generosity, an elite ethos in which honour attaches to acts of beneficence, an ideology of generosity to all comers, and a social system in which gift-exchange transactions remain structurally significant. In the early modern period in England (1400–1700) she shows that there was a relatively sophisticated law of generosity to defined guests, but increasingly there was separation between hospitality to the prosperous and alms given to the poor. Most of the other conditions of open hospitality were much less visible in England than elsewhere. Already a fairly extensive system of inns and ale houses had developed by the end of the sixteenth century. Hospitality was becoming commercialised and being taken out of the context of the household (Heal 1990: Ch. 5). Heal argues that this resulted from the existence in England of an economic and social structure which proved very responsive to the forces of the market, even to the marketisation of hospitality.

If then pre-capitalist societies contain a mixture of open and commercialised hospitality, liberal capitalism ushers in a much more commercialised pattern, linked especially to the railway. In London, for example, many grand hotels were constructed in the late nineteenth century. These were very much public places open to all with money, for wealthy men and women, to see and

147

be seen in. Such hotels necessitated new forms of rationalised organisation so that meals could be produced much more rapidly (see Mennell 1985: Ch. 6, on the innovations introduced by Escoffier). By the end of the century organised mass tourism was well on its way in Britain, as hospitality and travel became not merely commercialised but packaged and organised. Elsewhere Scott Lash and I show that if disorganised capitalism involves the dominance of non-material forms of production (especially images), then in many ways this is what tourism has always involved (Lash and Urry 1994). Does this therefore mean that tourism presages disorganised capitalism? Indeed is it therefore the 'industry' which is paradigmatic of disorganised capitalism as automobiles were of organised capitalism? If disorganised capitalism involves the predominance of culture, consumption, the global, the local and concern for the environment, then all these characterise contemporary travel and hospitality. Disorganised capitalism then seems to be the epoch in which, as tourism's specificity dissolves, so tourism comes to take over and organise much contemporary social and cultural experience. Disorganised capitalism then involves the 'end of tourism'. People are tourists most of the time whether they are literally mobile or only experience simulated mobility through the incredible fluidity of multiple signs and electronic images.

The purchase of images has become extraordinarily widespread and means that the purchase and consumption of visual property is in no way confined to specific tourist practices. Almost all aspects of social life have been aestheticised. This means that visual consumption can occur in many different contexts, cultures and so on. To take one paradigmatic example: the publicity material for the West Edmonton shopping mall in Canada demonstrates this very clearly:

> Imagine visiting Disneyland, Malibu Beach, Bourbon Street, the San Diego Zoo, Rodeo Drive in Beverly Hills and Australia's Great Barrier Reef . . . in one weekend and under one roof. . . . Billed as the world's largest shopping complex of its kind, the Mall covers 110 acres and features 628 stores, 110 restaurants, 19 theatres . . . a five-acre water park with a glass dome that is over 19 storeys high. . . . Contemplate the Mall's indoor lake complete with four submarines . . . Fantasyland Hotel has given its rooms a variety of themes: one floor holds Classical Roman rooms, another '1001 Nights' Arabian rooms, Polynesian rooms . . . .
>
> (Travel Alberta n.d.)

In recent years then visual consumption has become exceptionally more widespread and pervasive, although it seems that the 'new middle classes' lead the way in developing such roles of consumption (see Urry 1990; Featherstone 1991). This reflects what elsewhere has been termed social and cultural 'de-differentiation' (see Lash 1990b). The modern period was one of vertical and horizontal differentiation, the development of many separate institutional, normative and aesthetic spheres each with its specific conventions and modes of evaluation and with multiple separations of high and low culture, science and life, auratic art and popular pleasures and so on (see Urry 1990: 83–5).

Postmodernism involves de-differentiation. There is a breakdown of the distinctiveness of each sphere and of the criteria governing each. There is an implosion via the pervasive effects of the media and the aestheticisation of everyday life. Cultural spheres are much less auratic. There is a shift from contemplation of consumption, or from 'high culture' to the 'high street'. Some of the differences between the cultural object and the audience dissolve. And finally postmodernism problematises the relationship between representations and reality, since what we increasingly consume are signs or images: so there is no simple 'reality' separate from such modes of representation. What is consumed in tourism are visual signs and sometimes simulacrum; and this is what is consumed when we are supposedly not acting as tourists at all.

The significance of visual consumption can be seen in the pervasive tendency to produce 'themed' environments, such as the townscapes of elsewhereness found in the West Edmonton Mall. Eco (1986) terms these apparently real and authentic environments 'travels in hyper-reality'. The surfaces of such places appear more 'real' than the original. Eco summarises: 'Disneyland tells us that technology can give us more reality than nature can' (1986: 44). Two contexts in which such simulated reality is commonplace are shopping centres and world fairs. In both people are encouraged to gaze upon and collect the signs and images of many cultures – to act as tourists, in other words (Urry 1990: Ch. 7). This is made possible by the most extreme form of 'time-space compression', what one might term global miniaturisation.

Contributing to this proliferation of images has been the huge growth in choice for consumers. This can be seen by briefly considering the extraordinary development over the past few decades of the social practice of eating out. Twenty or thirty years ago this practice tended to be confined for most people to the holiday period. Apart from work canteens it was fairly rare for people to go out to restaurants for pleasure unless they were on holiday. Now however this practice has become exceptionally commonplace, having been taken to the furthest extreme in the US. There is now one restaurant for every 1000 people in the average American city, with perhaps 10,000 restaurants in Chicago, for example (Pillsbury 1990: 6). The number of restaurants in the US doubled between the 1960s and the 1980s (Pillsbury 1990: 103). Likewise there are said to be at least 100 different restaurant cuisines in the typical American city. As Pillsbury says: 'The great migrations, the acculturalization process, and the food technology explosion have brought exotic new foods to virtually all communities at low cost' (Pillsbury 1990: 130). Many of these new cuisines have been tried out first in California which has provided a kind of testing ground for cuisines even when they are apparently based on other regions of North America (see Pillsbury 1990: 86, on the very varied restaurant activity ratios in different American cities).

This range of consumer alternatives can also be seen in the extraordinary number of countries that can now be visited throughout the world, particularly because of the role of international agencies, such as the World Bank, the Inter-American Development Bank, the United Nations Development Programme, the Organization of American States and the European Community (Pearce 1989: 45–8). Choice can also be seen in the remarkable range of holidays that can now be taken even within say Britain. These include Xenophobic Weekends, Blearly Breaks, Murder Weekends, Bureaucratic Breaks, Soccer Weekends, City Breaks in Wigan, Boring Weekends in Grantham, and visits to 'Belfast – a Hibernian Rio'! And finally, over the past few decades there has been an incredible increase in the range of museums to visit, either while away or within one's own area. It seems that a new museum opens every week or so in Britain. Some of the more improbable museums worldwide include a pencil museum in Keswick, Auschwitz, the Leprosy Museum in Bergen, a sex museum in Amsterdam, a dental museum in London, a shoe museum in Street, a chemical museum in Widnes, a prisoner-of-war museum in Singapore, Granada's Coronation Street museum in Manchester, as well as a possible on Robben Island featuring Nelson Mandela's former prison cell (see Urry 1990: Ch. 6).

This proliferation of choice partly stems from certain kinds of resistance on the part of consumers. The mass holiday in which all consumers were treated as relatively similar has apparently declined in popularity, especially for younger, more affluent sectors of the population. Poon (1989), for example, talks of the shift from 'old tourism', which involved packaging and standardisation, to 'new tourism', which is segmented, flexible and customised. The Marketing Director of British Airways writes, for example, of 'the end of mass marketing in the travel business . . . we are going to be much more sophisticated in the way we segment our markets' (cited in Poon 1989: 94; see also Pearce 1989: Ch. 4).

In conclusion then, I will summarise how this shift away from mass packaged tourism might be said to reflect the rather broader change towards so-called 'post-Fordist' consumption. This can be seen in Table 9.2, together with examples drawn from the tourism industry.

CONCLUSION

Travel and tourism thus transform the modern and postmodern subject. This has been shown with regard to new technologies of transportation, novel ways of socially organising travel, the growth of an aesthetic reflexivity, the development of 'interpretation' in the travel industry, changes in the nature of consumption, and the 'end of tourism' per se. The contemporary subject inevitably engages in what we might call tourist practices much of the time. In postmodernity many spheres of social and cultural life are de-differentiated. Tourism is nowhere and yet everywhere.

Table 9.2 The shift to post-Fordist consumption

Post-Fordist consumption	*Tourist examples*
Consumers increasingly dominant and producers have to be much more consumer-oriented	Rejection of certain forms of mass tourism (holiday camps and cheaper packaged holidays) and increased diversity of preferences
Greater volatility of consumer preferences	Fewer repeat visits and the proliferation of alternative sights and attractions
Increased market segmentation	The multiplication of types of holiday and visitor attractions based on life-style research
The growth of a consumers' movement	Much more information provided about alternative holidays and attractions through the media
The development of many new products each of which has a shorter life	The rapid turnover of tourist sites and experiences because of rapid changes of fashion
Increased preferences expressed for non-mass forms of production/consumption	The growth of 'green tourism' and of forms of refreshment and accommodation which are individually tailored to the consumer (such as country house hotels)
Consumption as less and less 'functional' and increasingly aestheticised	The 'de-differentiation' of tourism from leisure, culture, retailing, education, sport, hobbies

10

REINTERPRETING LOCAL CULTURE*

GLOBAL AND THE LOCAL

In this chapter I will criticise two positions: that which suggests that processes of globalisation are producing economic, political and cultural homogenisation; and that which claims that what is most important about the contemporary world is the surprising emergence of locally distinct cultures. Both of these accounts are one-sided and instead what we need to analyse are the complex interconnections of *both* global and local processes. It is the *interconnections* between them which account for the particular ways in which an area's local history and culture is made available and transformed into a resource for local economic and social development within a globally evolving economy and society.

Deciphering these interconnections is complex and cannot be reduced to an examination of the economy on its own. In particular it involves analysis of the nature of social flows, of people, information, companies, ideas and images. Such flows do not take place in a vacuum but depend partly on cultural processes. These include certain tendencies towards globalised forms of culture but as we will see these do not necessarily produce cultural homogenisation. The following are some of the main forms taken by these global cultural flows: new forms of global communication including satellite technologies and massive media conglomerates which 'collapse space and time' (Brunn and Leinbach 1991); the development of international travel and of 'small worlds' little connected to nation-state relationships; the increasing numbers of international agencies and institutions; the development of global competitions and prizes; the emergence of a small number of languages of communication, most notably English; and the development of more widely shared notions of citizenship and of political democracy (see Lash and Urry 1994, for more detail).

I suggested earlier that what we need to consider are various flows. This

---

* This was first given as a lecture to The International Conference on Comparative Regional Studies, Tohuku University, Sendai, Japan, 1992. Discussions with Dan Shapiro have helped to develop the argument here.

thesis has been amplified by Appadurai who attempts to detail five different dimensions of such global cultural flows (1990). These dimensions move in non-isomorphic paths and challenge simple notions of a cultural centre and a subordinate periphery. They constitute building blocks for what Appadurai terms 'imagined worlds', the multiple worlds constituted by the historically situated imaginations of persons and groups spread across the globe. Such worlds are fluid and irregularly shaped.

The five dimensions of such global cultural flows are *ethnoscapes* – the moving landscape of tourists, immigrants, refugees, exiles, guestworkers and so on; *technoscapes* – the movements of technologies, high and low, mechanical and informational, across all kinds of boundaries; *finanscapes* – the movement of vast sums of monies through national turnstiles at bewildering speed, via currency markets, national stock exchanges and commodity speculations; *mediascapes* – the distribution of electronic capabilities to produce and disseminate images and the proliferation of images thereby generated; and *ideoscapes* – concatenations of images often in part linked to the ideologies of states or of movements of opposition (Appadurai 1990: 296–300).

This chapter is concerned with the interconnections between these various flows and the shapes that they take, and with the resulting economic and social organisation of particular towns, cities and regions especially within Britain. I shall presume the following. First, these flows in part derive from very particular places from which in a sense they derive – such as the financial flows which in the British case stem from the history, traditions and spatial form of the 'square mile' of the City of London (Lash and Urry 1994: Ch. 11).

Second, these flows impact upon particular towns and cities in often unexpected and counter-intuitive ways. There are many different kinds of flow as we have seen and the impact of their non-isomorphic shapes can produce distinct non-homogenised outcomes in particular places (see Bagguley *et al.* 1990).

Third, the effect of globalisation is often to increase local distinctiveness for one or more of the following reasons: the increased ability of large companies to subdivide their operations and to locate different activities within different labour markets located in different societies (see discussion in Bagguley *et al.* 1990); the breaking up of previously relatively coherent regional economies; the competition between local states for jobs, the growth of international differences and the localising of regional policy (see discussion in Harloe *et al.* 1990); the decreasing tendency for voting patterns to be nationally determined and the increased importance of 'neighbourhood' effects; the enduring significance of symbols of place and location particularly with the decline in the popularity of the international modern style of architecture and the emergence of local and vernacular styles; and the resurgence of locally oriented culture and politics especially around campaigns for the conservation of the built and physical environment.

Robins effectively summarises:

> Globalization is, in fact, also associated with new dynamics of re-localization. It is about the achievement of a new global-local nexus, about new and intricate relations between global space and local space. Globalization is like putting together a jigsaw puzzle: it is a matter of inserting a multiplicity of localities into the overall picture of a new global system.
>
> (1991: 34–5)

TRANSFORMING HISTORY AND CULTURE

I am mostly going to refer in this chapter to transformations in the interpretation of the history and culture of industrial Lancashire. Before doing so though I need to make a number of further points about the context in which such transformations took place.

Initially, it is important to note that in terms of employment creation, since most people in Britain work in services, it is the geographical location of service-sector enterprises which is of most significance for the distribution of employment. Further, even in the case of manufactured goods there is an increasing design element built into them. This means that a range of services are particularly pertinent to such manufacturing industry, that is, those services concerned with their design. One particularly important set of industries in contemporary Britain are so-called cultural industries which include music, television, cinema, publishing, leisure and tourism. Cultural industries are concerned in part with the re-presentation of the supposed history and culture of a place. Many authorities have begun to develop a specific strategy with regard to the arts and culture, with designated arts areas or corridors, as in Sheffield, Liverpool and Glasgow.

This in turn is related to the way in which many places in Britain have begun to develop policies designed to attract both tourists and incoming entrepreneurs and their employees to their area. Such policies have mainly involved developing the range of appropriate services available. And this in turn has partly at least involved efforts to re-present the history and culture of their area. The following are some of the reasons why this occurred in the 1980s, so much so that almost every town and city in Britain has now developed a 'tourism strategy'. The re-presentation of an area's history and culture is also seen as relevant to the attraction of new employees and managers.

First, there was the astonishingly rapid de-industrialisation of many towns and cities in Britain in the late 1970s and 1980s. This created a profound sense of loss, both of certain kinds of technology, factories, steam engines, blast furnaces and pit workings, and of the patterns of social life that developed around such technologies. The sense of loss was found in very many places, especially where the work had involved backbreaking and apparently heroic labour by men. The transformation of coal mines into museums in south Wales is perhaps the best example of this development (in 1994 the only pit now in south Wales is a museum).

Second, the costs of job creation in tourist and leisure-related services compared with manufacturing industry are very much lower (up to one-eighth). Moreover, local councils have been willing to engage in leisure and tourism projects because this is one area where there are funds available to initiate projects which may also benefit local residents. Funds have been available both from central government and from the European Community. Such facilities have been important not only in attracting visitors but also prospective employees and employers and in keeping them satisfied once they have relocated. One place in Lancashire where this has clearly happened is Wigan following the establishment of the Wigan Pier Heritage Centre. The Chairman of the North West Tourist Board argues that:

> The growth of the tourism industry has a great deal to do with the growth of every other industry or business: the opening up of the regions as fine places to visit means that they're better places to live in – and thus better places to work . . . a higher quality of life benefits employees.
>
> (cited in Reynolds 1988)

Third, this de-industrialisation mainly took place in the 1980s in northern towns and cities, especially within inner-city areas. It resulted in a para-doxically useful legacy of derelict buildings from the Victorian era. Some of these were intrinsically attractive, such as the Albert Dock in Liverpool, or could be refurbished in a picturesque heritage style, such as the White Cross Mill in Lancaster (on the Albert Dock, see Mellor 1991). A heritage style normally entails sandblasted walls, Victorian street furniture, replaced but 'authentically' appearing windows and brightly painted doors, pipes and balconies. Such derelict buildings have often been suitable for conversion to educational, cultural and leisure uses. Further, the preservation of such vernacular buildings has been particularly marked because of the mostly unappealing character of modern architecture in Britain. Modern buildings have been particularly unpopular, partly because many were built in the 1960s using concrete as the predominant building material (see Coventry city centre for example). The criticisms of such buildings expressed by Prince Charles resonate well with popular sentiment in Britain. Vernacular buildings by contrast appear very attractive to British people and well worth preserving. The novelist Margaret Drabble writes of:

> a sort of stubborn English philistinism about architecture and city life, encouraged by the wilder utterances of the Prince of Wales. Not for us the pride of Paris in its pyramid, in its brave and soaring arch; not for

us the multi-coloured panache of Stirling's Staatsgalerie in Stutt-
gart. . . . One of the reasons for our current architectural timidity lies
in the failure of post-war high-rise and deck-access council building

(1991: 33)

And this in turn raises a more general issue, namely the process of
conservation and its relationship to the symbols of history and culture. In
Britain there is an extremely well-organised movement for conservation in
many rural areas, towns and cities and this can exert a veto over certain kinds
of new building development. The strength of such groups varies considerably between different places. In 1980, for example, while there were
5.1 members of such societies per 1000 population in the UK as a whole, the
ratio was over 20 per 1000 in Hampshire and over 10 per 1000 in most of the
counties around London, in Devon and in Cumbria in the north-west of Britain
(Lowe and Goyder 1983: 28–30). Partly this variation varies in response to
where there is deemed to be a 'history and culture' worth preserving (see
Cowen 1990, on Cheltenham for example). But in some ways it seems that
almost anything can be seen as worth conserving, including in Lancashire a
slag heap from a coal mine! Preservation also need not be of a building – it
can be of a road layout or of the shape of an original building. In Lancaster,
for example, there has been a huge protest movement against the re-siting of
a Victorian market hall after the original had been destroyed by fire (the
distance involved was about half a kilometre).

There are two further points to note about such conservation. First,
normally conservation is sought in relationship to some aspect of the built
environment which is taken to stand for or represent the locality in question.
It is not merely that the object is historical, but that the object signifies the
place and that if the object were to be demolished or substantially changed
then that would signify a threat to the place itself. This can be seen in debates
in Morecambe in Lancashire and the planned refurbishment of the Winter
Gardens Theatre. There is an extremely energetic campaign to preserve this
theatre which in a sense has come to stand *for the town*. This semi-derelict
building has come to symbolise the town itself – if it is demolished then the
town itself is thought to have no viable future.

Second, there is nothing inevitable about conservation. It would be
perfectly posssible to permit many buildings to be destroyed and to build new
ones in their place. And this does of course happen, especially in the larger
cities in Britain. However, since the planning and building disasters in the
1960s this is often resisted by conservation groups, normally called civic
societies, many of which were established in the 1960s. These are normally
set up by those in professional and managerial occupations and may then
conflict with the interests of large-scale developers. The members of such
groups who may not necessarily originate from that particular town or city.
There appear to be relatively lower rates of geographical mobility among at

least the male professionals and managers in Britain. As a result they often develop a strong attachment to 'their place' – what is sometimes called the service class becomes 'localised' and this works its way into the formation of local conservation groups who energetically resist large-scale plans for office and retail development.

Although such civic societies may not literally be 'locals', they often articulate a strong sense of nostalgia for that place. They will suggest that there is a profound sense of loss of one's 'home' resulting from various economic and social changes. This in turn depends upon a particular structuring of the collective memory which is reinforced by various enacted ritual performances. However, much of the 'nostalgia' and 'tradition' of the place may in fact be invented by these conservation groups who articulate a set of particular aesthetic interests often based on the concept of 'community'. This gives rise to attempts to preserve otherwise derelict property such as the Albert Dock in Liverpool, and to favour any new building that is necessary, being built in the local style as opposed to the international architectural style of modernism. This localism or neo-vernacularism in architecture is often developed and encouraged by firms of local architects, the numbers of which have been rapidly growing in recent years.

LANCASHIRE

In this section I will consider some of the ways that history and culture are being used in the efforts to regenerate industrial Lancashire, an area located in the north west of England. This is where the first ever industrial revolution took place. The development of industry worldwide began initially in the cotton textile villages and towns of Lancashire in the late eighteenth century. This area therefore has first, a unique claim as the original site of industrialisation; second, it has the longest history of industrialisation anywhere in the world; and third, it has a culture which is almost literally built around manufacturing industry. For two centuries then the culture of Lancashire has been based upon the work relations of textile mills, coal mines and factories. The best known artist from the area, L. S. Lowry, made his name with his heavily urbanised and industrialised paintings, hardly the typical pastoral scenes of English landscape painting. It should also be noted that these towns and cities of industrial Lancashire were built close to rivers, often at the bottom of quite deeply cut river valleys. Surrounding them is a lot of impressively wild and attractive countryside, especially the Pennine range of hills.

So there is in Lancashire a unique history, an area that for two centuries has been moulded by industry. The main industries have been textiles, coal mining, textile engineering, linoleum and various sorts of engineering including aerospace. More or less all the towns are industrial. The main exceptions consist of those located on the coast. These became in the mid-to late-nineteenth century the very first holiday resorts for the lower middle and skilled working classes. Here developed the first *mass* resorts, including probably the most famous resort in the world, Blackpool. There is then a second kind of history to be found in the area, a history of mass leisure which has in a way become as representative of the area as has the cotton textile industry itself. A symbiotic culture therefore exists in Lancashire, of factory-based industry and of mass leisure, the two being heavily intertwined (see Urry 1990: Ch. 2 for more detail on the work–leisure interconnections in Lancashire).

The history of the twentieth century in Lancashire has been one of long-term decline for many of these textile towns. This has involved: the emergence of various new industries especially between the 1920s and the 1960s; the rapid de-industrialisation of the area from the 1970s onwards; the corresponding weakening of the seaside leisure industry from the 1960s onwards especially as foreign competition emerged from the Mediterranean region; and the unexpected emergence of industrial and urban tourism in the 1980s. What I am going to analyse briefly is the relationship between de-industrialisation on the one hand, and urban and industrial tourism on the other.

It is first worth pointing out that twenty years ago no one in Britain would have contemplated visiting industrial Lancashire *by choice*. It would have been travelled to only for business or for visiting friends. Likewise no one would have considered that it possessed a history that was in any way interesting. It was a 'place on the margin' of British life, a place rendered peripheral by virtue of global economic process (see Shields 1991, on the place-image of 'the north'). The culture of the area was not thought of as worth knowing about. It was 'up there', well away from the supposed centres of British public and artistic life which have for some centuries been based in the south east of the country, in the so-called 'home counties' surrounding London. To the extent that 'southerners' visited Lancashire it was to go to Blackpool and the other resorts – but even this was not that common and mostly undertaken to confirm prejudices about the 'uncivilised' northerners whose tastes were viewed as 'other', as not really English, as irredeemably uncultured.

George Orwell for example in *The Road to Wigan Pier* talked of a 'line north of Birmingham to demarcate the beginning of "the real ugliness of industrialisation"'. As a southerner, Orwell was conscious when travelling north in the late 1930s of 'entering a strange country . . . [which is] partly because of certain real differences which do exist, but still more because of the north–south antithesis which has been rubbed into us for such a long time past' (1959 [1937]: 106–7). Likewise he ridiculed the working class holiday camp. He talked of how muzak would be playing in the background 'to prevent the onset of that dreaded thing – thought' (cited in Hebdige 1988: 52).

The only exception to this generally unfavourable image of the north and particularly of Lancashire was the belief that most people in fact lived in warm-hearted 'working class communities'. It was believed that these were solidaristic, that they involved a great deal of mutual support and advice in times of trouble, that there were very close-knit contacts between family and neighbours, and that leisure was organised collectively rather than individually.

So these then are some components of the history and culture of Lancashire which have come to be reassessed in the past decade and a half. No longer is Lancashire seen as somewhere merely to pass through, as merely on the margins. The neighbouring city of Liverpool now attracts 20 million visitors a year; Manchester has recently enjoyed a huge revival of fortune, particularly artistically; and almost every town and city in Lancashire seeks both to attract visitors and permanent residents partly through repackaging its history and culture. In other words, what was seen as a set of characteristics which were peripheral to mainstream British life have now been reassessed. As working industry has disappeared so vast numbers of people seem to be fascinated by the memories of that industry and of the forms of life that were associated with it. Britain seems to be engulfed by a vast collective nostalgia in which almost anything from the past, whether an 'old master' or an old cake tin, is viewed as equally interesting and well worth visiting. The Director of the Science Museum in London has said of this growth in heritage that: 'You can't project that sort of rate of growth much further before the whole country becomes one big open air museum, and you just join it as soon as you get off at Heathrow' (quoted in Hewison 1987: 24).

There are now over half a million listed buildings in Britain; a new museum opens every fortnight including many with an industrial theme, more people visit museums and galleries than the cinema and three-quarters of overseas visitors to Britain visit a museum or gallery during their stay (see Urry 1990: 105–6).

One of the most interesting attempts to re-present history has taken place in Wigan in Lancashire, about which Orwell wrote his classic work *The Road to Wigan Pier* in the late 1930s. Incidentally, the pier had been used for loading coal – it was not a seaside pier. I noted above the way in which various local authorities have begun to see in tourist-related developments a way of both generating jobs directly and developing more general publicity about their area. The latter is designed to attract prospective managers and their families. Wigan has attempted to do this via a publicity booklet entitled *I've Never Been to Wigan but I Know What it's Like* (Economic Development, Wigan: undated). The first five pictures in black and white are of back-to-back terraced housing, mines and elderly residents walking along narrow alleyways. But we are then asked if we are sure that this is really what Wigan is now like. The following twelve photos, all in colour, demonstrate contemporary Wigan, which is revealed as possessing countless tourist sites, including the award winning Wigan Pier Heritage Centre, a colourful market and elegant shops, excellent sports facilities, attractive pubs and restaurants, and delightful canalside walkways. Selling Wigan to tourists is then part of the process of selling Wigan to potential investors, who are going to be concerned about the availability of various kinds of services for their employees.

What though is interesting about this is the way in which the industrial past is part of what gets sold. The Wigan Pier Heritage Centre attracts over one million visitors a year. It has unashamedly re-presented the industrial and social history of Wigan albeit in a way which is certainly somewhat sanitised. The set of buildings by the canal have been cleaned up and given a 'heritage' look. Moreover, that history also includes George Orwell and the famous book written about the town. So the history to be re-presented is complex. It is both the industrial and social history of Wigan and it is Orwell's visit to the town. There is for instance a bar in the Heritage Centre called The Orwell.

In Hewison's famous examination of the 'heritage industry' in Britain, Wigan Pier is his first port of call, the first representation of the past to be critiqued (1987). He condemns the way in which the agenda of heritage promotes a mythical English idyll of harmony and community and a romanticised and glamorised industrial past. The effect of this commodification of history systematically distorts attention from the present, from contemporary polarisations and conflicts. He draws a strong distinction between an authentic history, continuing and therefore dangerous, and a packaged heritage, past, dead and safe. The protection of the past conceals the destruction of the present. Indeed Hewison argues that if we are really interested in history then we may need to preserve it from the conservationists. Heritage is for him bogus history.

His arguments do have a a certain plausibility but there are some points to make in opposition, points revealed by the case of the Wigan Pier Heritage Centre. It is educational, even recreating something of the appearance of an old school room; it presents a history of popular struggles against employers and town bosses; it partly blames the employers for mining disasters; and it celebrates a non-elite culture as no longer marginal. Wigan Pier was organised by a Labour local authority and much of the text has been written by professional historians. It also attracts considerable numbers of local people as well as tourists and encourages a degree of active engagement rather than passive acceptance from the visitors. One might also note that most people's understanding of history is rather sketchy and ill-formed. It is not obvious that the Wigan Pier experience is worse than say reading historical novels. Mellor presents a robust defence of sites such as Wigan Pier:

> when you ask other visitors what they are doing there, it turns out many of them . . . are reminiscing. They do so, not simply in passive deference to Wigan Pier's own construction of Wigan life at the turn of the century, but actively using the displays, reconstructions, and discourses of the actors . . . as the point of departure for their own memories of a

way of life in which economic hardship and exploited labour were offset by a sense of community, neighbourliness and mutuality.

(1991: 100)

There is however one aspect of the representation of history involved in such sites of industrial heritage which is problematic. This is that heritage history is distorted because of the emphasis upon visualisation, on presenting visitors with an array of artefacts, including buildings, and then encouraging visitors to try to visualise the patterns of life that would have formed around those artefacts. This might then be termed an 'artefactual' history, in which a whole variety of social experiences are trivialised or marginalised (see Urry 1990: 112).

Finally, in this section I will consider the city of Lancaster that has been seeking to turn itself into a heritage city by re-using its history and culture. It seems that there are three preconditions that have to be met for the construction of a heritage city. First, there has to be legacy of a number of attractive and well-preserved buildings from a range of historical periods. In Lancaster's case these are medieval (a castle), eighteenth century (many town houses), nineteenth century (many mills and further town houses) and inter-war (art deco hotel). Second, such buildings would have to be used for purposes in some way consistent with their use as tourist sites. Currently much of the prison which possesses a magnificent Norman gate is not open to the public, and in fact is used as a prison, a use that conflicts with its potential as a tourist site. The third condition for Lancaster to become a plausible heritage city is that the buildings should in some sense have been significant historically, that they stand for or signify important historical events, people or processes. In one report Lancaster is thus described as:

an ancient settlement steeped in history, with Roman origins, an important medieval past. . . . Through the Duchy of Lancaster it has close associations with the Monarchy. . . . The city's many attractions, based on its rich history and fine buildings, together with its royal associations, combine for the promotion and marketing of Lancaster's heritage.

(cited Urry 1990: 118)

CONCLUSION

Thus I have endeavoured to set out some of the ways in which history and culture have been employed within some north-western towns and cities in Britain, employed as part of a strategy of urban regeneration. In conclusion though, it is important to note some of the constraints under which such places have been operating.

First, there have been enormous funding difficulties as the Conservative national government has attempted to minimise the role and scale of local government intervention (for details, see Pickvance 1990). Second, and related to this, have been the efforts by the same government to 'Americanise' urban policy, to find private sector solutions and to minimise the importance of infrastructure, of local government and of public planning (as most clearly shown in the Canary Wharf débâcle in the London Docklands; see Bianchini and Schwengel 1991). Ideas about economic regeneration have 'flowed' to Britain from the US.

The final constraint is that British towns and cities are poorly placed to compete successfully with some European cities which have been able to plan their use of history and culture in a strategic fashion. Public funding has been available to link together different elements particularly via a strategy which has provided extensive support both for the arts and for a public infrastructure. Glasgow in Scotland is probably the British city that has best been able to effect such a 'European' transformation especially through its newsworthy designation as the European City of Culture in 1990 (see Wishart 1991). But in general flows of attractive images of some European cities have weakened the competitive position of many British cities, even those which had a particularly rich reservoir of history and culture to mobilise. Global competition can be a demanding and relentless taskmaster!

11

TOURISM, EUROPE AND IDENTITY*

In this chapter I want to try to think through some of the implications of mass travel and tourism for the forms of social identity by which people organise and live their day-to-day lives. This is clearly a different concern from the standard impact studies on the one hand and the debates about tourism and international understanding on the other. I want to relate travel and tourism much more generally to the changing forms of culture that characterise contemporary society. Indeed I want to suggest first, that travel and tourism are extremely significant features of the modern world; and second, that current debates about the changing nature of 'Europe' cannot be undertaken without relating them to possible transformations of social identity that mass mobility brings about. This chapter is unashamedly conceptual and presents little empirical information.

I will begin by examining rather more carefully the concept of the 'modern' by quoting from the seminal work on this subject. Marshall Berman says that to be modern is:

> to find ourselves in an environment that promises adventure, power, joy, growth, transformations of ourselves and the world – and, at the same time, that threatens to destroy everything we have, everything we know, everything we are. Modern environments and experiences cut across all boundaries of geography and ethnicity, of class and nationality, of religion and ideology; in this sense, modernity can be said to unite all mankind.

> (1983: 15)

Berman then describes some of the processes integral to modern towns and cities which 'pour us into a maelstrom of perpetual disintegration and renewal', as well as some of the strategies that people employ in order 'to make oneself somehow at home in the maelstrom' (1983: 15, 345). And that, as many writers now illuminate, is particularly difficult. The current epoch

---

* This was first given as a lecture to a *Tourism in Europe* Conference held in Durham Castle in 1992.

is one of expanding horizons and dissolving boundaries, of 'collapsing space and time' (Brunn and Leinbach 1991), of globalisation through transformed informational and communicational flows, and of the erosion of territorial frontiers and clear cut national and other social identities. Particular identities around place become seriously disrupted by such global change – there is a disengagement of 'some basic forms of trust relation from the attributes of local contexts' (Giddens 1990: 108).

What however this account does not address is one particular set of social practices which are central to the modern experience that Berman discusses in the nineteenth century, and to the recent transformations of space and time that contemporary theorists have analysed in the late twentieth century, namely, the social practices of travel and tourism. Is it really sensible to consider, as Berman does, that it is pedestrian strollers (*flâneurs*) who can be taken as emblematic of the modern world? It is surely rather train-passengers, car drivers and jet plane passengers who are the heroes of the modern world. And it is the social organisation of such *long-distance* travel which is the characteristic feature of modernity. In some ways the 'social organisation of the experience of modernity', beginning of course with Thomas Cook's, is as important a feature of modern Western societies as is the socialised production of manufactured goods.

When Berman for example talks of crossing boundaries of geography and ethnicity, when we anticipate adventure, joy, growth and so on, these should be seen as centrally bound up with mobility, especially for pleasure. Travel may be enjoyable in its own right, it may involve liminal spaces permitting less structured forms of social interaction and enabling the cultures and environments of many other places to be encountered, consumed and collected. The scale of this is enormous and has three types of immediate effect. First, on the places which such visitors travel to, which come to be remade in part as objects *for* the tourist gaze. Their built and physical environments, their economies and their place-images are all substantially reconstructed. Second, on the places from which visitors come from which effectively export considerable amounts of income, images, social and cultural patterns and so on. And third, via the construction of often enormous transportation infrastructures which may have effects, not only on the places just mentioned, but also on all sorts of intermediate spaces close to runways, motorways, railway stations and so on.

Thus travel and tourism are important industries and have significant effects on many places. But more significantly they are centrally important to the *very* nature of modern societies. Such modern societies are unique for the scale of such flows of short-term mobility. In the rest of this chapter I want to think through some of the issues involved in investigating the wider cultural impact of such huge flows of visitors, the impact upon the very forms of social identity available in the modern world.

I will begin with Morley and Robins, who talk of the 'need to be "at home"

164

in the new and disorientating global space' (1990: 3). There are two points to emphasise: first, that the disorientating global space is in part the product of massive global flows of tourists; and second, that such flows disrupt the very sense of what is a person's home. In what sense then can spatial meanings be attached or developed in which: 'the space of flows ... supersedes the space of places'? (Henderson and Castells 1987: 7). That space of flows consists in part of tourists and means that many places are constructed around attracting and receiving large numbers of visitors. This is true, not just for obvious places such as Brighton and Benidorm, Stratford-upon-Avon and San Sebastian, but also for cities such as London and New York, Paris and Berlin. When some such cities are described as 'cosmopolitan' this means that they receive very large numbers of tourists. Their nature as a specific place in part results from their location at the intersection of various *global* flows, not just of money or capital, but of visitors.

Watts notes the importance of investigating how people define themselves, how identities are produced 'in the new spaces of a post-Fordist economy' (1992: 123). How are identities constructed amidst the processes of globalisation and fragmentation, especially when part of the image of place is increasingly produced for actual or potential visitors? Identity almost everywhere has to be produced partly out of the images constructed for tourists.

Furthermore, it is not just that places are transformed by the arrival or potential arrival of visitors. It is also that in an increasing number of societies, particularly in Europe, people are themselves transformed. The right to travel has become a marker of citizenship. It is important to consider what this does to conventional conceptions of citizenship based upon the notion that rights were to be provided by institutions located *within* territorially demarcated nation-states (see Held 1990). A novel kind of 'consumer citizenship' is developing with four main features.

First, people are increasingly citizens by virtue of their ability to purchase goods and services – citizenship is more a matter of consumption than of political rights and duties. Second, people in different societies should have similar rights of access to a diversity of consumer goods, services and cultural products from *different* societies. Third, people should be able to travel within all societies as tourists and those countries that have tried to prevent this, such as Albania, China and some Eastern European countries in the past, have been seen as infringing the human rights of foreigners to cross their territories. Fourth, people are viewed as having rights of movement across and permanent or seasonal residence in whichever society they choose to visit as a stranger, for whatever periods of time.

Thus citizenship rights increasingly involve claims to consume other cultures and places throughout the world. A modern person is one who is able to exercise those rights and who conceives of him or herself as a consumer of other cultures and places. What though will happen to such notions with the future changes in Europe after 1992, the opening of the Channel Tunnel in 1994 and the increased mobility between the formerly relatively separate East and West Europes? Currently about two-thirds of international tourism occurs to or within Europe. In particular what will be the effects of mass mobility, dependent upon such consumerist notions of citizenship, upon the multiple forms of social identity within Europe?

Social identities emerge out of imagined communities, out of particular structures of feeling that bind together three elements, space, time and memory, often in part in opposition to an imagined 'other' such as a neighbouring country. However, massive amounts of mobility may transform such social identities formed around particular configurations of space, time and memory. This can be seen by briefly considering each of these terms.

'Spaces' of a neighbourhood, town or region may become overwhelmed by visitors so that locals no longer feel it is their space/place any more. So many visitors pass through, visually appropriating the space and leading locals to feel that they have 'lost' their space. Visitors are viewed as the 'other'. However, it should be recognised that some places *only* exist because of visitors, that the very place, the particular combination of landscape and townscape, could only exist because of visitors, such as the Lake District (see Chapter 13). Visitors are in a sense as much local as are 'real' locals.

The second element is time. Tourism normally brings about some striking changes in the organisation of time: attractions are here today and gone tomorrow; there are representations of different historical periods placed in unlikely juxtapositions; tourism involves extensive time-travel; and time is speeded up so that sufficient attractions can be accumulated in the prescribed period. Time seems to be organised in terms of the interests of the large leisure companies and of their clients. But two points should be noted: first, that some spaces, like Blackpool, only exist for *locals* because of the particular emphasis on being modern, being up-to-date, being almost ahead of time; and second, that some tourists increasingly wish to slow down time, to participate in sustainable or responsible tourism, which may not be the kind of time that locals feel is their time (see Chapter 14).

And finally, memory. One kind of dispute is over history: whose history should be represented and whose history should be packaged and commodified? Visitors are likely to seek a brief comprehensible history that can be easily assimilated – heritage rather than history as it is normally conceptualised. However, it should be noted that social memories are in fact *always* selective and there is no real memory to counterpose to the supposedly false memory of the visitor. The memories of 'locals' will be as selective as those of visitors.

What then can we say about international tourism and social identity? As a general claim the suggestion in the literature that tourism facilitates international understanding seems very dubious. However, international tourism does surely have two relevant effects. First, it produces international familiarisation/normalisation so that those from other countries are no longer

166

seen as particularly dangerous and threatening – just different and this seems to have happened on a large scale in Europe in recent years. Second, there is the generation of cosmopolitanism amongst at least some travellers. Living in the modern world is taken to a new level with cosmopolitanism, with a willingness of people to open out to others who live elsewhere. Cosmopolitanism involves an intellectual and aesthetic stance of openness towards divergent experiences from *different* national cultures. There is a search for and delight in contrasts between societies rather than a longing for uniformity or superiority. Hannerz talks of the need for the cosmopolitan to be in 'a state of readiness, a personal ability to make one's way into other cultures, through listening, looking, intuiting and reflecting' (1990: 239).

Hebdige likewise argues that a 'mundane cosmopolitanism' is part of many people's everyday experience, as they are world travellers, either directly or via the TV in their living room. He argues that: 'It is part of being "taken for a ride" in and through late-20th century consumer culture. In the 1990s everybody [at least in the "west"] is more or less cosmopolitan' (1990: 20). I would further argue that contemporary societies have initiated a distinctive kind of cosmopolitanism, an aesthetic cosmopolitanism dependent upon certain scopic regimes. The following is a model of such an aesthetic cosmopolitanism:

Table 11.1 Aesthetic cosmopolitanism

---

1 Extensive patterns of real and simulated mobility in which it is thought that one has the *right* to travel anywhere and to consume at least initially all environments.

2 A *curiosity* about all places, peoples and cultures and at least a rudimentary ability to map such places and cultures historically, geographically and anthropologically.

3 An *openness* to other peoples and cultures and a willingness/ability to appreciate some elements of the language/culture of the place that one is visiting.

4 A willingness to take *risks* by virtue of moving outside the tourist environmental bubble.

5 An ability to *locate* one's own society and its culture in terms of a wide-ranging historical and geographical knowledge, to have some ability to reflect upon and judge aesthetically between different natures, places and societies.

6 A certain *semiotic* skill – to be able to interpret tourist signs, to see what they are meant to represent, and indeed to know when they are partly ironic and to be approached coolly or in a detached fashion.

In the late eighteenth and early nineteenth centuries a similar kind of cosmopolitanism developed amongst the British upper class who were able to expand their repertoire of landscapes for visual consumption. Barrell summarises the importance of their mobility throughout Europe:

> the aristocracy and gentry were not . . . irrevocably involved . . . bound up in, any particular locality which they had no time, no money, and

no reason ever to leave. It meant also that they had experience of more landscapes than one, in more geographical regions than one; and even if they did not travel much they were accustomed, by their culture, to the *notion* of mobility, and could easily imagine other landscapes.

(Barrell 1972: 63; see also Zukin 1992a: 224–5)

Overall then I am concerned here with the issues of social identity, of local, regional, national and European identities, and ask what is the role of mobility and cosmopolitanism in forming and reproducing such identities. In conclusion I will briefly consider some possible changes that are likely to take place in Europe in the next few years as a result of changes in mobility.

First, we can note the contemporary importance of Europe within international tourism: in 1990 the world's top ten destinations were: France, USA, Spain, Italy, Austria, Hungary, UK, Germany, Canada and Switzerland; in 1991 there were some 429 million international tourist arrivals worldwide of which 275 million occurred in Europe, a 41 per cent increase over the decade. Seventy per cent of international visits by Europeans were *not* on inclusive tours but were by so-called 'independent travellers'; and 80 per cent of leisure travel in Europe is by car. The 'richer' countries in the EC dominate the European tourism industry in absolute terms, accounting for about three-quarters of both expenditure and employment. But the 'poorer' countries gain disproportionately and tourism is one of the main industries which produces a net flow of resources from north to south in Europe.

The following summarises the main developments in mobility patterns in Europe in the 1990s:

1 *Changes in companies* Europeanisation of leisure companies; investment in Eastern Europe; breakdown of nationally regulated and protected travel industries; tour operators to operate more across borders; stricter consumer protection laws.
2 *Changes in travel* abolition of internal frontiers; exchange of health provision; Channel Tunnel; high-speed trains in Europe; deregulation of airlines and the weakening of the power of 'national carriers'; hub airports in Europe; longer-distance car holidays; moves towards a single currency and savings of foreign exchange dealing; elimination of immigration controls for intra-EC traffic; probable abolition of duty-free sales.
3 *Changes in places* spectacular resort development as regions and nations compete for a larger share of the European market; increased competition by cities to establish themselves as 'European'; a greater specialisation of place and image; increased marketing of 'Europe'; and threats to regional/national identities; importance of 'Europe' as signifying 'history and culture'; fewer gains for 'poorer' Mediterranean Europe.
4 *Changes in types of tourism* growth of 'globally responsible tourism'; of overseas second homes/timeshare; some more EC support given to

peripheral regions especially via a 'Europe of the regions'; diversification of rural areas away from agriculture towards tourism etc.; growth of city centre tourism given that international tourists tend to keep inland; further growth of historical/cultural tourism; large increases in tourism amongst the young and the old.

In the current debates about the nature of Europe, we need to consider the following: changing European institutions, such as the apparent weakening of the powers of individual nation-states; a possible Europe of the regions; the relationship of Europe to Islam; the growth of Europe-wide institutions of the media; and the efforts to construct a European homeland. But at the same time we need to investigate the massive and growing patterns of short-term mobility within Europe. It is inconceivable that new or reinforced conceptions of social identity can be formed without both actual and imagined journeys around Europe playing an important role. In his influential book on nationalism, Anderson analyses the importance of 'imagined communities', of investigating the rituals, the media and patterns of travel by which people came in different supra-national territories to imagine themselves as members of a *single* nation (1983). He argues that nations are: '*imagined* because the members of even the smallest nation will never know most of their fellow-members, meet them, or even hear of them, yet in the minds of each lives the image of their communion' (1983: 15). Anderson notes the importance of travel in this process, quoting Victor Turner on the importance of real and metaphorical journeys between times, statuses and places as being par-ticularly meaning-creating experiences (cited in Anderson 1983: 55). I want to suggest something similar here: that in the current reworkings of social identity, of the changing relations between place, nation and Europe, travel is an element which may be of great importance in constructing/reinforcing novel identities. The development of a possible 'European identity' cannot be discussed without considering how massive patterns of short-term mobility may be transforming dominant social identities.

Moreover, these mass forms of mobility involve tremendous effects upon the places visited, which almost all become locked into a competitive struggle for visitors. One consequence is the emergence of a new Europe of competing city-states, where local identities are increasingly packaged for visitors. And one way in which such competition between city-states takes place is through the identity of actually 'being European'. Such a place-image conventionally entails the establishment of various cultural and other 'festivals', the desig-nation of artistic quarters, the development of areas of outdoor cafés and restaurants, the preservation of old buildings and street layout, the re-development of river and canalside waterfronts and the use of the term European as standing for 'history' and 'culture' for marketing that particular place (see Clark 1992, on the tradition of communal celebrations in Europe).

But there is an interesting paradox here. Part of what is involved in towns and cities becoming more European is that places should demonstrate at least some signs of local distinctiveness. Robins refers to this as 'the importance of place marketing in placeless times' (1991: 38). This will of course often entail the use of an area's heritage: 'Even in the most disadvantaged places, heritage, or the simulacrum of heritage, can be mobilized to gain competitive advantage in the race between places' (Robins 1991: 38). But there are of course competing heritages waiting to be captured by various kinds of organisations. There will be contestation over whose heritage is being conserved and how this relates to local people and their sense of what is important to remember. Robins notes that in the north of England there is a struggle taking place between the working-class, industrial image of the region, and a new image which emphasises enterprise and opportunity, proclaiming that 'Andy Capp is dead – Newcastle is alive' (1991: 39). However, it is clearly impossible to eliminate entirely the industrial history of the area; Robins notes that Beamish in the north-east of England has become a European recognised tourist site while there are numbers of cultural projects designed to recreate the area's working-class heritage and to show how it contributed to a particular regional identity (1991: 40–1).

In the reworking of the relationships between a European identity and regional and local identities, the role of travel and its collective forms of organisation seem particularly salient and currently underexamined. Mass mobility is probably one of the main factors that will determine whether a European identity will emerge; and it is a crucial factor in transforming local identities. Robins clearly summarises the dilemmas involved here:

> The driving imperative is to salvage centred, bounded and coherent identities – place identities for placeless times. This may take the form of the resuscitated patriotism and jingoism that we are now seeing in a resurgent Little Englandism. Alternatively . . . it may take a more progressive form in the cultivation of local and regional identities or in the project to construct a continental European identity.
>
> (1991: 41)

Part IV
CONSUMING NATURE

12

THE TOURIST GAZE AND THE ENVIRONMENT*

INTRODUCTION

This chapter is concerned with the implications of recent developments in tourism for especially the 'physical' environment. It will be shown that there are some striking changes taking place in how the environment is being 'read', how it is appropriated, and how it is exploited, and that these changes increasingly depend upon the economic, social and geographical organisation of contemporary tourism. By the year 2000 this will be the largest industry in the world, in terms of employment and trade, and it is already having profound environmental consequences. These stem, first, from the fact that much tourism is concerned with in a sense visually consuming that very environment; second, from the enormous flow of people carried on many different forms of transport which enable tourists to gaze upon often geographically distant environments; and third, from the various transformations of the environment which follow from the widespread construction of tourist attractions and from the incredible concentrations of people into particular places. The emergence of new technologies of transportation and of mass hospitality have transformed the environmental consequences of the world's current population. Because of the enormous scale of tourism, the carrying capacity of the earth and of its relatively finite resources is substantially reduced below what it would have been without that tourism.

To appreciate the scale of developments I will briefly outline some of the global developments in tourism. First, there are over 400 million international arrivals a year (in 1989). This compares with merely 60 million in 1960. There are between three and four times that number of domestic tourists worldwide. International tourists are increasing by 4 to 5 per cent per annum and will have risen at least 50 per cent by the year 2000. International tourists currently spend $209 billion a year, generate at least 60 million jobs and fill

* This first appeared in *Theory, Culture and Society*, 1992, vol. 9. Reprinted with permission of Sage Publications Ltd. I am very grateful for the comments of Sarah Franklin, Ann McAleer and the Lancaster Regionalism Group. I am also grateful for examples provided by Michaela Gardner.

10.5 million hotel beds. Moreover, there will be significant increases in the world's population over the next few decades, something like 93 million a year. Tourism will expand at a much faster rate than this increase in population. It grows with income, since there is a high income elasticity of demand, and as a result of new forms of publicity through the media. For example, the number of visitors to the Mediterranean, currently the world's most successful destination region, is predicted to rise from 100 million in 1985 to 760 million in 2025. Two obvious environmental effects will be the increased use of fossil fuels to fly people there, as long-haul holidays become widespread, and intense shortages of clean water especially with the probable climatic changes in the region.

Although these are fairly clear environmental effects many others are much more ambiguous. This is in part because what is viewed and criticised as environmentally damaging in one era or one society is not necessarily taken as such in another. For example, the rows of terraced housing thrown up during industrialisation are now viewed not as an environmental eyesore but as quaint, traditional and harbouring patterns of human activity well worth preserving. Another example is the steam railway, which in the nineteenth century was seen as an environmental disaster but is now viewed as benign, traditional and particularly attractive as it belches filthy smoke into the atmosphere. 'Reading' nature is therefore something that is learned; and the learning process varies greatly between different societies and between different social groups within any society. Of course, there are environmental disasters but they are relative to a particular configuration of a society and 'its' environment. Configuration here refers both to the relationship between a society and 'its' environment, and to the manner in which this difference is culturally constructed within that environment.

With regard to the former aspect, there are four main ways in which societies have intersected with their respective 'physical environments': *stewardship* of the land so as to provide a better inheritance for future generations living within a given local area; *exploitation* of land or other resources through seeing nature as separate from society and available for its maximum instrumental appropriation; *scientisation* through treating the environment as the object of scientific investigation and hence of some degree of intervention and regulation; and *visual consumption* through constructing the physical environment as a 'landscape' (or townscape) not primarily for production but embellished for aesthetic appropriation.

These are very much ideal types and any particular situation will involve some mixture of two or more. Furthermore, although there is a loose historical ordering in the emergence of these different configurations of society and the environment, all four are to be found in contemporary societies. This chapter is concerned to establish that visual consumption is relatively separate and to examine some implications of this for the other three forms of relationship. I have so far used the term 'environment' as though this is fairly clear. It is

174

not of course and this becomes evident as soon as we start to consider its visual consumption. I shall use the term 'environment' to cover either the physical setting alone (whether this is or is not built), or the physical setting and the forms of its cultural appropriation.

An example of the latter can be seen in the development of the Western concept of 'landscape'. This began as a technical term standing for natural inland scenery; then it came to mean a particular tract of land seen from a specific point of view as though it were a picture; and finally it came to mean the whole natural scenery (Barrell 1972). The concept of landscape is important both for the history of art and for the history of those places which were thought to possess remarkable or distinctive landscapes (see Hefferan 1985, on the creation of landscape within English Romanticism; Pemble 1987, on the Mediterranean; Green 1990, on the area surrounding Paris in the early nineteenth century; and Barrell 1972, 1980).

This is not then a simple question of the physical environment. Zukin argues that 'the material landscape was mediated by a process of cultural appropriation, and the history of its creation was subsumed by visual consumption' (1991: 7). Green argues that it was in the nineteenth century that nature came to be 'hegemonised by a definition of the external world as scenery, views, perceptual sensation' (1990: 3). Nature as landscape was, then, a historically specific social and cultural construction. In particular, there is the irony that something as apparently important as nature 'has largely to do with leisure and pleasure – tourism, spectacular entertainment, visual refreshment' (Green 1990: 6).

In the eighteenth century, the aristocracy and gentry possessed exceptional power to determine the character of their landscapes for visual consumption. In particular, the physical environment that they encountered contained the working poor. But in the representations of such environments, in the landscape paintings, the poor came to be transformed into part of the landscape itself (see Barrell 1980). This can be seen even in the case of Constable. The representation of the poor changed over his lifetime in that the figures came to be placed more and more in the distance, becoming an almost invisible element of the distant landscape.

The upper class was, moreover, mobile and this helped them develop the cultural capital necessary for judging and discriminating between such different environments. Barrell argues that such an upper class: 'had experience of more landscapes than one, in more geographical regions than one; and even if they did not travel much, they were accustomed, by their culture, to the notion of mobility, and could easily imagine other landscapes' (Barrell 1972: 63).

By the later nineteenth century the upper middle and middle classes were also becoming increasingly mobile, travelling not just to spa towns, seaside resorts and areas like the Lake District in Britain, but further afield to the Mediterranean, especially to Italy and the French Riviera (see Pemble 1987).

They brought back memories, souvenirs and, increasingly, photographs of landscapes lit by qualities of quite unfamiliar heat and light. In the twentieth century such landscapes have, of course, helped to generate an even more extensive 'Mediterranean passion' among much of the population of Western and Northern Europe.

Everyone in the 'West' is now entitled to engage in visual consumption, to appropriate landscapes and townscapes more or less anywhere in the world, and to record them to memory photographically. No one should be excluded except for reasons of cost. To be a tourist, to look on landscapes with interest and curiosity (and then to be provided with many other related services), has become a right of citizenship from which few in the 'West' are formally excluded.

There is thus a 'democratisation' of the tourist gaze, something well-reflected in the anti-elitist and promiscuous practices of photography (see Sontag 1979). Such practices give shape to travel. Much tourism becomes in effect a search for the photogenic, it is a strategy for the accumulation of photographs (Urry 1990: Ch. 7). This means that as photographic technologies and practices change and develop so the kinds of sights to be photographed also change. Thus what people look for in the landscapes and townscapes that they photograph are not given and fixed but alter over time. In particular, new techniques of colour photography have increased the demand to travel to and record landscapes which are free from various kinds of visible pollution, such as machinery, motorways, power stations, workers, polluted water, smog, derelict land and so on (see Williams 1973; Cosgrove 1984; Urry 1990: 97–8). Technical developments have made this possible for many people. So as the means for recording people's memories have been democratised, this has further boosted the development of tourism, particularly the visiting of places where environmentally unpolluted landscapes can be viewed and captured. And yet, of course, such places are increasingly polluted in another sense, through the huge numbers of visitors all seeking to photograph rather similar scenes (often from formal or information viewing points). So photography has heightened the contradictions involved in the relationship between tourism and the environment. It has increased the attractions of particular kinds of unpolluted landscapes and hence of demands to protect or conserve such environments; and it has in turn done much to worsen such environments through increasing the numbers and concentration of visitors all seeking to capture particularly memorable views.

There is an interesting piece of research conducted on photographing one particular tourist mecca, Durham in north-east England. The research showed that tourists were in fact rather disappointed by their photographs of the cathedral and castle from Prebend's Bridge (see Pocock 1982). It was thought that their memories of the view were richer and fuller than their photographs, which had as C. Day Lewis once wrote the quality of 'dead accuracy' (cited in Pocock 1982: 364). And indeed it may be that such images always disappoint but that, of course, does not stop people continuously seeking new images of place. Indeed it may be that it is because of that disappointment that people continuously seek ever-new images and hence ever-new places to visit and capture.

However, this raises much more general questions concerning broader changes in economic and social life of contemporary societies. These changes have been characterised by Harvey as involving 'time-space compression' (1989). This refers to the way in which changes in the organisation of capitalist labour-time have transformed space, suppressing all sorts of differences between places. Events and processes are increasingly interdependent. Simple narratives are implausible. Everything depends upon developments elsewhere as the nineteenth and twentieth centuries have brought about a plethora of new technologies of transportation and communication which have subdued and unified space, producing many imagined or metaphorically 'small' worlds (see Lodge 1983).

Harvey notes five effects of time-space compression. First, there is the accentuation of volatility and the ephemeral in products, fashions, ideas, values, technologies and so on. As Marx and Engels famously wrote, 'all that is solid melts into air' (1964) and this characterises modern consumerism and its deleterious environmental consequences. Second, there is the emphasising of instantaneity and disposability, or what Toffler termed the 'throwaway society' (1970). Not only material goods but also values, lifestyles, relationships and attachments to place can all be easily disposed of. Third, short-termism is encouraged or, as Lyotard remarks, the temporary contract is everything (cited in Harvey 1989: 291). Long-term conservation becomes difficult to contemplate where everything is judged in and by the present. Fourth, it is signs or images which most exemplify time-space compression. A world-wide industry produces and markets images, not only for products, but also for people, governments, places, universities and so on. There is an extraordinary transitoriness, and an extraordinary number, of different images, including in recent years those of nature and the natural. Fifth, certain of these images resulting from time-space compression involve the production of simulacra: replications of originals more real, or hyper-real, than the original (Eco 1986). Almost everything can now be reproduced, including apparently authentic ancient buildings as in Quinlan Terry's neo-classical Richmond; or 'natural' features of the landscape, such as the pink and white terraces which were located above Lake Rotomahana in New Zealand and are to be recreated elsewhere a century after they were destroyed by a volcano (Urry 1990: 146). One might also suggest that tourist souvenirs particularly well illustrate these characteristics of time-space compression. It is as though the paradigm case of ephemerality, disposability, temporariness, images and simulacra, is the material culture involved in the consumption of visual tourist signifiers.

But such developments in turn produce responses. Harvey argues that the 'collapse of spatial barriers does not mean that the significance of space is decreasing' (1989: 293). The less salient the spatial barriers the greater the sensitivity of capitalist firms, of governments and of the general public to variations of the environment across space. Harvey says that: 'As spatial carriers diminish so we become much more sensitised to what the world's spaces contain' (1989: 294). The specificity of place, of its workforce, the character of its entrepreneurialism, its administration, its buildings, its history, its environment and so on, become important as spatial barriers collapse. And it is this context that further explains just why places increasingly seek to forge a distinctive image and to create an atmosphere of environment, place and tradition that will prove attractive to capital, to highly skilled prospective employees and especially to visitors (see Harloe *et al.* 1990). Indeed, the heightened interest in the environment, both physical and built, partly stems from the fact that people, politicians and prospective employers are all concerned both to make places seem different from each other and to make them consistent with particular contemporary images of environment and places, particularly those of nature.

Two interesting examples from Australia illustrate this point. First, Game (1990) shows how an attempt was made in the mid-1980s to construct Bondi Beach as an international tourist attraction based on the famous but run-down Pavilion. It was argued that the 'natural' site of Bondi was not in itself sufficient, but that it had to be produced as memorable and as standing for 'Australia', that it was truly part of an international tourist industry. However, this failed for a number of reasons. It was argued by the 'local community', mainly in fact recent in-migrants, that Bondi belongs to 'Australia' and therefore not to any commercial interests, and that since Bondi is 'nature' and that since no one can own nature, so no one can (or should) own Bondi. The potential developers, by contrast, argued that since Bondi belongs to the world it needs 'international' tourist facilities, but that a strong emphasis should be placed on reinforcing or even constructing the local particularity of Bondi-ness at least for visitors. In other words, the developers sought to combine the global and the local in the site that stands for 'Australia', the nation.

Morris (1990b) provides a similar analysis of Sydney Tower, a cultural symbol in Australia dating from 1981. She argues that what was symbolically different about this tower was that it celebrated tourism as a means of becoming modern rather than as an end in itself. In particular it interpellated Sydney residents as 'citizen/tourists', becoming at one with 'real' tourists in their gaze on Sydney, and becoming simultaneously the living objects of that gaze (see Urry 1990, on the tourist gaze). But by the late 1980s much of the tower had changed and it had become not a spectacle of Sydney and its history but merely an indicator of other places that visitors might travel to. Indeed, Morris notes that the Sydney skyline is now one of the Pacific Rim, not of Europe and the Eiffel Tower (1990b: 12).

In the next section I shall consider the ways in which an apparently heightened interest in protecting the environment has stemmed from the growth of visual consumption through tourism. Following this I shall show some of the complex ways in which it might be thought that tourism adversely affects the environment. Finally, I shall consider some of the characteristics which render an environment attractive or unattractive to visual consumption through the tourist gaze. I shall suggest that such a gaze can take a variety of forms which will fall very differently on different places and environments.

TOURISM AND THE ENVIRONMENTAL CONSCIOUSNESS

There are a number of ways in which mass tourism has helped to broaden concern for both the physical and the built environment. First, tourism enables a much wider range of environments to be gazed upon. This has been especially marked with the growth of car and air transport, compared with the railway which tended to funnel visitors into particular centres and resorts. People have become able to compare and contrast different landscapes and to develop some of the cultural capital necessary in order to make appropriate judgements of taste. Car transport in particular enables people to be much less channelled in their movements through particular landscapes. They can come across unexpected eyesores or indeed unexpected and unplanned landscapes or townscapes. Of course, all forms of transport necessitate a substantial infrastructure and this may itself be the eyesore!

Second, different environments can be much more effectively compared than was possible in the past. This is because of the 'globalisation' of the tourist gaze, at least for those in the 'West' and for some of those living in the Pacific Rim. This globalisation is a further demonstration of time-space compression. It occurs through actual travel, often now to much more distant places; through simulated travel as in shopping centres, world fairs and touristic-historical spectacles such as the Australian Bicentenary (see Morris 1990a on the last of these); and most spectacularly through armchair travel which permits almost everywhere in the world to be seen and compared with anywhere else (Urry 1990). Images of appropriate environments can now be much more readily conjured up, evaluated and compared, often through people's own photographs or through programmes seen on the TV/VCR.

Third, both the interest in environment and the growth of tourism stem from the increased importance of visual consumption, or more generally of an 'aesthetic' judgement rather than one based on reason and discourse (Lash 1990b). This in turn is related to the shift in the predominant economic structure in Western societies, from the relations of production to those of consumption (see Abercrombie 1990; Morris 1990a). Central to people's experience of such societies are the dynamics of consumption, and such consumption is based on aesthetic judgements, especially in relationship to the consumption of the environment. This is in turn related to the widespread development of what elsewhere I call the 'romantic tourist gaze'. Larger numbers of people seek, in their visual consumption, solitude, privacy and a personal, semi-spiritual relationship with their environment, whether this is physical or built. The romantic tourist gaze thus feeds into and supports attempts to protect the environment. (Walter (1982) illustrates this with reference to Stourhead Park in Wiltshire, see p.137 of this book)

Fourth, the increase in the proportion of people with higher levels of education, with professional/managerial jobs and who are older, are all leading to increases in concern for the environment and in certain kinds of tourism. In particular these factors are heightening the attraction of both visiting and protecting the countryside. In the UK there have been huge increases in the membership of various countryside conservation organisations: between 1971 and 1987 that of the National Trust increased by 505 per cent, the Royal Society for the Protection of Birds by 539 per cent, the Royal Society for Nature Conservation by 281 per cent, and Friends of the Earth by 2850 per cent (Urry 1990: 96). The countryside is attractive to such groups and this reflects the anti-urbanism of the environmental movement. The countryside appears to be 'closer' to nature; there is a relative absence of people; there is a non-mechanical environment; and the environment is unplanned, complex and labyrinthine. And yet, of course, there is little that is natural about Westernised forms of agriculture in the countryside; in order to achieve solitude it is necessary to travel long distances to by-pass congested sights; the environment is highly mechanised and one only avoids such mechanical sights through the construction of very selective 'landscapes'; and little in the environment is unplanned since in some respects agriculture is one of the most rationalised of industries and subject to extensive external regulation. Moreover, the effects of environmental conservation in the countryside has by no means unambiguous consequences for other social groups. As Flynn, Lowe and Cox point out:

> Most towns and villages have an amenity or preservation group, concerned with safeguarding the character and physical appearance of the locality from any unpleasant developments. By the 1970s, twenty-five years of rural planning had thus succeeded in recasting protected dormitory villages and middle-class enclaves whose residents' demands were often at odds with those of the indigenous population.
>
> (Flynn *et al.* 1990: 10)

Further, there are important changes taking place in contemporary tourism which both reflect an increased environmental consciousness and further develop such a consciousness. The mass-production, mass-consumption packaged holiday to Mediterranean resorts seems to be declining in popularity as people's tastes are becoming more differentiated and selective.

Instead there are expansions in long-haul holidays, and in rural, urban, industrial and even green tourisms. Increasingly, people seem to be attracted by a much wider range of objects upon which to gaze. This has mixed environmental effects. On the one hand, it reduces, at least relatively, some of the problems of congestion that I will discuss further below. On the other hand, the broadening of people's tastes means that the effects of tourism, both good and bad, are spread across a much wider range of places. In the UK there is hardly a village, town or city which does not now have the promotion of tourism as one of its key objectives. And this is increasingly true worldwide.

The case of Spain is one of the most interesting here since, on the face of it, there could hardly be a clearer case of somewhere where tourism has been an unmitigated environmental disaster (see Hooper 1990; Hopkins 1990, on the following). There are, however, some rather contradictory points to note about its pattern of development:

1 it did not experience the long period of industrialisation found in all of its northern neighbours – there were therefore relatively few areas which were environmentally damaged in the way experienced by the industrial regions of Northern Europe;

2 the country has jumped from a mostly pre-industrial to a post-industrial society in about three decades in the post-war period;

3 the industry which brought about this striking transformation has been tourism which generated the foreign exchange to cover the trade gap as the economy took off – in 1988 tourism was responsible for about 10 per cent of economic activity and employment;

4 the development of tourism has, moreover, had a significant redistributive effect as it has mainly been those from the richer countries of Northern Europe who have travelled to the Mediterranean basin and, apart from the British, they have spent quite a lot while there;

5 the environmental effects on the Spanish Mediterranean coast and the Balearic islands have been devastating, and to some extent this is also true on the Atlantic coast which is more popular with the Spanish themselves;

6 however, this environmental effect has been confined to the relatively narrow coastal strip and most of Spain has remained relatively untouched (with, for example, more rare species than in any other European country);

7 there are now major efforts being made to develop tourism in the rest of Spain because of the declining attractiveness of its standard product, the cheap mass-produced beachside holiday (in part resulting from the visually unattractive nature of the Mediterranean coastline);

8 this will, though, result in new forms of environmental decline inland,

181

especially with the kind of large-scale developments favoured by Spanish entrepreneurs that, paradoxically, may not be particularly attractive to potential visitors from Northern Europe where there is more sensitivity about the environment;

9 the Spanish government is attempting to move the Mediterranean area upmarket through the ecologically draconian 1988 Shores Act which bans construction near the shoreline and enables the demolition of any buildings which do not have proper planning permission.

Thus the environmental implications are more complex than they might otherwise seem. It certainly does not follow that encouraging tourists to travel into inland Spain is necessarily going to benefit either the environment or the Spanish people. One might argue the reverse, that minimum damage would be exerted by keeping the visitors to the Mediterranean coast and by actually preventing them from moving inland. However, that would have had socially selective consequences since only the richer visitors would be able to buy property inland enabling them to escape the coast.

One of the common criticisms made of many tourist developments such as those on the Spanish coast is that they are 'artificial' and have involved the production of an entirely constructed environment (often with buildings of the direst architectural quality). However, the Spanish example should make us wary of jumping to the conclusion that such artificial developments are necessarily undesirable. An interesting example cited by Jill Tweedie is that of Portmeirion, a beautiful fantasy village built on a north Wales peninsula which is designed only for tourists (Tweedie 1990). It has two particular virtues: first, it is very attractive and works as a set of buildings in a striking physical location, although it is entirely 'artificial' and 'postmodern' before its time; and, second, visitors to the area are concentrated into this 'honeypot' and do not bother people living in the surrounding villages. Tweedie summarises: 'tourists may wander, gawp, shop and relax without elbowing a single local off his rocker. . . . The locals, 80 of them, just work there and retire of an evening to the peace of their own real villages' (1990).

However, many tourists would in fact also like to visit those 'real villages'. Recent research on tourism in rural Wales revealed that what people claimed to like best was 'ordinary' relatively well-preserved countryside rather than specific themed attractions (Jones 1987). Such views reflect the growth of so-called 'green tourism' which began in Switzerland, West Germany and France and is found in Britain in Dorset, Northumberland, Herefordshire and Cumbria. Its task is to ensure the conservation of areas and their associated wildlife. Its emphases are small-scale, local control, modest developments using local labour, buildings in 'traditional' style, the emphasis on personal contact with visitors, the eating of local produce, encouraging the understanding of the area's ecology and heritage, and the setting of limits to the growth of such developments so as to avoid a tourist mono-industry.

One example of where green tourism would have had a significant impact is in the case of reforestation. Tourists have shown particular hostility to the 'modernistic' planing of coniferous forests which are believed to have deleterious environmental and social consequences: the loss of 'indigenous' wildlife including birds of prey, reduced employment levels and the elimination of wild, open and 'romantic' moors (see Shoard 1987: 223–5). This example suggests that if tourists were able to exert greater pressure to protect the environment then open moorlands and deciduous forests would have been more effectively preserved and the modernised planting of rows and rows of conifers would not have been allowed. So one effect of more tourists may be to improve the campaigning for an improved environment, especially to the extent to which a kind of 'green tourism' consciousness becomes more common. It is because of tourism that many national parks have been created and without them many animal and plant species would have disappeared (see Hamilton 1990).

Finally, it is worth considering briefly why many people want to gaze upon such a wide range of environments, that is, why are people willing to take greater risks with regard to foreign food, language, air transport, foreign customs, pollution and so on? Does the development of tourism in the past two decades suggest greater personal risk-taking and hence a re-skilling of everyday life? Is there some paradoxical connection here between disempowerment in relationship to nuclear radiation and other forms of chemical pollution and a re-skilling in various other aspects of everyday life? As Beck argues, our senses have become inadequate to assess certain forms of risk, there has been a 'disempowerment of our senses', so that people have been reduced to 'media products' and need to accept 'the dictation of centralised information' (Beck 1987: 156). So it is argued that as the atomic danger (war and power) has made everyday life 'headless', so people have instead become risk-takers in other contexts (crime, fast driving, drugs, exotic food, foreign travel, etc.). Certainly these are new ways of using one's senses which according to Beck have been disempowered. He talks of 'the end of perceptiveness and the beginning of a social construction of risk realities' (Beck 1987: 156).

In conclusion then, part of the process by which tourism is spreading worldwide is the very growth of an environmental consciousness. People, it seems, increasingly search out and compare different places, particularly in terms of the perceived character of the physical and built environment. Places that have been subject to modernisation, of their agriculture or forestry, industry or leisure, are normally unsought after by visitors, except in the case of major cities. One element of this tourism is to help heighten an environmental consciousness and, indeed, in some cases to improve aspects of the physical environment (even arguably in the case of Spain). In the next section I shall consider the obverse side of many of these points. The growth of the romantic gaze, which celebrates 'nature', is helping to spread tourism worldwide and is therefore contributing to widespread environmental deterioration (see Romeril 1990 on the following).

TOURISM AND ENVIRONMENTAL DAMAGE

In the 1970s the Greek Orthodox Church recommended a new prayer:

> Lord Jesus Christ, Son of God, have mercy on the cities, the islands and the villages of this Orthodox Fatherland, as well as the holy monasteries which are scourged by the worldly touristic wave.
>
> (Cited in Crick 1988: 64)

Thus tourists are increasingly seen as major polluters of the environment, by comparison with the locals who are taken as signifiers of authentic forms of life. This comparison is not, of course, fully justified because of the enormous impact of the different farming practices of 'locals' upon environmental quality (see Lowe *et al.* 1990, in the case of the UK). Nevertheless, tourists have increased the risks for those already living in particular places. The heightened sensitivity to the environment, with 52 per cent of those in the UK considering it to constitute a serious problem facing the country, has the effect that tourism is also increasingly viewed as a major environmental issue (Phillips 1990). The deleterious environmental consequences of tourism take a number of different forms:

1 Congestion and infrastructural strain

In Venice the intense problems of transportation and basic services have recently been even further aggravated by a huge influx of East European visitors, particularly on day trips. There has been a successful campaign waged by residents to prevent EXPO 2000 being located in the city because it is already viewed as completely full. In the Lake District the National Park Officer argues that the area cannot take any more than the current 16–18 million visitors a year. He has suggested that a tourist tax should be levied on visitors (see Tighe 1990, for a rejoinder from William Davis, Chairman of the English Tourist Board at the time). Similarly, in Malta the lack of any public regulation, combined with a desire to expand the number of tourists, has resulted in intense problems of congestion. The number of tourists rose 30 per cent in one year (see Kelly 1990).

One reason why the environmental consequences are likely to be intense is because of the geographical concentration of tourists. For example, 86 per cent of the tourists who used to visit Yugoslavia stayed in the coastal resorts. This not only intensifies the problems of ensuring good infrastructural services, such as the provision of clean water, but produces further problems: damage to the natural habitat of coastal marine life, the building of inappropriate and unsightly high-rise hotels (as currently in Turkey); the

184

distorting of the local patterns of employment, especially because of the seasonal nature of many tourist flows and social strains because of the cultural differences between 'hosts' and 'guests' (see Turner and Ash 1975; Smith 1978).

2 Changes in farming patterns and in the resulting appearance of the landscape

In Chianti in Tuscany, there has been a growing dispute over what British visitors call 'Chiantishire'. Recently, the Chianti Foundation has been founded with the aims of preventing further foreign investment in the area and the 'purging' of 'contaminating elements'. Foreign smallholders, in particular, have been criticised since they do not know how to run vineyards properly. The result has been that local culture, farming practices and the appearance of the countryside are in danger of being seriously altered (see Johnston 1990). In the Lake District the reduction in farm subsidies is threatening the viability of upland sheep farmers and hence of the particularly distinctive landscape that flocks of Herdwick sheep have produced over the centuries.

3 The siting of large tourism developments in environmentally sensitive areas

Examples here include the development of skiing complexes such as that at Aviemore in Scotland or the extraordinary development of 'industrial skiing' in the Alps (see Kettle 1990). These mountains extend into seven countries but now support a permanent population of only 12 million. However, the temporary population is ten times as large and rising fast. The Alps have been reconstructed as 'a single-commodity colony of lowland Europe. That commodity is . . . "industrial skiing"' (Kettle 1990: 7). There are now an extraordinary 40,000 ski-runs in the Alps, produced by the ripping up of forests, the obliteration of pastures, the diverting of rivers and the concreting over of valleys.

In Malta large areas of farming land have been turned over to tourist developments. On the island of Gozo, Malta's only remaining area of 'wilderness' has been sold to a Swiss company which is going to build 600 holiday villas there (see Kelly 1990). Interestingly, the Maltese government has just appointed their first Secretary for the Environment, and he has made a modest reduction in the scale of this proposed development. There is little doubt that mass tourism in relatively small areas like Malta (now receiving 1 million overseas visitors a year) results in serious environmental damage in countries without a strong and environmentally conscious state. And this will in turn result in an area's declining attractiveness to more prosperous visitors. However, arguments against mass tourism are commonly socially selective and imply that such visitors are unable to appreciate the more subtle features about a place. Kelly writing on Malta talks of the mass English visitors not being 'particular about tasteful surroundings or holidays that reflect the country's character' (1990). Selbourne likewise inveighs against 'Club Yob' in Corfu which has been devastated by the arrival of large numbers of young working-class men from Britain who, it is claimed, sometimes do not even appreciate which island they are visiting (1990). Selbourne notes that:

> Prices are too low [*sic*] and development has been too rapid, with greed the spur and profit the all-consuming aim, at whatever the cost to the ancient spirit of the place and its ravishing, ravaged beauty. . . . It is a vicious circle that has left Corfu at the mercy of the more brutish of British tourists.

There are two points to note about criticisms of mass tourism on environmental grounds. First, such a critique involves an expression of social taste which may well connote social superiority over the mass tourists who are thought to be causing environmental deterioration. It is therefore a form of class and generational politics (as in the Selbourne example above), or of racial/national politics (as in the opposition to Japanese mass tourism developments in Australia: see Morris 1990a). Such a viewpoint often rests on what I term the romantic tourist gaze, the solitudinous contemplation of an undisturbed nature, which has been fostered by a particular social class. Walter argues that:

> professional opinion-formers (brochure writers, teachers, Countryside Commission staff, etc.) are largely middle class and it is within the middle class that the romantic desire for positional goods is largely based. Romantic solitude thus has influential sponsors and gets good advertising.

> (Walter 1982: 303; and see Ch. 8)

Second, to advocate that areas should be conserved from the ravages of tourist development suggests that it is clear what is meant by 'conservation'. But of course all environments are in part 'person-made' and thus one cannot simply employ the concept of the 'natural' to demarcate that which should be conserved. Conservation is not an unambiguous notion with precise environmental implications. There are at least three kinds of conservation. One of these can be called aesthetic conservation – to conserve an environment in accordance with pre-given conceptions of beauty and the sublime, conceptions which often depend upon what is being contrasted with the environment in question (see Green 1990). A second conception is that of scientific conservation – to conserve in accordance with current scientific thinking on which elements of the physical environment are worth preserving and with how such elements should be so protected. A third conception is that of cultural conservation – to conserve the particular patterns of life of those living in a given area and to prevent outside interventions. The problem is that these different notions may well stand in stark contrast with one another, and this is especially so in the face of greatly increased demands to visit particularly attractive environments. For example, change is a crucial part of all apparently 'natural' processes so that attempts at literal 'conservation' on aesthetic or cultural grounds will contradict what is understood as scientific conservation.

Furthermore, aesthetic notions of the environment themselves change and recently have come to depend upon particular developments in the nature of the mass media. For example, with regard to the countryside, Daniels and Cosgrove point out that the rural landscape is like a 'flickering text . . . whose meaning can be created, extended, altered, elaborated and finally obliterated by a touch of a button' (1988: 8). Such aesthetic notions of conservation have also been important in the construction of various rural 'themed' environments consisting of a pastiche of artefacts, sounds, textures, photographic images and so on. These may appeal to visitors to the countryside but they obviously involve a highly constructed nature and almost certainly will produce environmental damage, especially from the viewpoint of scientific conservation. This damage, relative to a particular construction of nature, will result both from a contrived construction of rural themes, and from marked increases in the number of visitors which will, for example, affect the indigenous flora and fauna.

And yet, even scientific conservation is not a fixed notion since what is supposedly 'indigenous' is not an absolute. The species found within any given area change, depending upon climate, atmosphere, migration, land use and so on. There is no absolute nature – it is historically and geographically relative. And yet relative to that particular nature, certain sorts of changes, such as those produced through tourist developments, *are* environmentally damaging. There is, therefore, not absolute damage but damage relative to a specific historically and geographically given nature.

TOURISM AND THE VISUAL CONSUMPTION OF THE ENVIRONMENT

In the final section I shall set out a number of different ways in which an environment is seen as inappropriate for visual consumption through the tourist gaze. This will then reveal some of the characteristics that render an environment suitable for that gaze, as well as some of the different forms taken by that gaze.

First, there is the environment which is visually contaminated because matter is out of place, there is 'technological landscape guilt' (see Thayer 1990: 2). Material objects are present which can be interpreted as 'inappropriate'. Examples would include the viewing of a nuclear power station on an attractive coastline (such as Heysham nuclear power station on Morecambe Bay), or factory buildings in an otherwise charming river valley (as in much of the Basque country), or farm buildings next to a high technology science park and so on. In response to this problem many owners of tourist-related services have developed techniques of 'visual resource management', to disorganise, hide or screen out inappropriate technologies (see Thayer 1990).

However, it should be noted that there are some environments which are enjoyed by people almost because they contain interesting juxtapositions of landscape and building (as in much city tourism). Cultures vary as to the degree to which pastoral landscapes devoid of 'modern' technologies are appreciated (see Thayer 1990: 5). Also, as buildings age, some become viewed as metaphorically 'part of the landscape', such as the Ribblehead viaduct on the Settle–Carlisle railway or the Albert Dock on the waterfront at Liverpool.

Second, there are environments which are seen as dangerous, as unnecessarily risky, because they are believed to be polluted. This pollution can take either or both of two forms. On the one hand, there is physical pollution, in particular of air or water, which makes it seem dangerous to be present in a particular location. However, the judgement of what is 'risky' here is very much dependent on context. Being a tourist seems to involve some striking changes in what is perceived to be risky. For example, visitors to an area may be willing to risk illness, through eating contaminated foods (such as local shellfish) or having sexual relations with strangers, because of the forms of exotic visual consumption that place such activities in a different context from what is normal and everyday. It is claimed that tourism is a liminal state in which conventional calculations of safety and risk are disrupted. Other kinds of physical pollution though, such as breathing in the relatively harmless steam produced by coal-fired power stations, will almost certainly render an area as inappropriate for the gaze of tourists.

On the other hand, there is social pollution. There are believed to be individuals or social groups in a particular location whose beliefs or actions are seen as 'polluting'. Some examples include alcoholics, the homeless, prostitutes, drug users, pick-pockets, dangerous drivers, teenage gangs and even other tourists. The result is to make certain places seem contaminated and unsuitable for visual consumption. However, quite striking changes can occur in the perception of such 'pollutants', even sometimes with such groups becoming part of the exotic or 'traditional' attractions of a place. This seems to be occurring with regard to the Aboriginal peoples in Australia. On the occasion of the Bicentenary, the Australian government found it necessary to initiate some hasty measures to compensate the Aborigines for years of neglect (see Morris 1990a). This was apparently because tourists and journalists were increasingly finding that Aboriginal culture and practices are no longer 'polluting' but are part (or even the most important part) of the exotic attractions of Australia. In New Zealand, of course, there has been a longer process of transforming the Maoris into an object of visual consumption.

Third, the environment is viewed as commonplace, as too much like everywhere else. There is nothing that potential visitors find remarkable, which sets off that place from many others and especially from the views and scenes that people experience in their everyday life. A crucial aspect of the tourist gaze is that there is a dichotomy drawn between the ordinary and extraordinary (see Urry 1990). Obviously all sorts of sites/sights can be extraordinary, including places that are merely famous for being famous. But environments which are not visually distinct in some way or other are very unlikely to be consumed. But it does not follow from this that only physical phenomena possess such an aura of distinctiveness. Both physical and person-made phenomena can generate awe, that moment that takes the breath away (such as seeing Glencoe in the Scottish Highlands or the Clifton suspension bridge in Bristol for the first time). However, it should be noted that this perception historically changes from period to period (as with the current attraction of old railway stations and sidings); and that sometimes it is the very unchanging nature of a particular environment which makes it para-doxically remarkable (as with an apparently unending desert).

It should also be noted that attempts to conserve a particular area because of its special environmental quality may end up with the area being made so distinctive for visitors that it becomes over-run. This is currently a matter for debate in the Cairngorms in Scotland, the most significant area of wild land and woodland over 3,000 feet in the UK. It has been proposed that the Cairngorms should be protected through being designated as a national park (see Clover 1990). However, it has been argued against this that such a proposal would create a tourist 'honeypot', much like the Lake District in north-west England. To designate somewhere as a national park is to generate a kind of magnet, sucking in potential visitors who otherwise might visit many different places in the Scottish Highlands. It is also worth noting that one of the current environmental problems in the Cairngorms is that the native pine forests are not regenerating satisfactorily because of the large deer population. Yet visitors to the area might in fact prefer to see large herds of deer. However, the herds are only there because of deer-stalking by the landowners and their friends. More pine forests and fewer deer would appear to be a more environmentally sound policy but it is not necessarily the one that environmentalists might pursue.

Finally, there are those environments which are in some sense historically inappropriate. The reference here to history may seem strange but it is important to understand that landscapes are not only visible in space but are also narratively visible in time (see Folch-Serra 1990). Or as Lynch asks, 'what time is this place?', or rather, 'what time is this environment?' (Lynch 1973). Environments will be visibly consumed if they appear consistent with that 'time'. This is what people mean by authenticity, that there is a consistent relationship between the physical and built environment and a given historical period. An example of where a rural landscape does not seem authentic is where it seems too 'modern', too planned, lacking hedgerows, winding paths, mixed tree and plant vegetation and an element of surprise. The 1950s holiday camp, by contrast, was based upon looking modern, often being built in a functionalist manner devoid of ornamentation and anything traditional (see Ward and Hardy 1986: Ch. 5, on the design of Prestatyn holiday camp for example). However, it should not be concluded from this that people's sense of what is and is not authentic about an environment is in fact historically accurate. This is very well shown by Sharratt in the case of the apparently authentic medieval environment of Canterbury Cathedral (1989: 36–8). But in fact almost all the windows in the cathedral have been reconstructed much more recently, such as the south window (in 1972) and much of the north (in 1774), and the first miracle window is made up of scraps of old and new glass. Likewise Christ Church Gate dates from a restoration begun in 1931 and the twin turrets were replicas from 1937. Sharratt notes that: 'the videos and snapshots . . . are recording images of replicas, constructed appearances' (1989: 38), which are hardly more authentic than those taken of the wholly simulated environment of the neighbouring Pilgrim's Way Centre, something that is part of the much maligned heritage industry (see Hewison 1987). Such centres are in part maligned because they are thought to produce passive consumption, with visitors having little real understanding of the exhibits or the forms of life being represented.

This is connected to what Sharratt goes on to discuss, namely, the development of 'the present image economy', where past objects and images are 'now seen, looked at, predominantly if not exclusively, as potential mental souvenirs, as camera material, as memorable "sights"' (1989: 38). There is thus the development of a widespread and colonising tourist gaze. This has the effect of transforming environments, many of which are reconstructed for visual consumption. However, Sharratt further distinguishes between a number of different elements or types of such a gaze. Putting these together with the distinction I have drawn elsewhere between the romantic and collective tourist gaze, generates the forms shown in Table 12.1 (Urry 1990).

These are to be seen as ideal types and many tourist situations will involve complex combinations of these different tourist gazes. It is also necessary to note that these forms do not exhaust the different types of tourism. In particular, different tourist practices vary along three further dimensions: the spatial, that is the diverse types of travel and mobility involved; the temporal, that is, the length of time and the prospective/retrospective dimensions; and the institutional, that is, the overlap between tourism and other related forms of activity, such as shopping, sport, culture, hobbies, education and partial residence in an area. On the last of these I have elsewhere argued that there is

Table 12.1 Forms of the tourist gaze

Romantic	Solitary Sustained immersion Gaze involving vision, awe, aura
Collective	Communal activity Series of shared encounters Gazing at the familiar
Spectatorial	Communal activity Series of brief encounters Glancing at and collecting of different signs
Environmental	Collective organisation Sustained and didactic Scanning to survey and inspect
Anthropological	Solitary Sustained immersion Scanning and active interpretation

a process of de-differentiation taking place between tourism *per se* and these various other social practices, so much so that there is what one might describe as a colonising tourist gaze which has considerable implications for the quality of the environment within which these other services are provided (see Urry 1990).

The last point above is also particularly relevant to the environment. It is likely that people who live for part of the year in a tourist area, through possession of a 'second' home, will be particularly concerned about the environmental conservation of that area. They will tend to see themselves, perhaps over more than one generation, as being especially concerned for the careful stewardship of an area. Shurmer-Smith (1990) shows how wealthy summer tourists with second homes in the Ile de Moine are more 'local' in their orientation than are the apparently 'real' locals. And yet, of course, the phenomenon of the second home causes particularly severe environmental problems of a different sort, especially for those who are year-long residents, often on very modest incomes, who, for example, cannot ensure that their children are able to continue living in the area in question because the housing has been taken by second-homers.

What now needs to be undertaken is further research to demonstrate just how the social organisation of these different gazes impact upon various physical and built environments. This is a very complex issue, in part because many of the existing environments are themselves experiencing rapid but not always very perceptible environmental change (see Lowe *et al.* 1990 on British agriculture and the environment). But in relationship to such environments and the diverse modes of their visual consumption, such complexities derive from three crucial aspects of tourism.

First, tourism is fundamentally concerned with visually consuming the physical and built environment and in many cases the permanent residents who are its inhabitants. This has the consequence that environments, places and people are being regularly made and re-made as tourist objects, a process which often involves active participation by the state (see Morris 1990a, on how many Australians went from being 'tourists' to being 'toured'). Tourism is thus inseparable from the environment, although that environment has many other uses, including agriculture especially.

Second, to talk of visual consumption is to suggest that tourists use up or devour the very places and environments that they seek to gaze upon. Many people want to visit relatively undamaged environments and yet that is more or less impossible. As Wheatcroft says: 'We are all caught without escape in the tourist trap' (1990). It is very difficult to implement policies that would induce large numbers of people not to travel to places because of the undesirable environmental consequences. They know just how many other people are already on their way to any particular environment. And they also know that if they wait longer then the environment in question may have been totally destroyed, either directly or more indirectly through the construction of apparently contrived sites of 'staged authenticity'. In the absence of the kind of draconian solution favoured by the economist Mishan (1969), to abolish all international air travel, it is hard to see how the individual choices of millions of different consumers are going to be appropriately constrained. This is further reinforced by the very widespread involvement of local and national states who view the encouragement of tourism as a major component of economic strategy (see Leong 1989, on national tourism as an element of post-war nation-building).

Third, as tourist practices spread even more widely throughout populations that had not previously been active participants, so the demand for new forms of visual consumption and their environmental costs are going to increase markedly. It is very hard to see how it is going to be possible to regulate access *and* to maintain divisive forms of restricted access and not cause other environmentally undesirable consequences. Geoffrey Wheatcroft, for example, suggests that: 'a policy of moderate Nimbyism is the only hope of preserving our healing contact with Nature' (1990). So far neither private enterprise nor competing states have been able to develop collective solutions which would mitigate the profound effects of millions of individual tourist decisions. And that is partly because of the exceptional environmental dilemmas involved in tourism, as are strikingly revealed in the Spanish example discussed above. It is not entirely fanciful to suggest that tourism produces some of the *most* difficult of contemporary environmental issues.

13

THE MAKING OF THE
LAKE DISTRICT*

In some ways it would seem easy to account for why 17 million visits are made to the Lake District each year. It contains many very well-established tourist sites, a surprising variety of attractions from spectacular mountains to quaint hamlets, and a wealth of historical and literary associations. It also has a coherent identity which makes marketing it relatively straightforward both in Britain and in many countries in the First World.

But explaining this pattern of visiting is not so straightforward as it might seem. To continue to draw people to this place rather than to many others involves continuous work, both in terms of marketing but much more generally in terms of 'cultural production'. There is nothing obvious or inevitable about why huge numbers of people would voluntarily choose to visit this particular place, a place that up to the eighteenth century was seen as the very embodiment of inhospitability (see Crawshaw 1994a, 1994b). In the *Short Survey* of England in the 1630s it was described as 'nothing but hideous, hanging Hills' (cited in Ousby 1990: 130), while a century later Daniel Defoe famously described Westmorland as 'the wildest, most barren and frightful of any that I have passed over' (cited in Nicholson 1978: 25). Visiting the Lake District has not been undertaken simply because it exemplified nature. It was in some sense natural in the early eighteenth century but at the time the hills and mountains represented 'unhospitable terror', rather than the kind of nature which drew people to it. The Lake District appears to be the very embodiment of nature, an area that naturally exists and requires no external factors to ensure its continued successful existence. But this is misleading. The area had to be discovered; then it had to be interpreted as appropriately aesthetic; and then it had to be transformed into the managed scenery suitable for millions of visitors. This particular leisure pattern has not been the inevitable consequence of the Lake District's 'natural' scenery.

Up to the eighteenth century the Lake District was barely known about; it

* This chapter was produced as part of the ESRC project on 'Tourism, Nature and the Environment', 1992–4 (R00023–3172); the research officer was Carol Crawshaw. I am very grateful for her contribution to the argument here.

was a poor area, with few large houses and with little literature written in English. It was not part of England until it was both visited in significant numbers and some of those visitors began to write first in a somewhat mannered picturesque style and then in what is known as English Romanticism. Nicholson summarises: 'the Lake District does not come into English literature until it was discovered by visitors from the outside world' (1978: 33). It was that literature produced by visitors which served to develop a place-myth around the area which we now identify as the 'Lake District'. Such a myth could not have developed without visitors and without the literature that some of those visitors produced and others read. Also it could not have developed without some of those writers becoming definitive of a standard English literature. Thus the development of the Lake District as possessing a particular place-myth only occurred because of visitors and writers and of the incorporation of Romanticism into what has come to be known, taught and revered as English literature (see Shields 1991, on the concept of the place-myth).

The interconnections between travel patterns and artistic activity is well shown by Holderness who argues that London theatres since the Elizabethan period have partly served a national and international tourism market (1988). They only developed and became successful because large numbers of visitors from outside London were drawn to them. Shakespeare himself belonged to a class of entrepreneurs that 'helped to establish a cultural pattern in which every spectator is encouraged to become a tourist: who may well undertake a lengthy journey to a metropolitan theatre, who is required to attend at the dramatic event with reverence' (Holderness 1988: 10).

In the case of what we now call the Lake District, this only in a sense became part of England when many visitors, including artists and writers, began to travel to it, particularly from the metropolitan centre. These visitors turned the 'Lake District' into part of England particularly through the development of a particular kind of place-myth. The area came to be visited because a place-myth developed about this otherwise barren and inhospitable place. This was a noteworthy example of what became a strikingly significant characteristic of the late eighteenth century onwards, namely the rapid proliferation and circulation of myths of place. It seems to be a characteristic of 'modernity' that social spaces develop which are wholly or partly dependent on visitors, and that those visitors are attracted by the place-myths that surround and constitute such places (Lash and Urry 1994: Ch. 10). These may include places which are central to a society, such as London or Stratford-upon-Avon, as Holderness discusses (1988), or places which are otherwise peripheral, 'places on the margin' (Shields 1991). Examples of such place-myths which emerged in the late eighteenth and early nineteenth centuries in England included various country houses such as Blenheim and Chatsworth; certain ruins such as Stonehenge or Fountains Abbey; and resorts such as Brighton where royal scandal helped to concretise such a myth (Ousby 1990; Shields 1991).

The emergence of multiple competing place-myths itself stemmed from the striking shift in the nature of travel which Adler has documented between the sixteenth and eighteenth centuries (1989a). She demonstrates that before the eighteenth century travel had been based upon discourse and especially upon the sense of the 'ear'. This gradually shifted as 'eyewitness' observation became more salient but travel was still viewed as involving the documentation of information. However, this emphasis upon the eye as opposed to the ear was soon to receive a different inflection. By the eighteenth century mere travellers could not anticipate their observations becoming part of the scientific or scholarly understanding of the world. Mere travel to a place did not provide that sort of authority. The 'scientific' knowledge of 'nature' (and civilisation) came to be structurally differentiated from travel which thus entailed a different discursive justification. This came to be organised around connoisseurship as both works of arts and buildings, and then landscapes, became the object of comparative aesthetic evaluation. Travel itself became something of a 'performed art' in which good taste could be demonstrated by the places visited and by the aesthetic judgements made (see Barrell 1990, on correct taste in landscape painting in the eighteenth century). And Adler suggests that over the eighteenth century:

> travellers were less and less expected to record and communicate their observations in an emotionally detached, impersonal manner. Experiences of beauty and sublimity, sought through the sense of sight, were valued for their spiritual significance to the individuals who cultivated them. . . . In its aesthetic transformation, sightseeing became simultaneously a more effusive passionate activity and a more private one
>
> (1989a: 22)

She goes on to note the significance of the Rev. Gilpin's 'picturesque tours' in which travellers were enjoined to seek 'amusement' in the ways in which natural landscape was added to the other 'things' that an aesthetically trained eye might hope to grasp (Adler 1989a: 22). The amused eye in the eighteenth century turned to nature and to those places which had previously repelled visitors since they were not in any sense foci of aesthetic judgement. As an aesthetic judgement came to fix upon nature so it turned to those places, such as the 'Lake District', which had previously done nothing to attract the eye of the connoisseur. The eye turned to nature but this was the eye of the amused visitor not the scientific enquirer; and it was an eye that sought out places partly in terms of myth and image. In the rest of this chapter I will consider how such place-myths developed within this rapidly circulating sign-system in 'modern' England about the area that came to be known as the Lake District. This place-myth sought to fuse together a literary shrine similar to Stratford-upon-Avon *and* a shrine to nature – *Wordsworth's Guide to the Lakes* combining both elements (Wordsworth 1984; Ousby 1990; Andrews 1989). And this was a place-myth which established a discursive structure for being in, seeing and experiencing nature which was then taken as appropriate for reading and experiencing many other landscapes (see Chapman 1993: 195–6).

Such a place-myth is of course socially selective since only some people are drawn to a place by such myths. Not everyone visits, nor do visitors come from all social groups to the same degree, nor do all groups feel the same regret at not visiting. In the eighteenth century the Lake District came to be popular with writers and artists. In the nineteenth century the emergent professional and managerial class began to visit in large numbers, especially for walking, as we shall see, and later for climbing which began as a sport for professional men (see Milner 1984). Nowadays the area is still more popular with the middle-aged, with those in professional and managerial occupations, with white people, with car-owners, and those who prefer relatively 'quiet recreation' (see Crawshaw 1994b). The working class, ethnic minorities, those without a car are less likely to be drawn to the Lake District, less seduced by its place-myth, although rock climbing and various water sports are popular with a wide variety of younger social groups (see Milner 1984, on the broadening of the appeal of rock climbing from about 1900 onwards).

The predominant mode of experiencing the Lake District is summarised by a participant in a focus group discussion: '"To me, it is hills and mountains and lakes and water and peace and tranquillity"' (Crawshaw 1994b: 11). But this response to 'nature' is something that has to be learnt. Finding pleasure in 'dead' scenery involves acquiring a fair amount of cultural capital. We do not really know how people learn how to enjoy such experiences; and these focus group interviews suggest that people are not directly attracted to the Lake District precisely because of its literary and artistic associations. In such interviews almost no one referred to such associations and indeed visitors often seemed unaware of many of them (see Crawshaw 1994b: 13).

However, it is those writers and artists, beginning with Gilpin, who have provided us with the kind of language and vocabulary by which places are appreciated for their visual appeal. Lying behind individual perceptions of the Lake District are more systematic discourses of landscape, countryside, scenery and sight which have authorised and legitimated particular activities and ways of seeing, particularly those involving walking and 'quiet recreation' in the open air (Wallace 1993). Such discourses are socially and historically variable. The Lake District has both been transformed as a consequence of the development of such discourses and it has come to play an iconic role, especially because of the Lake poets, Ruskin and, indeed later, Beatrix Potter. However, such discourses and their related place-myths are not simply unchanging and eternal. The collapse of the attractiveness of the English seaside resort demonstrates that there can be rapidly changing social and cultural processes involved here; place-myths can evaporate or become outmoded or be replaced (see Shields 1991, on the changing place-myth of Brighton, for example).

One particular way that such myths can change is because of the flows of visitors; that too many or too few people arrive, or they are people whose social characteristics are inconsistent with or indeed directly opposed to the particular place-image. In the case of some English seaside resorts their place-myth of youthfulness, fun and repositories of excitement have been undermined by the declining numbers of people attracted to them and by the fact that an increasing proportion of visitors are elderly and are hence inconsistent with the place-image.

The place-myth of the Lake District suffers from the opposite problem, of huge numbers of visitors flowing especially to the so-called honeypots and the sense that many of the small urban centres are periodically overwhelmed. It is widely thought that at particular times in specific spaces, too many people are drawn into the Lake District and that as a result the enjoyment and pleasure of many visitors is reduced. Recent debates have occurred as to whether physical or financial systems of controlled entry to parts of the area should be introduced. In certain valleys the flows of visitors are regulated by deliberately restricted numbers of car parking spaces. There are various efforts made to channel, restrict and focus the flows of visitors, both to preserve aspects of the physical and built environment, and to enhance the enjoyment of those who are visiting, even if some of these initiatives entail modes of regulating the body in surprisingly restrictive ways. Much of the Lake District countryside involves its construction through discourses as a relatively 'passive landscape' (see Macnaghten and Urry 1993). This problem, of overcrowding and consequential surveillance and regulation, is particularly acute in the area because of two elements of the Lake District's place-myth.

First, there has been an emphasis placed upon what elsewhere I have termed the romantic tourist gaze, on the lakes and mountains constituting a positional good, a shrine to nature that individuals wish to enjoy in solitude or at least with relatively few others present. The emphasis here is upon a semi-private, quasi-spiritual relationship with the signifiers of 'nature' (see Chapter 8). This relationship with nature is established through walking in the countryside with relatively few other visitors being even visible, let alone nearby. In Chapter 8 I noted how Walter distinguishes between the physical carrying capacity of a place and its perceptual capacity (1982). During much of the year the perceptual capacity of some parts of the Lake District is met earlier than its apparent physical capacity; its perceptual capacity resulting from the pervasiveness of a romantic gaze which emphasises the more or less solitary, and peripatetic, appropriation of its supposedly unique 'nature'. Other countryside features such as caravans, allotments, groups of travellers, dairies, environmental protestors, traffic jams, pig farms, theme parks and so on are inconsistent with this gaze.

The second feature of the place-myth is the belief that the Lake District is particularly suited to 'quiet recreation', and that certain kinds of noisy activities are inappropriate. In other words, that this shrine to nature is constructed not just visually but also aurally, that only certain kinds of noise are somehow appropriate to the place – birdsong, steamers, tractors, cars – quite where low-flying aircraft or military gunfire fit into this is unclear! This means that too many people in general or too many people doing the wrong kinds of thing and making the wrong kinds of noise also reduce the area's carrying capacity. Recent debates over the speed limit of boats on Lake Windermere demonstrate the significance of these notions. There is a proposal to limit the speed on the lake to 10 m.p.h. and hence to prevent the very noisy boats that pull water skiers, as well as to limit certain other water sports. What is involved here is an objection both to the noise of the speed boats (although cars are responsible for far worse noise pollution in the Lakes) but also a distinction of taste against younger men and women who engage in such water sports. Their practices demonstrate that not all visitors to the Lake District do in fact embrace the dominant place-myth organised around the 'romantic' (and quiet) tourist gaze. In Chapter 8 I suggested that there is in tourism a 'collective' gaze based upon conviviality and collective activity and this will not necessarily produce the same response to what others perceive as over-crowding. A focus group participant observed: 'There were loads of day trippers in Bowness today. They are not looking for peace and quiet. They are looking for the high life' (Crawshaw 1994b: 18; and see Crawshaw 1994a). The Lake District demonstrates a clash between two forms taken by the tourist gaze, the romantic and the collective; in each case, the gaze is not simply visual since other activities stimulating non-visual senses are also involved (see Urry 1992, on the critique of the ocular in both social theory and travel literature, as well as Buzard 1993).

So I am concerned here to consider some of the reasons why the Lake District draws people to it, to problematise what might appear to be obvious. I will now show that it is not possible to understand the tourist attractions of the Lake District without relating its history to much more general processes of cultural and social development within England and to the variety of contending images of place and region that have been found during the last couple of centuries of English development. I will also show that it has been visitors from elsewhere that have produced *the* Lake District. Its very existence as a social space has resulted from the central role of visitors since the late eighteenth century. This most literary and artistic of sceneries is also one of the most visited so that it is tourism which has literally *made* the Lake District out of the 'wildest, most barren and frightful' of landscapes (Defoe, cited in Nicholson 1978: 25).

It is important to note some interesting parallels with the emergence of a 'spectacle of nature' which developed in early to mid-nineteenth century France. Green argues that nature is not a universal but is something that is historically and culturally constituted. In particular, a relatively new conception came to be hegemonic in the nineteenth century, that is, nature as understood as 'scenery, views, perceptual sensation' (1990: 3). And this new conception resulted from the development of travel and tourism. Green argues: 'Nature has largely to do with with leisure and pleasure – tourism, spectacular entertainment, visual refreshment' (1990: 6).

Green connects this spectacle-isation of nature with changes taking place within Paris itself. Before the industrialisation of France Paris became a modern city: that is, for Green, it had novel *visual* characteristics. There were spectacular street scenes bathed in new forms of lighting; arcades and shops demonstrated a fashionable consuming gaze; a male gaze developed within the recently built public spaces; and new ways emerged of environmentally viewing the diseased and dangerous parts of the city. The Marquis de Salvo described the capital in 1846: 'tumult, a mass of objects which every day reproduce the sensations of the day before: the sight of beautiful shops, richly-decorated cafes, elegant carriages, lovely costumes, lovely women . . . and all this kaleidoscope which changes, stirs, bemuses' (cited in Green 1990: 75).

However, this metropolitanism did not remain spectating only at Paris itself. There was a prolonged 'invasion of surrounding regions by and for the Parisian spectator' (Green 1990: 76). Two particular patterns of leisure and recreation in the 1840s onwards facilitated this invasion, the short trip out of the city and the increased ownership of houses in the country. These combined to produce what Green terms 'metropolitan nature'; that is, nature as spaces located relatively distant from the city and turned into places to be viewed for leisure and recreation through an individualised rejuvenating experience of nature (see Williams 1973). Green summarises some of the advertising for houses in the country in nineteenth century Paris:

> The language of views and panoramas prescribed a certain visual structure to the *nature* experience. The healthiness of the site was condensed with the actual process of looking at it, of absorbing it and moving round it with your eyes. Environmental values were here articulated in relation to visual modes of consumption that enabled the visitor simultaneously to look at 'the picture' and plunge into sensation.
>
> (1990: 88)

He also shows in the case of Barbizon, on the edge of the forest of Fontainebleau, the role of the burgeoning artists' community. Its growth had the effect both of producing appropriate pictorial images of metropolitan nature, and of actually leading the 'colonisation of rural space' (1990: 120). It was part of that very process by which the 'cultural hegemony of metropolitanism' was effected in the context of a rapidly developing tourist industry (1990: 128).

Some similar themes and processes are evident in the case of the Lake District, particularly after the growth of rail travel in the mid-nineteenth century (the 'rash assault' of the railway arrived in Windermere in 1847). However, its location far away from the centres of power in England, namely,

London and the south-east, meant that the kind of metropolitan nature that developed was rather different from that in Paris. In some ways the Lake District has always been a curious zone of transition between England and Scotland, a kind of anglicised, tamed and accessible version of Scotland. It has never been like the 'real' English countryside in the 'home counties', the more obviously 'metropolitan nature' which surrounds London. Hewison (1993) summarises: 'The wilder parts of Wales, Scotland and the Lake District offer grandeur, but Britain's imaginative heartland is a patchwork of woods and fields, small villages and distant spires. It is Samuel Palmer's Kent, Constable's Suffolk, John Piper's Oxfordshire'.

The Lake District countryside is rugged, spectacular and disturbing; it has been predominantly shaped by upland farming, especially sheep farming; there have been relatively few large landowners and stately houses built in the area; typical countryside sports are not those of the south; and it is land of evident hardship where working, walking, sightseeing, and now even driving involve a serious degree of effort. Unlike Scotland it has not been owned by very large landowners (except around the perimeter) and it has not provided a leisure resource only for the super-rich. As a consequence it has been more accessible, especially in the twentieth century to car owners, even though the majority of the land remains in private ownership (in fairly small units).

I will not provide here a lengthy account of the emergence of Lake District tourism since that has been developed in various other places (see, for example, Nicholson 1955; Bicknell and Woof 1983; Andrews 1989; Murdoch 1990; Ousby 1990; Buzard 1993; Wallace 1993). Some of the key moments were: the poet Gray's visits in 1767 and 1769; Arthur Young's visit in 1768 and his subsequent practical proposals for 'enabling the spectator to command . . . the luxuriant beauties and striking views'; Gilpin's visit in 1772 and his subsequent elaboration of the picturesque; Thomas West's guidebook in 1778 with its account of various viewing stations and of the desirable use of the Claude glass; the appearance of various satires such as the Revd James Plumptre's *The Lakers* in 1797; the discovery of Buttermere and the popular fascination with the story of the Maid of Buttermere; and Wordsworth's *Guide to the Lakes* in 1822 with its elaboration of the sublime and the picturesque and their subsequent transcendence by Romanticism.

There are I think four key points to emphasise in this history. First, most of these writers of the Lakes were initially visitors and not locals. They then wrote in such a way that popularised the area and encouraged many other visitors. This was achieved through developing the terminology by which nature could be characterised. Such a terminology later became applied to all sorts of other places but was initially formulated in the Lakes. The categories were applied elsewhere, often to imply that visitors were out-of-place and spoiling the 'romantic' sense of nature that people had learnt from the Lake District. This area was 'made' out of these visitors and of their struggles to convey the pictorial, experiential and emotional responses which their encounters with nature appeared to engender.

Second, although some of what was conveyed by the Romantic poets was universal, concerned with the living force of nature and its power to console, uplift and ennoble, other elements were much more localist. Coleridge, Southey and of course Wordsworth came to be known as the 'Lake poets'; their growing fame and the popularity of the area becoming indissolubly linked. And this was in an area which had previously lacked any celebrities who had made their mark in English life. The Lake poets became such celebrities and hence themselves were major tourist attractions. As early as 1802 Coleridge's residence in Keswick was being noted as an additional attraction of the area; while by the 1840s it is thought that Wordsworth was receiving 500 visitors a year at Rydal Mount (Ousby 1990: 180). After their deaths the Lake poets were transformed into literary shrines and memorialised in a fashion similar to the bardolatry at Stratford-upon-Avon (see Holderness 1988). But even more than this their greater effect was in the construction of a 'literary landscape'. This is clearly pointed out for example in some of Wordsworth's own poems which indicate the kinds of experiences and feelings likely to be engendered as one walks over certain routes in the area (Ousby 1990: 182; Newby 1991).

Third, what also thus came to be established in the Lake District was a particular way of relating to its presumed 'nature' through walking and this has established a widespead cultural pattern which supposedly exemplifies good taste. Wallace argues that the following factors transformed the material and ideological shape of walking: transport changes from the late eighteenth century onwards, especially the turnpikes and then the railway, which gradually removed the association of walking with necessity, poverty and vagrancy; the diversity of modes of transport which enabled people to compare and contrast different forms of mobility and to see the virtues of slower ways of overcoming distance; agricultural changes which threatened existing rights of way so that visitors in particular were keen to ensure that they remained open through regular usage; and the development of a new ideology, the 'peripatetic', which represented excursive walking as a cultivating experience capable of renovating the individual and society (Wallace 1993: 1–17). She argues that walking: 'preserves some portion of local topographies against widespread, nationalizing physical changes and, by extension, partially preserves the sites in which the ideal values of agrarian England were supposed to have flourished' (1993: 12).

Walking gradually came to be viewed as a positive choice. Since ordinary people did not now always need to walk so walking travellers were not necessarily thought of as poor. Nor were women walkers not going on a pilgrimage deemed to be necessarily disreputable. Hewison (1993) nicely makes this point:

when Shakespeare's King Lear leaves court to wander on the heath, he does not meet bobble-hatted hikers in sensible boots enjoying a refreshing tramp across the moors. He is among the naked, the starving and the mad, the excluded of society in this hostile wilderness.

During the nineteenth century there was an increasing appreciation of how aesthetic choice was one of the main readings of why people went walking voluntarily. There was an extensive growth in excursive walking – and this resulted from the increasingly widespread belief that walking as travel had personal and social benefits. Moreover, this was a disciplined and organised mode of walking well-reflected in Wordsworth's choice of the term *The Excursion* (see Wallace 1993: Ch. 3). This he uses to refer to the walking tour. The walker does not wander aimlessly or in a socially disruptive fashion. The wanderer returns continually along paths that have already been walked. This ensures connection and stability and in particular there is the intention to return. Wallace interestingly discusses the notion of the 'wanderer' in Wordsworth; that it is not a withdrawal from community but a deliberate, directed labour undertaken to remake the individual and the home (1993: 122).

This conspicuous example set especially by Wordsworth and Coleridge stimulated pedestrian activity by their contemporaries and then by many other relatively affluent men in the nineteenth century. The distances walked by the intellectuals of the period were prodigious: William Hazlitt claimed to walk 40 or 50 miles a day; De Quincey walked 70 to 100 miles a week; and Keats apparently covered 642 miles during his 1818 tour of the Lakes and Scotland (Wallace 1993: 166–7). By the middle of the century 'the very highest echelon of English society regarded pedestrian touring as a valuable educational experience' (Wallace 1993: 168). It had become particularly associated with 'the intellectual classes' who had begun to develop quite complex justifications, a 'peripatetic theory' based upon the way that the pedestrian is re-created with nature. Some of the key texts in this analysis are Hazlitt's 'On Going on a Journey' in 1821; Thoreau's 'Walking' in 1862; Robert Louis Stevenson's 'Walking Tours' in 1881; and Leslie Stephen's 'In Praise of Walking' in 1901 (Wallace 1993: 172–3). They explore the impact of Wordsworth's justification for walking although they differ as to the degree to which 'the peripatetic' necessarily connects people back to local communities or remains a much more private activity. Later in the century parallel justifications began to be advanced for rock climbing in the Lakes, an activity which became transferred from the Alps where it had originated (see Milner 1984).

Fourth, issues of conservation have always been part of the discourse surrounding the Lake District, Ousby noting the early protest in 1802 against a particular development of Pocklington's Island (1990: 190). However, in the early years of the nineteenth century most writers, including Wordsworth, were arguing for the interests of visitors so that they could enjoy an unspoiled nature; but by 1844 and Wordsworth's public letters on the Kendal and Windermere Railway the threats of 'mass tourism' were much more apparent. Ousby summarises Wordsworth's distinction of taste, one repeated two decades later in Ruskin's diatribe against the 'stupid herds of modern tourists':

> The Kendal and Windermere letters throb with a horrified vision of 'cheap trains pouring out their hundreds at a time along the margins of Windermere', of the industrial towns being able to send as many weekend excursionists to the Lake District as they did to Scarborough, of 'wrestling matches, horses and boat races without number' and of pothouses and beershops run by 'the lower class of innkeepers'.
>
> (Ousby 1990: 192)

In particular Wordsworth argues that while we may all appreciate the ordinary countryside, the Lake District is distinct. It demands a different eye, one in which we are not threatened or frightened by the relatively wild and untamed nature. This is not something that can be appreciated briefly, through what in Chapter 12 I termed the 'spectatorial' glance. It requires according to Wordsworth 'a slow and gradual process of culture' (cited in Ousby 1990: 194), what I would call an 'environmental' and 'anthropological' scanning of nature and culture.

But Wordsworth also views the 'tourist' as a symptom of larger changes taking place in English society, of those external forces which were beginning to undermine integral rural communities at the end of the eighteenth century (Buzard 1993: 25). Wordsworth saw these forces as inducing a kind of fall from a state of affairs in which social life was organic and natural. Buzard's analysis of Wordsworth's 'The Brother' (1799) brings out how the tourist is a synecdoche for the power of external forces to undermine integral communities:

> It signifies . . . the beginning of modernity, characterized alternately as a time when formerly integral cultures fall within the reach of encroaching impersonal networks of influence, or as a time when one stops belonging to a culture and can only *tour* it.
>
> (Buzard 1993: 27)

But Buzard also notes that for all Wordsworth's criticisms of these processes his poem (and those of various contemporaries) does not entirely escape the 'lure of aestheticization, bearing an unmistakable likeness to standard and satirizable touristic views of rural settings' (1993: 27). This seems to a more general feature – that the conservation of the Lake District in the nineteenth century increasingly employs terms and expressions which are similar to the ways in which the travel industry itself characterises such places. In the making of the Lake District there is an increasing coalescence of the cultural and the commercial. Each feeds into the other as the Lake District place-myth is developed and enormously elaborated. The language of Romanticism plays a burgeoning role in the discourses of both promotion *and* conservation.

I have so far discussed some of the processes affecting Lake District tourism up to the middle of the nineteenth century. There was though another set of relevant influences and that was the changing place of the countryside more generally in English life as England forged ahead as the first and most spectacularly successful industrial power. Wiener has famously asked: 'Why did hostility to industrial advance persist and even strengthen in the world's first industrial society? Why did such hostility so often take the form of rural myth making?' (1981: 7). He talks of British modernisation being a struggle between a northern and a southern metaphor with the former losing out and becoming characterised as the merely 'provincial', separate from and inferior to the metropolitan centre in London. There have been a number of strands to this southern anti-industrialism in England. First, there has been the attraction of the past and the denigration of the new and especially the denigration of the new industry of the north (as in the industrial revolution). Many commentators have asserted that England was and should be viewed as an overwhelmingly 'old country' (see Wright 1985). Second, there has been the more specific idealisation of the old countryside and a profound anti-urbanism which has never been seriously dislodged although England has always been the most urbanised of European and north American countries. Stanley Baldwin famously stated: 'England is the country, and the country is England' (cited in Lowenthal 1991: 205); note the paradox in England of the way the army often is able to present itself as the agent preserving the countryside from unwelcome developments. Third, since the countryside was depopulated at a very early stage through the enclosure movement it has not been denigrated as 'barbaric' and 'idiotic' as occurred in other countries. From the eighteenth century onwards the countryside as pastoral came to represent a particular ideal of England. It was the *towns and cities* outside London that came to be viewed as the merely 'provincial'; while the countryside of the north has been partially colonised by the south, in a way similar to that around Paris (Wiener 1981: Ch. 4).

Lowenthal argues that it is this English countryside that has ultimately served to constitute national identity, given that many bases of such identity are lacking in England/Britain compared with elsewhere. He argues:

One icon of heritage has a distinctly English cast. That is the landscape. Nowhere else is landscape so freighted as legacy. Nowhere else does the very term suggest not simply scenery and *genres de vie*, but quintessential national virtues. . . . Peopled and storied in all the arts, rural England is endlessly lauded as a wonder of the world.

(Lowenthal 1991: 213)

Lowenthal cites many commentators who have argued for the importance of the English landscape to British identity (see Hewison 1993, on the 'deep-seated identification between the landscape and national identity'). G. K. Chesterton's homage to the (southern) English village proceeds as follows:

> That solid look of the village; the fact that the roofs and walls seemed to mingle naturally with the fields and the trees; the feeling of the naturalness of the inn, of the cross-roads, of the market cross . . . in a real sense the Crown Jewels. These were the national, the normal, the English.
>
> (Cited in Lowenthal 1991: 213)

Lowenthal also notes that this English village and countryside is a 'consummate artefact', a 'vast museumised ruin' (1991: 217). And even when there is too much countryside, so to speak, this is to be offset by orderly control. All land seems to require human supervision – in England nature cannot be left to its own devices. Hence with the 'set-aside' arrangements every piece of land must be cared for by someone, especially by landowners and farmers. Lowenthal notes how it is the southern English countryside which has been owned and managed by relatively few large and medium-sized landowners and farmers; and it has also been seen as *the* 'proper place for proper people to live in' (Newby 1990: 631). It is of course a racial landscape, one which is presumed to be white. The photographer Ingrid Pollard describes the English countryside as a 'landscape of fear'. Captions next to her photographs of the English countryside include: 'I wandered lonely as a black face in a sea of white' and '. . . and what part of Africa do you come from? inquired the walker'.

The Lake District, although white, is not of course a southern landscape. So when it has been appropriated within what Wiener terms the 'southern metaphor' there has had to be a complex transformation. This rather exotic and intimidating landscape has been turned into one that is safe both for being viewed and for certain relatively novel kinds of sport, especially the climbing and walking that became fashionable in the nineteenth century, as we saw above.

Wiener suggests that it was around 1900 that the southern metaphor had become dominant in England. This: 'went together with the devaluation of both the locales of, and the qualities that had made, the industrial revolution. Such places and such characteristics became "provincial"' (1981: 42). Working-class and lower middle-class suburbs were therefore characterised as provincial, as far away from the metropolitan centre. The countryside occupied a rather different and diverse location. Much of the countryside came to be be viewed as a kind of honorary part of the metropolitan centre. Horne summarises:

> Things that are rural or ancient are at the very heart of southern English snobberies, even if they occur in the North. *Provincialism is to live in or near an industrial town to which the industrial revolution gave its significant modern form.*
>
> (1969: 38)

Wiener also notes that this incorporation of the rural takes both an elite form and a more populist, socialist version, Williams best representing this alternative reading of rural Britain (1973).

I will now suggest what are some of the main characteristics of the metaphors of north and south using Shields' characterisation of the contrasting cultural constructions of the north and south of England (I have slightly amended this from Shields 1991: 231).

Table 13.1 The north and the south

North	South
Periphery	Centre
Working class	Economic and social elites
Bleak countryside	Tamed countryside
Industry, factories	Stockbroking, management
Rugged leisure pursuits	High culture, the 'season'
Wet and colder climate	Warmer climate
'Gemeinschaft'	'Gesellschaft'
Neighbourliness and emotional community	Social institutions, money, power

Shields emphasises that these are cultural constructions, which have in part developed from the literary and journalistic writings of the nineteenth century (Dickens, Mrs Gaskell, Disraeli), and which have then been reinforced by cultural output during the twentieth century (D.H. Lawrence, Arnold Bennett, George Orwell, post-war British realist cinema and theatre, *Coronation Street* and so on). What this cultural construction does is to transform differences of social class into a cultural geography. These different 'places' have become metaphors for different social classes *and* for the process by which a landed, financial and managerial ruling class working in London and living in the south-east has dominated the rest of Britain and has partly remade the countryside through its metropolitanism. The terms which are used to characterise the 'north' constitutes a spatial discourse which privileges the centre, London, and reinforces the north as an economic, cultural and social periphery around that core (see Shields 1991: Ch. 5 for detailed analysis of these contrasting place-images). To demonstrate the power of these images which exemplify such domination consider George Orwell's comments in *Homage to Catalonia* on his return to 'southern England, probably the sleekest landscape in the world':

The industrial towns were far away, a smudge of smoke and misery. . . .
Down here it was still the England I had known in my childhood: the

206

railway cuttings smothered in wild flowers, the deep meadows where the great shining horses browse and meditate, the slow-moving streams bordered by willows, the green bosoms of the elms, the larkspurs in the cottage gardens . . . all sleeping the deep, deep sleep of England.

(Orwell 1938: 314)

Ousby notes how Orwell, the self-questioning intellectual and journalist, unselfconsciously slips into a conventional tourist imagery of England and especially of its southern rural charms (1990: 2). This suggests that what Ousby terms the 'tourist map of England' is singularly powerful and all-encompassing, and it certainly swept Orwell into its seductive charms (see Chapter 10 on Orwell and the place-image of Wigan).

In conclusion I will consider the relationship of the Lake District to this 'tourist map', and more generally to the variety of available place-images, especially that of the north. First, the area is located a fair distance from many of the well-known industrial towns of the north and could not be viewed as simply part of the 'provincial' north. However, such a perception depends upon 'forgetting' the fact that surrounding the Lake District to the south and west are a string of once-significant industrial towns which are in many senses marginal to the margins of England (Barrow, Cleator Moor, Workington, Whitehaven). Chapman on the basis of some ethnographic materials summarises the hyper-marginality of this west Cumbrian area as follows:

This area is emphatically not part of the Lake District. . . . The great majority of the British population knows little or nothing about this area. . . . The existence of the area is, most importantly, scarcely acknowledged by most people who frequent 'the Lakes'. . . . Hundreds of thousands look out over it, from the summits of Lakeland peaks, but their eyes are on the horizon.

(1993: 197)

He describes walking into Cleator Moor wearing breeches, boots, brightly coloured socks, orange waterproofs and a rucksack. Instead of feeling intrepid, as one is permitted to do on descending a modest Lakeland mountain into Ambleside or Keswick, he felt acutely out of place. He was wearing what would be seen as fancy-dress in Cleator Moor – he had literally walked *out* of the Lake District which he characterises as:

the *locus classicus* of high-minded and privileged leisure, wealthy, rural and beautiful, a national playground for the healthy and the thoughtful, with stone-built hotels in parks of rhododendron. West Cumbria, and Cleator Moor particularly, represents a desolate and unregarded landscape of industry declining, industry departed and high unemployment.

(Chapman 1993: 205–6)

This hyper-marginality is further demonstrated by the location of the most dangerous of Britain's nuclear installations on this west Cumbrian coast, at

Windscale/Sellafield, only a few miles from what many locals and visitors deem to be the most 'unspoilt' and 'natural' parts of the Lake District. These 'places [right] on the margin' of modern Britain hardly figure in most people's geography of the north or indeed of the Lake District, although they are part of the county and tourist board area of Cumbria. Given the proximity to Sellafield the comments from focus group participants as to the cleanness and freshness of the air are striking: '"You can see the purity of the air by the lichen that grows on the trees. . . . If there is a tree and it was so polluted there wouldn't be anything growing on it"' (Crawshaw 1994b: 12). Chapman nevertheless effectively shows that the marginality of west Cumbria is well-reflected in the debates over the future of Sellafield. He argues that the generally pro-Sellafield views of local people (that is, those living 'outside' the Lake District) are consistently misunderstood and mis-reported by national TV and press (1993: 211–17). He suggests that many local people consider that Sellafield fits rather well into the west Cumbrian economy (and is indeed apparently cleaner than previous industry) but not of course into the Lake District economy which it would totally eliminate if there was a significant nuclear accident.

Second, the Lake District, while geographically in the north, it is not quite of the north. It is almost an honorary part of the south-east and that is mainly because of the particular forms of elite leisure that were established in the area. The Lake District is rather like Nice, Madeira, the Alps, the Dordogne – places significantly made as part of the English south-east and of its white metropolitanism. Shields argues with regard to leisure that 'one does not go to the "North" for high culture but for hiking, fishing, or for the British version of "unspoiled nature"' (1991: 231). However, although this general point is important the Lake District occupies a special location here because of the way that it provides a particularly striking social and physical setting for various kinds of activity. The Lake District has a place-image which derives both from the 'north' but also from the 'south', a hybrid. This hybridity stems from the way that the bleak wild countryside has been mostly tamed for visitors: it has been tamed by its art and literature which have become canons of English culture; by the mainly middle-class outdoor leisure practices; and by its compactness and array of accommodation services. It has continued to connote good taste, the various leisure activities found in the area being more common amongst both middle-class and service-class people, especially men (see Savage *et al.* 1992: Ch. 6, those employed in 'education, health and welfare' particularly favouring climbing, camping, and rambling/hiking). Recent research by Squire brings out the attraction of Beatrix Potter tourism to women visitors in the Lakes – and how the buying of souvenirs from the National Trust shop can be considered to be in appropriate taste (1993).

The Lake District is a hybrid nature: on the one hand, like highland Scotland, it is wild and threatening; and on the other hand, like the *home* counties, it is small, pretty and inviting. It is not a wilderness experience but it does contain some extremely wild and inhospitable scenery. Yet that is located within walking distance of attractive valleys and quaint little villages. One focus group respondent suggested: '"The Lakes is contained wilderness. It has been contained and produced in a certain way"' (Crawshaw 1994b: 12). The sublime and the picturesque are almost coterminous. Hence it is the contrasts that attract. As another respondent said: '"It is a unique part of the country. One can't get away from that fact. There is nowhere else you could find this sort of contrast in such a stark, clear juxtaposition"' (Crawshaw 1994b: 15). The scenery like the weather is continuously changing. The Lake District then is a kind of mirror image of how English people might see England itself, that is, as small, accessible and containing a wide diversity of experiences and sceneries. It is a nature of contrasts, not a nature that appeals through the unending scale of a particular feature.

The Lake District is like other parts of England in another sense. Although some of it is wild it is at the same time a highly managed landscape. In focus group one discussion participant said that: 'My father's family have just been here and they thought it was great. They said "it's so neat and tidy" as if that was their idea of beautiful. That is what the Lake District is. It is very neat and tidy.'

This tidiness results from the long period of control over development, so that ownership of land by farmers or leisure-based industries has been heavily compromised. Capitalist enterprise has been regulated even though most land has remained in private ownership. This managed landscape has resulted from a very restrictive planning regime (since the National Parks Act in 1949), and from ownership of about one-quarter of the area by a voluntary association, the National Trust, which has come to assume an almost hegemonic role in the area. The Lake District is highly managed and almost manicured with extremely little derelict land, litter or graffiti. It is the exact opposite of unmanaged wasteland. It has been gentrified. Lowenthal notes the way that farmers are highly circumscribed in what they are able to do since they have now become 'museum custodians . . . scenic stewards for tourism' (Lowenthal 1991: 217). It is a landscape that could be described as the 'consummate artefact', a place where nature could not be left to its own 'natural' devices. As one respondent in focus group discussion said: '"it feels very civilised. Wherever you go it still feels civilised"' (Crawshaw 1994b: 17).

This relates to Strathern's more general point (1992). It is clear that in contemporary England there is a greatly enhanced emphasis upon the importance of nature – to value the natural, to be attracted by images of nature and to seek to implement nature conservation under the impact of green and new age philosophies. But Strathern notes that these emphases are fundamentally mediated by culture – it is this which has in a way rescued nature. But this in turn has the effect of producing: 'the conceptual collapse of the differences between nature and culture when Nature cannot survive without

Cultural intervention' (1992: 174). The Lake District particularly exemplifies the role of this cultural intervention. It has had to be rescued from itself. Culture has been necessary to save nature in the Lake District and to produce a very distinct and 'civilised' place for consumption (especially for the white service class). It is a place that is simultaneously valued for its culture and civilisation *and* for its naturalness and relative wildness. It is a hybrid landscape.

14

SOCIAL IDENTITY, LEISURE
AND THE COUNTRYSIDE*

INTRODUCTION

A large body of literature has developed which suggests that over the past decade or two there has been a striking transformation in the nature of people's social identity, and that this is the consequence of massive changes in the organisation and culture of contemporary societies. It is argued that because of organisational and cultural changes individuals have been changed. Different kinds of people are required by the kind of society which is emerging at the end of the century.

The most visible literature is that concerned with the supposed shift to 'postmodernity', a term now routinely employed in public discourse to refer to a variety of changes in architecture, the arts, culture and social life more generally. Although the term had been in use in literary criticism since the 1960s it was only after the publication of Jencks' book on postmodern architecture in the late 1970s that it came into public debate in the UK (see Jencks 1991). It thus more or less coincided with the election of the Conservative Government in 1979. There has been a complex interrelationship of two kinds of analyses. On the one hand, there is the examination of 'postmodernity', with its claims about the playful and pastiched intertwining of culture and commerce; and on the other, there is the study of so-called 'Thatcherism', with its apparent ambition to 'marketise' most aspects of social and cultural life.

At the same time there have been some other debates in the 1980s which have focused on various transformations of economic and political life rather than on culture, such as the shift from 'Fordist' to 'Post-Fordist' society, from 'organised' to 'disorganised capitalism', from an 'industrial' to a 'post-industrial' society, or from an 'industrial' to an 'information' society (for further analysis see Lash and Urry 1994). In each case it is suggested that a

* Unpublished; prepared as part of a Leisure and the Countryside project funded by the Monument Trust, 1994. I am grateful for the comments of my collaborators: Gordon Clark, Jan Darrall, Robin Grove-White and Phil Macnaghten, as well as Kevin Hetherington for prompting me to think about 'new sociations'.

211

particular form of society rooted in the earlier part of this century is being transformed, and that one element of that transformation comprises changes in individual subjects, that different kinds of people are produced or required by the new type of society. In particular, it is now suggested that contemporary Western capitalism no longer 'needs' entrepreneurs with a strong 'Protestant ethic' (for whom time is money, who believe that work is a religiously inspired duty and who save and invest for the future). Instead what is needed are 'hedonists', who consume now rather than save for the future, who enjoy their leisure rather than their work, and for whom identity is derived from consumption rather than from work (see Keat *et al.* 1994).

At the same time there has been a further debate concerned with the more general and long-term nature of the 'modern' experience. Although there is much dispute about when the modern period began (the scientific revolutions of the sixteenth and seventeenth centuries, or the 'enlightenment' of the eighteenth century, or the modern urban-industrial civilisation of the nineteenth century), it is widely agreed that modern societies are strikingly different from traditional or pre-modern societies. The debates on these differences are very wide-ranging, involving archaeologists, anthropologists, historians, geographers, economists, sociologists, cultural analysts and so on (see Lash and Friedman 1992 for a recent relevant collection).

For my purposes the most interesting debate concerns the nature of the 'modern' city. It is often now argued that a number of such cities developed in the middle to late-nineteenth century, beginning with Haussmann's extraordinary rebuilding of Paris during the Second Empire (and followed by London, Vienna, Berlin and Chicago). The following features of late nineteenth century Paris are important to note: the destruction of medieval buildings and street layout; the building of elegant boulevards which allowed the rapid movement of traffic; the siting of a monument to be gazed upon at the end of many such boulevards; the development of new public spaces, arcades and cafés, where people could be 'private while in public'; the tremendous mixing of people, many of whom were discovering new forms of leisure; and the emergence of certain sites for tourism for the mass of the population, as almost coming to define what it is to be a tourist. Berman writes that: 'All these qualities helped to make Paris a uniquely enticing spectacle, a visual and sensual feast . . . after centuries of life as a cluster of isolated cells, Paris was becoming a unified physical and human space' (1983: 151; see also Urry 1990: 136–40).

Such debates have significant implications for the analysis of tourism and leisure in general and for countryside leisure in particular. Indeed in many ways the very notion of 'leisure', as a finite set of activities done in specialised sites for specific periods of time, is itself a quintessentially 'modern' activity. Also in pre-modern societies it would not occur to most people that they might travel to the countryside for 'leisure'. Indeed as with the development of the city as an object of the 'tourist gaze' (beginning in a way with nineteenth century Paris), so the countryside had also to be transformed into an object fit for the gaze of very many visitors and not to be viewed as merely a working environment from which people would escape as soon as they could (as seems to be mainly the case in contemporary Japan; see Chapter 13 on the making of the Lake District).

This last point brings out how people's wish to visit an interesting city ('romantic Paris') or an attractive countryside (the 'picturesque Cotswolds') is not in any sense 'natural'. It is something that is socially constructed and depends in particular upon developing what we can term 'cultural desire' for particular kinds of townscape or landscape. The development of this desire depends upon at least four factors.

1 The availability of sites/sights to visit as a result of developing appropriate forms of transportation/accommodation/refreshment, etc. This depends on the development of new forms of capital and organisation particularly concentrated within specific geographical locations. Two important examples in Britain include the growth of thousands of small boarding houses in nineteenth century Blackpool which provided cheap accommodation away from home for the industrial working class of Lancashire (see Walton 1978); and the development of Thomas Cook's, beginning with the first 'packaged tour' in 1841, to the facilitating of mass tourism in Britain and across Europe particularly to the Alps (see Brendon 1991, and Chapter 9). It should also be noted that certain kinds of landscape, such as areas of wilderness, are often culturally desired because they are not widely available and remain partly inaccessible.

2 Social groupings with an appropriate aesthetic, such as for particular styles of vernacular architecture or for certain kinds of countryside or what came to be known as a 'landscape'. In the case of the latter, Harrison talks of the development of a 'countryside aesthetic' which seems to have developed amongst parts of the professional middle class in the nineteenth century. She says that 'an educated and cultured few began to regard the countryside as a source of spiritual renewal and inspiration' (see 1991: 21). It also came to be believed in the inter-war period that 'mountains and moors' would do people more good than other kinds of countryside.

3 The existence of a broader cultural emphasis which spreads through significant parts of the wider society and which emphasises the desirability of certain kinds of leisure activity. In relationship to the countryside, literary and artistic figures have played a particularly important role in spreading the idea that visiting wild and remote landscapes is socially desirable and an expression of good taste. Michael Dower thus argued that: 'We must discriminate, fitting each feature and region to the creation it can best satisfy, gathering the crowd into places which can take them, keeping the high, wild places for the man [sic] who seeks solitude' (1965; see also Crawshaw 1994a, 1994b). Harrison summarises the effects of this English Romanticism:

For poets like Wordsworth and Coleridge, the only right and proper
way to enjoy the countryside was to walk through these landscapes
in solitude and contemplative mood and thereby to achieve a new
sense of solace, consciousness and spiritual awareness.

(1991: 21; see also Ousby 1990, on the development of the
'literary landscape'; Wallace 1993, on the 'peripatetic')

4 The notion of a landscape has come to play a centrally important role in
structuring this general desire for the countryside. Cosgrove summarises
how the idea of landscape is individualistic and visual:

the landscape idea was active within a process of undermining
collective appropriation of nature for use. It was locked into an
individualist way of seeing. . . . It is a way of seeing which
separates subject and object, giving lordship to the eye of a single
observer.

(1984: 262; more generally on the role of vision in tourism, see
Urry 1992)

Williams in his classic work *The Country and the City* (1973) points out
that what we think of as the rural 'landscape' is normally devoid of farm
machinery, workers, telegraph wires, electricity pylons, motorways, derelict land, polluted waters and, we may add, nuclear power installations and
other tourists, although all of these are of course common in rural areas.
The 'landscape' is essentially unpeopled.

In the next section, attention will be directed more specifically to the issue
of how identity is being transformed in the late twentieth century according
to postmodern analyses. After this I will return to how such debates relate to
the development of leisure in the countryside and analyse some aspects of
the self less recognised in the postmodern argument.

IDENTITY AND POSTMODERNISM

One way of understanding the changes which are to be analysed here is in
terms of time. Roughly speaking the modern period at least from 1750
onwards was defined in terms of the organisational and experiential importance of clock-time (see Adam 1990). This was associated with a number of
features: that time is money, that one should be careful with the passing of
time; that industrial relations are systematically structured around clock-time,
around efforts to extend or contract the working day and week; that a modern
person is aware of and oriented to the passing of time; that time is a resource
which is to be organised, regulated and distributed; that leisure as well as
work is organised and regulated by the clock; that people have a temporal
identity orientated to the future and especially to long-term planning through
marriage/career; that pleasures are systematically deferred because there is

confidence about the future; that there is no pronounced nostalgia for the past and its artefacts; that cultural texts have a narrative structure with a beginning, a middle and an end; and that long-term historical processes of social improvement are conceivable and realisable (see Lash and Urry 1994: Ch. 9).

The modern person embraces most of these features with the entrepreneur possessing a strong 'Protestant ethic' being a kind of paradigm case. It should however be noted that the cultural movement of 'modernism' in the early years of this century involved the rejection of some of these characteristics (Joyce's *Ulysses* being the classic modernist novel).

Also there is some overlap between the emergence of clock-time and the shifting from a mainly oral to a mainly written culture (see Ong 1982). Much nineteenth and twentieth century culture was written, with the huge growth of cheap books and daily newspapers doubling every fifteen years or so, the general keeping of written time-keeping records including transportation timetables, the widespread written documentation of citizens through registering births, deaths, marriages, taxation, travel and so on and the general use of written signs to indicate routes, location, leisure facilities, tourist sites and so on (see Lash and Urry 1994: Ch. 9; also Hoffman-Axthelm 1992, on the modern process of establishing identity via one's passport).

Recently though it has been argued that this kind of modern society is undergoing dramatic transformation. Some analysts consider that we are moving into a hyper-modern situation (see Giddens 1991a), others that society has become postmodern (see Bauman 1992). Three particular aspects have been analysed.

First, and briefly, it is argued that this predominant written culture is under extreme threat from a more visual and aesthetic culture which is appreciated in a much less detached, formal and distanced manner. This in turn is linked to the way in which the symbolic boundaries between, on the one hand, art, high culture and the academy, and on the other, everyday life and popular culture are dissolving. As the architect Venturi has famously written, we should 'learn from Las Vegas' in the development of a playful and pastiche style of 'roadside eclecticism' (see 1977; and Featherstone 1991, more generally). Postmodernity is in effect a post-cultural condition if culture is to be taken to imply aesthetic or moral standards imposed by an elite.

Second, it is argued that postmodernity ushers in much more open and fluid social identities, rather than the traditionally fixed identities of the modern period. Indeed it is sometimes argued that the very idea of identity is itself a mythical construction. Kellner summarises:

> It is thus claimed that in postmodern culture, the subject has disintegrated into a flux of euphoric intensities, fragmented and disconnected, and that the decentred postmodern self no longer experiences anxiety . . . and no longer possesses the depth, substantiality, and coherence that was the ideal and occasional achievement of the modern self. . . .

Postmodern theorists claim that subjects have imploded into masses, that a fragmented, disjointed, and discontinuous mode of experience is a fundamental characteristic of postmodern culture. . . . In these theories, identity is highly unstable and has in some postmodern theories disappeared altogether . . . where 'The TV self is the electronic individual *par excellence* who gets everything there is to get from the simulacrum of the media: a market identity as a consumer in the society of the spectacle.'

(1992: 145; see also Featherstone 1991)

Thus one particular leisure activity, watching TV, is central to these claims about postmodernity. These analyses do not consider the rather older topics of the biased content of the media. Indeed no longer is there thought to be a class bias but there is rather a media bias. Postmodern theorists are concerned with form, and particularly with the breaking up of the 'representational realism' and the simple narratives of TV. So in postmodern TV – such as Miami Vice, MTV, Max Headroom, advertisements which have in some ways become more pleasurable than the programmes, coupled with the widespread use of the VCR (see Cubitt 1991) – the signifier has been liberated and image takes precedence over narrative, the aesthetic is dominant, and the viewer is seduced by the free play of an excess of images. In Baudrillard this argument is carried to its extreme – that culture has disintegrated into pure image without referent or content or effects (1981). This flatness or depthlessness is said to produce a waning of affect, that postmodern selves are without depth and substance, they are superficial and one-dimensional, and there is no self beyond appearances, beyond the playful adopting and discarding of multiple life-styles or fashions, so much so that it has been said that there is no fashion, only fashions (see Ewen and Ewen 1982, on how there are no rules, only choices).

Third, it is argued that clock-time no longer provides the basis of time in modern society, and that there is a shift towards what we can term 'instantaneous' time. It is suggested that the future is dissolving into the present, that 'we want the future now' has become emblematic of a panic about the 'future' and a search for the instantaneous (see Adam 1990: 140). This partly results from how geographically distant events are brought into our everyday lives. Events often of an appallingly tragic character are dramatically brought into people's everyday experience. There is thus a literal time-space *compression* as this collage of disconnected stories intrude and shape everyday life. And instantaneously people are 'transported' from one tragedy to another in ways which seem out of control. This then seems to be a world so full of risks and where there is little likelihood of even understanding the temporally organised processes which culminate in the newsworthy tragedies that are routinely represented each day.

These effects are in turn connected to the development of the so-called three-minute culture, that those watching TV/VCR tend to hop from channel to channel and they rarely spend time in following through a lengthy programme. Indeed many programmes are now made to mimic such a pattern, being made up of a collage of visual and aural images, a stream of 'sound bites', each lasting a very short time and having no particular connection with those coming before and after. This instantaneous conception of time can be characterised as 'video-time' (see Cubitt 1991). Instantaneous time dissolves the future – 'I want the future now' as the T-shirt expresses it. Thus as a result of the need for instantaneous responses, particularly because of the telephone, telex, fax, electronic signals and so on, the future appears to dissolve and it no longer functions as something in which people appear to trust.

Three significant consequences follow from this development of instantaneous time. First, the objective time of modernity gradually gives way to a set of personalised, subjective temporalities which are self-generated and involve what Giddens calls 'life-calendars' (Giddens 1991a: Ch. 6). Trust and commitment over time are less geared to institutions and more to how individuals create their own subjective time of life plans. This relates to the way in which individuals are increasingly detached from wider social institutions, of generations, place, kinship, and rituals of passage which traditionally gave sense and order to social life (Giddens 1991a: 146–8). Morality is progressively viewed as a private matter, less related to social roles, even that of the monarchy, and an externally imposed structuring over time. The self and its structuring over time is increasingly privatised.

Second, the lack of trust in the future means it is increasingly likely that gratification will not be deferred. The following are some indicators of a less pronounced culture of waiting and the spread of instantaneous time. There are the increased rates of divorce and other forms of household dissolution as well as the marked rise in the willingness of, especially, women to undertake affairs within marriage. Likewise Conservative critics have suggested that there is a reduced sense of trust, loyalty and commitment of families over generations. Family relationships are more disposable. More generally, products and images are increasingly disposable in a 'throwaway society' in which there is a strong emphasis upon the volatility and ephemerality in fashions, products, labour processes, ideas and images. There is a heightened 'temporariness' of products, values and personal relationships, where the 'temporary contract' is everything. This in turn relates to an accelerating turnover-time and the proliferation of new products and of flexible forms of technology. There is a decline in long-term jobs and careers and an increased tendency for short-term labour contracts. The growth of 24-hour trading means that investors and dealers never have to wait for the buying and selling of securities and foreign exchange. There are extraordinary increases in the availability of products so that one does not have to wait to travel anywhere in order to consume some new style or fashion (see Toffler 1970; Lasch 1980; Harvey 1989: 299, on the 'emporium of styles'; Lawson 1989).

Third, this emphasis upon instantaneous time means that the time-space paths of individuals are desynchronised. There is a greatly increased variation in different people's times. They are less collectively organised and structured as mass consumption patterns are replaced by more varied and segmented patterns. There are a number of indicators of such time-space desynchronisation: the increased significance of grazing, that is, not eating at fixed meal times in the same place in the company of one's family or workmates; the growth of 'free and independent travellers' who specifically resist mass travel in a group where everyone has to engage in common activities at fixed times; the development of flexitime, so that groups of employees no longer start and stop work at the same time; and the growth of the VCR which means that TV programmes can be stored, repeated, and broken up, so that no sense remains of the authentic, shared watching of a particular programme. This in turn may well be linked to the emphasis placed on so-called quality time by those whose lives demonstrate exceptionally complex time-space paths. It is precisely because of the very high levels of time-space desynchronisation between two or more people that efforts may be made to ensure short but sweet moments of uninterrupted interaction between people, such as the romantic dinner or the short break holiday.

We have so far connected instantaneous time to a lack of confidence about the future. But there is another side to this and that is the remarkable appeal of the past. Once upon a time such nostalgia was formally confined to particular times and places. Now it seems nostalgia is everywhere, engulfing almost every experience and artefact from the past, even the 'dark satanic mills' of the industrial revolution or 1950s' juke boxes. Lowenthal characterises such nostalgia as 'memory with the pain taken out' (1985: 8). And Hewison has argued that Britain has come to specialise not in manufacturing goods but rather in manufacturing nostalgia or heritage (1987). And such institutionalised heritage functions to deflect attention in a systematic way from the forms of social deprivation and inequality in the present. This nostalgia is for an idealised past, for a sanitised version not of history but heritage. Lowenthal suggests that there is almost a mental complaint:

> Once the menace or the solace of a small élite, nostalgia now attracts or afflicts most levels of society. Ancestor-hunters search archives for their roots; millions throng to historic houses; antiques engross the middle class; souvenirs flood consumer markets. . . . 'A growing rebellion against the *present*, and an increased longing for the past', are said to exemplify the post-war mood.
>
> (1985: 11)

Michael Wood likewise suggests that until the 1970s nostalgia trips were 'surreptitious and ambivalent' because people did not want to lose their hold on the present and a modernist belief in the future. But: 'Now that the present seems so full of woe . . . the profusion and frankness of our nostalgia [suggests] . . . a general abdication, an actual desertion from the present' (1974: 346). There are a number of aspects identifiable here: the loss of trust in the future as it is undermined by instantaneous time and the proliferation of incalculable risks; the belief that social life in the present is profoundly disappointing and that in important ways the past was preferable to the present – there really was a golden age; the increased aesthetic sensibility to old places, crafts, houses, countryside and so on, so that almost everything that is old is thought to be valuable whether it is an old master or an old cake tin; the need nevertheless for a certain re-presentation of the past – to construct a cleaned up heritage look suitable for the gaze of tourists; the interpretation of history through artefacts, an artefactual history, which in part conceals underlying social relations; an increased significance of pastiche rather than parody as the past is sought through images and stereotypes which render the 'real' past unobtainable and replace narrative by spectacle; and the belief that once something is 'history', that once the past has been turned into a commodity, it is made safe, sterile and shorn of its capacity to generate risk and danger, subversion and seduction (see Lowenthal and Binney 1981; Lowenthal 1985; Wright 1985; Hewison 1987; Vergo 1989; Corner and Harvey 1991; Walsh 1992).

So far then I have argued that postmodernity involves three sets of processes: the visualisation of culture, the collapse of stable identities, and the transformation of time. In conclusion to this section I will briefly consider what the implications are of this for places, beginning with Zukin's recent analysis of a postmodern *urban* landscape. She says:

> we sense a difference in how we organise what we see: how the visual consumption of space and time is both speeded up and abstracted from the logic of industrial production, forcing a dissolution of traditional spatial identities and their reconstitution along new lines . . . a dream-scape of visual consumption.
>
> (1992b: 221; see also Harvey 1989, on time-space compression)

She talks of how property developers are able to construct new landscapes of power, dreamscapes for visual consumption that are simultaneously stages, sets within which consumption takes place. Such constructed landscapes pose significant problems for people's social identities which have historically been founded on place, on where people come from or have moved to. And yet postmodern landscapes are all about place, such as Main St. in Euro-Disney, or the themed Mediterranean village at the Metro Centre near Gateshead. But these are places which are consumed. They are not places that people come from or live in, or which provide a sense of social identity. Place is simulated. Postmodernisation then involves the conquest of space by instantaneous time. As Meyrowitz says: 'Our world may suddenly seem senseless to many people because, for the first time in modern history, it is relatively placeless' (1985: 309).

This in turn is linked to transformations in the nature of citizenship. People who live in a particular place have enjoyed certain rights and duties by virtue of that residence. Citizenship has not only been a matter of national rights and duties but also a matter of locality. Various citizenship services were provided locally, including those concerned with certain types of leisure. These were mainly provided for local people and it was presumed that people had rights which were general and access was not to be regulated by price. It is important not to be too sentimental about such public leisure provision since there were a number of *de facto* inequalities built into such provision, particularly surrounding gender. Nevertheless, part of the post-war settlement did involve the idea of public leisure facilities provided to those citizens living in each place.

More recently though this has been transformed in Britain under the combined onslaught of postmodernity and Thatcherism. The changes involved include: the attacks on local government expenditure and the efforts to reduce the range of discretionary spending by authorities; the encouragement to privatise leisure provision; the emphasis being placed upon tourist developments in local areas; the increased emphasis upon people as consumers of services rather than as having more general rights by virtue of local residence; the increased perception of culture and the arts as economically justified and part of an area's economic development strategy; the transformation of the visual appearance of an area so as to make it marketable for tourism rather than a site for leisure; and the increased importance of place-marketing so that places come to be transformed into images. These changes might be characterised as a shift from political-citizenship to consumer-citizenship, or from public leisure to private tourism.

I have so far set out the postmodern position fairly uncritically. It is however a partial and too general analysis since two important aspects of social identity are under-examined in this account. Both relate to issues of leisure and tourism and will be discussed in the next section in the context of a more detailed analysis of the countryside and leisure.

IDENTITY AND THE COUNTRYSIDE

The first point to note follows from the argument above which suggests that there is a 'de-traditionalisation' of social life, that people's tastes, values and norms are increasingly less determined by 'societal' institutions such as education, family, culture, government, the law and so on. One effect of such a stripping away of the centrality of such traditional institutions is that individuals and groups are more able to envisage establishing their 'own' institutions, relatively separate from those of the wider society, what I will term 'new sociations' (see Hetherington 1990).

Such 'new sociations' are not like those of traditional communities since they are joined out of choice and people are free to leave. People remain members in part because of the emotional satisfaction that they derive from common goals or experiences. Membership is from choice and many people will indeed enter and exit from such sociations with considerable rapidity. They provide important sites whereby new kinds of social identity can be experimented with. They can empower people, they provide safe social spaces for identity-testing, and they may provide a context for the learning of new skills.

Such institutions can be classified along a number of dimensions: the degree of *decentralisation* of power from 'the centre'; the degree of *formal* specification of the organisational structure; the level and forms of participation at the *local* level; the types of *actions* that may be entered into by the membership; and the degree to which the membership is *reflexive* about whether the institution is appropriately organised. Examples of such non-traditional institutions include tenants' associations, newer political pressure groups, bird watchers, youth cults, environmental groups, baby-sitting circles, communes, operatic groups, women's groups, allotment associations, leisure enthusiasms, conservation societies, war games, one-off political organisations (such as Greenham Common), railway preservation societies, groups of travellers and so on.

Hoggett and Bishop characterise at least some of these enthusiasms as forms of 'communal leisure', although it should be noted that they are not leisure organisations in the sense of being 'non-work' (1986). Such new sociations involve high levels of working for each other through a complex system of mutual aid reinforced by 'norms of reciprocity'. New sociations have three main characteristics. They are *self-organised*, a feature which is often strenuously reinforced when threatened. Second, they are *productive* of various kinds of output, artistic, written, sporting, spoken, visual and so on. And third, these products are largely *consumed by the membership* itself and do not enter either a marketplace or the state (Hoggett and Bishop 1986: 40). Obviously, campaigning sociations are somewhat different from this but even here much of the productive activity is in fact directed to the membership itself. Hoggett and Bishop suggest that 'group members see the overall identity and character of their group as a product to be consumed' (1986: 42). These sociations are not just passive individualistic leisure activities but depend upon 'communication, giving, creating and aesthetic enjoyment, the production and reproduction of life, tenderness, the realisation of physical, sensuous and intellectual capacities, the creation of non-commodity use-values' (Gorz 1985).

Another way of expressing this is to point to the social nature of much consumption, something I was particularly keen to emphasise in Chapter 8. A recent study of a somewhat unusual leisure practice, hot-rodding, brings this out particularly clearly. Moorhouse is interested in this as an enthusiasm, a hobby or an activity which mobilises people's intense collective interest (1991; see also Abercrombie 1994: 53–5). There are a number of social levels

221

of such an enthusiasm: a core of professionals who build and drive the cars and who write and communicate about the activity; amateur enthusiasts for whom hot-rodding is a central life-interest but who have other jobs; an interested public with a considerable background knowledge; and the general public. Although hot-rodding has been subject to commodification, there remains an interesting tension between this and the virtues of amateurism which are particularly emphasised by the non-professionals. Moreover, what one may term the 'organic intellectuals' of hot-rodding particularly emphasise the values of community, hard work and skill, and indeed see these as opposed to market principles. They particularly criticise the dangers of commercial interest and note how the professional hot-rodders depend upon the existence of large numbers of amateurs who have been responsible for many innovations in their enthusiasm. Moorhouse in fact argues that the preservation of skills and arcane knowledges amongst the enthusiasts is actually necessary for the very commodification of the enthusiasm itself (1991: 226). Abercrombie suggests that this collective consumption around various enthusiasms demonstrates reservoirs of expertise, skill and the authority of the 'collective consumer' (1994: 55).

The 'countryside' is the location for, or the object of, many of these enthusiasms and sociations, especially those concerned with various kinds of conservation, sport and hobbies. It is a field [sic] of struggle between many of them; and the struggles occur not just over overt policy but also over the very nature of the organisations themselves and the conception of 'the countryside' that is being contested. Such new sociations also conflict with two other sets of institutions present within rural areas. On the one hand, there are 'traditional institutions' which appear to be 'naturally' part of the countryside and able to speak authoritatively on its behalf. These include the family, church, agriculture, property and land, although increasingly some of these institutions are behaving in much less 'traditional' ways. And on the other, there are the new leisure/tourism companies which view the country-side as merely one of many other sites for profitable development and which may be unbothered by the fact that once the countryside has been transformed into a certain kind of leisure resource it can never be restored to its previous condition.

The countryside is thus a remarkably complex social system in which various new sociations are particularly significant. There are conflicts be-tween these new sociations (war games versus naturalists) as well as between them, among the traditional institutions and the new leisure companies. All these organisations are concerned in part with different kinds of so-called leisure and the range of potential conflicts is immense.

These conflicts have become more marked since the 1960s, partly because of the increased number of such sociations. And one particular category of such sociations has become especially significant, namely those concerned with conservation. This growth of various kinds of conservation began with the first great conservation battle in England in the post-war period, in 1962, over the archway at Euston station (for details on these examples, see Walsh 1992). This was then followed by many other conservation conflicts, particularly in smaller towns and cities and then in the countryside. Not that the objectors were always successful; during the 1970s an incredible 350,000 buildings were demolished in the UK. However, the main point to note is that of the conservation groups currently operating in Britain nearly half were founded in the period since 1970 (examples include Heritage in Danger, 1974, Society for the Interpretation of Britain's Heritage, 1977, National Piers Society, 1980, and so on). Likewise Lowe and Goyder noted in 1983 that the environmental movement more generally boasted two to three million members, and that its size had doubled since 1970 and quadrupled since 1960. The late 1960s and early 1970s showed a huge increase in the rate of formation of conservation and environmental groups. Lowe and Goyder note: 'The membership statistics of groups, however, show no dramatic increase until the early 1970s, when most groups experienced rapid growth and there was a large crop of new groups' (1983: 17).

The membership of the main countryside environmental groups increased even more strikingly during the 1980s when there was a veritable 'green tide' (Harrison 1991: 161; Lowe and Flynn 1989). By the early 1990s, despite electoral setbacks, it is calculated that one in ten people living in Britain is a member of an environmental organisation; nearly a quarter of the population are 'active greens' (compared with 14 per cent in 1988); 40 per cent are in some sense green consumers; and an astonishing 34 per cent of an MP's mailbag will consist of letters on environmental issues (Worcester 1993).

The pattern of local amenity society development is similar. So although by 1939 there was a network of about 30 CPRE (Council for the Protection of Rural England) branches, there was little further growth until the 1960s. But between 1960 and 1975 the number of such local groups increased from 300 to 1250, with the membership rising from about 20,000 to over 300,000 (Lowe and Goyder 1983: 88–9). The geographical distribution shows that there was high amenity society membership in the Home Counties surrounding London, Devon, North Yorkshire and Cumbria, with low membership in Scotland, the Midlands, much of the Pennine area in the north, and most of south and north Wales. Survey data for the 1980s show a rapidly increasing concern for changes taking place within the countryside, although interestingly tourism and visitors are apparently not directly blamed (Harrison 1991: 161–2).

On the face of it this huge increase in concern about one's local environment is not straightforward to explain. First, the geographical variation in the density of membership in the early 1980s is not directly proportional to any obvious measure of environmental quality. Nor does it seem to be systematically related to distance from major conurbations, nor to the nature

223

of the perceived threats to particular areas. Nor is it easy to explain in terms of the kind of postmodern dystopia analysed in the previous section. There it was noted that aspects of contemporary culture involve a depthlessness and a flattening of affect as places are transformed into images. How come then that large numbers of people come together to form new institutions to conserve place, at the very same time that postmodern processes are leading to a shallow and depthless placelessness?

Resolving this paradox requires us to consider the second limitation of the postmodern analysis presented above. This has already been hinted at when it was noted that one particular dimension of these new institutions is that their members are to varying degrees able to reflect upon the very form of organisation itself. Many of the activists in environmental, feminist and conservation movements are deeply self-reflective about their organisation and will seek to institutionalise processes that, for example, prevent hierarchy, or limit the power of particular categories of membership, or embody certain principles at meetings. In other words, it is part of the process of 'de-traditionalisation' that individuals have to be more reflexive and are forced to reflect upon the organisation that they have formed or have joined, with whether it is meeting their needs, with whether they should attempt to change it through expressing 'voice', or whether they should 'exit'.

There are three further points about this reflexivity. First, reflexivity is not simply a question of individual self-consciousness. Also crucial are various ways in which it is embodied within institutions. Elsewhere it has been shown that major differences between advanced economies depend upon the particular kinds of institutionalised reflexivity that are to be found (see Lash and Urry 1994: Ch. 4, on the differences between Anglo-American, German and Japanese systems). Giddens likewise has shown that lying behind the cult of the private, inner self, detached from various traditional institutions is a whole panoply of other organisations and sociations which institutionalise a kind of privatised reflexivity. Central to these are the discourses of therapy which begin with continuous self-observation and monitoring. Giddens states that therapy: 'is an experience which involves the individual in systematic reflection upon the course of her or his life's development. The therapist is at most a catalyst who can accelerate what has to be a process of self-therapy' (1991a: 71). Therapy is then a methodology for life-planning and represents the way in which the lifespan is separated from traditional moral and other concerns.

However, the second point is that one of the most important aspects of this reflexivity is in relation to nature and the environment. The awareness of the shift from what Beck calls an 'industrial' to a 'risk' society entails a kind of universalisation of human experience in which the catastrophic consequences of scientific and technological systems have become particularly apparent (1992). A number of transformations have recently occurred in the way that people consequently see the relationship between humans and nature. For example, it is now thought that nature is not something which is to be viewed as waiting to be tamed or mastered, but rather should be protected and nurtured. Various animals, even some plants and people as yet unborn are viewed as having rights to a quality of the environment no worse than that currently enjoyed. The 'earth' itself has rights and this means that almost any proposal for change in a local environment can be resisted by this new environmental discourse. The countryside in particular has become exceptionally contested because of the permeation of this institutionalised reflexivity about nature and environmental quality. Contestation occurs not just over the environment but about what is to count *as* the environment. The countryside is at the very centre of such conflicts.

Yet, furthermore, part of the very process by which this institutionalised reflexivity has developed about such environments is because the countryside is a place of leisure and travel. It is partly because of travel that many people have developed the capacity to reflect upon environments, to develop the kind of understanding which enables them to know what unspoilt places should look like, what the air should smell like, what the water quality should be, what an aesthetically pleasing environment should appear like, and so on. The paradox is that travel, leisure and tourism have helped to produce this very capacity to reflect upon and to contest threats to 'nature', these threats including of course the impact of too many visitors (this argument is further developed in Lash and Urry 1994: Part 4).

Third, such reflexivity is not of course simply spread throughout the population as a whole. Concern for the environment appears to be most marked amongst those with non-manual occupations, and especially those doing professional-managerial work. This group is often now conceptualised as a 'service class'. Savage *et al.* argue that middle class formation is based around three kinds of assets: property, bureaucracy and culture (1992). At different times and in different places these assets result in a relatively cohesive and effective service class; elsewhere they do not. Two particular contingent factors affect that process, the role of the state and the impact of gender differences. In the recent period they suggest that a quite marked division between the 'managerial' and the 'professional' middle class has developed. This division is reflected in cultural differences and the differential possession of cultural assets is part of the process by which classes are actually constituted as such.

Savage *et al.* develop this argument via the analysis of a large data source on the consumption patterns of the middle classes (1992: Ch. 6). They show that those working in 'education, health and welfare' public services are particularly high consumers of the following: opera, plays, climbing, skating, tennis, classical concerts, table tennis, contemporary dance, camping, rambling, yoga, museums, galleries; they are especially low consumers of fishing, champagne, vodka, whisky, gin, golf, snooker, Spanish holidays, bowls and rock concerts! (1992: 108). Savage *et al.* characterise this an 'ascetic' life-style which they also show is particularly common amongst those who stayed on in education into their twenties. Such a group is actively engaged with new forms of 'body culture', resulting from a reflexivity about the self in the form of fitness and health and concerned with the preservation of bodily rather than financial assets. This group are major users of the countryside and members of environmental organisations.

Interestingly though Savage *et al.* go on to suggest that they are acting as a kind of vanguard for a new 'healthy' life-style to be sampled at least by those who could afford much more costly leisure pursuits. Savage *et al.* summarise:

> What were once the practices of an 'alternative' middle-class minority resisting materialism and the dictates of professionalized medicine have now been adopted on a large scale by those with much greater economic resources. However, in the process it has not replaced other cultural practices but sits alongside them as another one to 'sample'. A 1960s-style counter-culture has been transformed into a 1990s-style post-modern cultural conformity.
>
> (1992: 113)

Two points should be noted about this insightful argument. First, this healthy life-style is one which through increased reflexivity affords greater significance to the 'natural' as opposed to 'culture'. Both the body and the environment may be attributed spiritual importance particularly if nature is viewed as a 'whole'. The countryside plays a particularly important role in providing the site for some of these healthy activities and in particularly symbolising how nature is not being appropriately nurtured. Second, it is odd to describe postmodern culture as 'conformist'. It is more that many different 'cultures' are eclectically sampled; it is that there are less clear-cut 'traditional' boundaries specifying appropriate forms of leisure activity. Savage *et al.* themselves note that many professionals are caught up in both pursuing a healthy life-style and in disproportionately consuming champagne, port, whisky, restaurant meals and so on (see 1992: 114, on the 'health-with-champagne' life-style as they dub it!).

We have already noted that a strong distinction is drawn between the professional and the managerial middle class. The latter appear to be more rooted in career and organisational loyalty, rather than in professional mobility. Savage *et al.* summarise the managerial middle class as follows:

> They seem more prone . . . to seek 'escape' in the form of modified versions of country pursuits earlier adopted by the landed aristocracy. For the managers at least the pursuit of a cleaned-up version of the 'heritage' or 'countryside' tradition . . . seems apposite.
>
> (1992: 116)

They disproportionately consume whisky, brandy and champagne and

226

participate in all sorts of shooting, coarse fishing, squash and golf.

Not surprisingly there are considerable variations in these social patterns by age (with the young particularly resistant to bridge, bowls, fishing and Rover cars!); by gender with professional/managerial women being disproportionately keen on yoga, keep fit/dancing, riding, health club membership, ballet, skating and drinking vermouth; and by region (with London as easily the most distinctive with a most disproportionately high consumption of jazz, ballet, dance, rock concerts, museums, and champagne).

However, despite these variations, Savage *et al.* argue that there are three broad middle-class life-styles, the ascetic, the postmodern and the indistinct. Each has a clear social base: the ascetic among public sector welfare professionals; the postmodern among private sector professionals and specialists; and the indistinct among managers and government bureaucrats. Each has significant and different consequences for the countryside.

During the 1980s the first two styles became more culturally important. First, this was because social and demographic trends increased the numbers in their respective social bases, and those bases became more varied by age, gender and place. And second, these are not hermetically sealed cultural styles. They impact upon each other and broadly speaking the postmodern has cast its shadow over the other two, although it should not be viewed as the only cultural pattern in contemporary society.

This argument has been recently extended by Harrison with regard to the countryside (1991; drawing partly on Urry 1990). She argues that it is through the willingness to transgress the cultural norms of 'group', whether this be age-group, gender, race, class or neighbourhood, that a service class impinges most clearly upon the culture and leisure of many other groups. Harrison discusses how this 'decentring' of identity leads to the transgression of boundaries through play, the casting on and off of identities and the opportunities to engage vicariously in other people's lives:

> Theme parks, medieval fayres and feasts, pop festivals and 'living' museums provide the opportunities to temporarily adopt identities which have new meanings for their participants. As part of postmodernism this dismemberment of group norms allows people to lead eclectic lives 'unshackled by the legacy of tradition or collective expectation' and to respond freely to the market place. But in turn, these consumers are fickle in their loyalties and demand is less easy to satisfy or control.
>
> (Harrison 1991: 159)

Indeed one final point should be noted here and that is to consider whether the 'countryside' as such can be unproblematically 'commodified' through the marketplace. What can be suggested is that there are in fact three 'countrysides' which are competing for dominance in the 1990s; and that there is an important cultural emphasis upon the eclectic sampling of all three.

These conceptions of the countryside coincide with distinctions drawn by Lefebvre in his major work on 'the production of space' (1991; see Ch. 1).

The first category is that of 'spatial practice', the countryside as a distinct space produced by the logic of the market. This results in a rapidly commodified countryside which experiences the rapid churning of demand and supply typical of industrial and urban areas. The second notion is that of 'representations of space'. These are the ideologies of space associated with the countryside, such as the conceptions of 'Englishness' or 'Scottishness' as revealed by particular rural images. And the third is that of 'representational spaces', the complex symbols and notions which entail opposition or hostility to dominant conceptions. This sees the countryside as a 'heterotopia', a place of dark corners, mystery, a labyrinth, with changing meanings and poignant memories. This last notion entails a countryside that should not be planned or homogenised, that should not be 'interpreted' and which should allow the visitor to stumble across unexpected meanings and memories. The countryside is of course all three of these conceptions. There are enduring conflicts between them, and between interests concerned to implement or to conserve one or other such conception.

CONCLUSION

Thus it is clear that what takes place in the countryside cannot be separated off from much wider changes in economic, social and cultural life, particularly those changes which occur within what might appear to be distant towns and cities. Elsewhere I have discussed the important role played in British culture of those employed in the media, arts, advertising and design; so-called cultural intermediaries (Urry 1990: 90–1). Such groups tend to have a very strong commitment to fashion, to the rapid and playful transformations of style (see Featherstone 1991). They are particularly alert to new popular styles, they are keen to market the 'new', and they move styles around from the avant-garde to the popular, the popular to the avant-garde, the popular to the jet-set and so on. There is a stylistic melting-pot, of the vulgar and the tasteful, the new and the old, the natural and the artificial, high culture and popular culture, and of multiple national, regional and ethnic styles. Anything can become stylish; and everything can go out of style. It is clear that such groups have been particularly active in generating the postmodern life-style analysed in the previous section.

This postmodern instantaneous eclecticism is of course immensely liberating since people and places can escape the dead weight of multiple traditions and generate their own new sociations. But it is also a dystopia, ravaging people and places, especially as the new developments of the 1980s have rapidly gone out of fashion with the style-wars moving developments elsewhere, because of the 'churning' of demand. This churning of demand in the countryside under the impact of the various conditions analysed in this chapter may 'leave no stone unturned'. But in the twenty-first century there may well be a very different countryside 'visited', if that remains still the correct term, by very different kinds of people. It is doubtful that much will remain of the countryside as a 'representational space', of mystery, memory and surprise. Such places may well have by then been literally consumed, used up, wasted, dissipated.

BIBLIOGRAPHY

Abercrombie, N. (1990) 'The privilege of the producer', in R. Keat and N. Abercrombie (eds) *Enterprise Culture*, London: Routledge.

Abercrombie, N. (1994) 'Authority and consumer society', in R. Keat, N. Whiteley and N. Abercrombie (eds) *The Authority of the Consumer*, London: Routledge.

Abercrombie, N. and Urry, J. (1983) *Capital, Labour and the Middle Class*, London: Allen & Unwin.

Adam, B. (1990) *Time and Social Theory*, Cambridge: Polity.

Adler, J. (1989a) 'Origins of sightseeing', *Annals of Tourism Research*, 16: 7–29.

Adler, J. (1989b) 'Travel as performed art', *American Journal of Sociology*, 94: 1366–91.

Aglietta, M. (1979) *A Theory of Capitalist Regulation*, London: New Left Books.

Aitken, H.G.J. (1960) 'The economy, management and foreign competition', in G. Roderick and M. Stephens (eds) *Where Did We Go Wrong?: Industrial Performance, Education and the Economy in Victorian Britain*, Lewes: Falmer.

Allheit, P. (1982) *Alltagswissen und Klassenbewusstsein, Arbeitspapiere des Forschungsprojekts 'Arbeiterbiographien'*, Bremen: Bremen University.

Altvater, E. (1973a) 'Some problems of state interventionism I', *Kapitalistate*, I: 96–116.

Altvater, E. (1973b) 'Some problems of state interventionism II', *Kapitalistate*, II: 76–83.

Anderson, B. (1983) *Imagined Communities*, London: Verso.

Anderson, K. and Gale, K. (eds) (1992) *Inventing Places*, Melbourne: Longman Cheshire.

Andrews, M. (1989) *The Search for the Picturesque*, Aldershot: Scolar.

Appadurai, A. (1990) 'Disjuncture and difference in the global cultural economy', *Theory, Culture and Society*, 7: 295–310.

Arcaya, J. (1992) 'Why is time not included in modern theories of memory?', *Time and Society*, 1: 301–14.

Ardener, S. (ed.) (1993) *Women and Space*, Oxford: Berg.

Bachelard, G. (1969) *The Poetics of Space*, Boston: Beacon Press.

Bagguley, P., Mark-Lawson, J., Shapiro, D., Urry, J., Walby, S. and Warde, A. (1990) *Restructuring. Place, Class and Gender*, London: Sage.

Banaji, J. (1976) 'Summary of selected parts of Kautsky's *The Agrarian Question*', *Economy and Society*, 5: 2–49.

Baritz, L. (1960) *The Servants of Power*, Westport, Conn.: Greenwood Press.

Barnes, T. and Duncan, J. (eds) (1992) *Writing Worlds*, London: Routledge.

Barrell, J. (1972) *The Idea of Landscape and the Sense of Place 1730–1840*, Cambridge: Cambridge University Press.

Barrell, J. (1980) *The Dark Side of the Landscape*, Cambridge: Cambridge University Press.

Barrell, J. (1990) 'The public prospect and the private view: the politics of taste in eighteenth century Britain' in S. Pugh (ed.) *Reading Landscape: Country–City–Capital*, Manchester: Manchester University Press.

Barrett, M. *et al.* (eds) (1979) *Ideology and Cultural Production*, London: Croom Helm.

Barry, B. (1965) *Political Argument*, London: Routledge & Kegan Paul.

Barry, B. (1970) *Sociologists, Economists and Democracy*, Chicago: University of Chicago Press.

Barry, B. and Hardin, R. (eds) (1982) *Rational Man and Irrational Society*, Beverly Hills: Sage.

Barthes, R. (1972) *Mythologies*, London: Jonathan Cape.

Baudrillard, J. (1981) *For a Critique of the Economy of the Sign*, St Louis: Telos Press.

Bauman, Z. (1987) *Legislators and Interpreters*, Cambridge: Polity.

Bauman, Z. (1992) *Intimations of Postmodernity*, London: Routledge.

Beck, U. (1987) 'The anthropological shock: Chernobyl and the contours of the risk society', *Berkeley Journal of Sociology*, 32: 153–65.

Beck, U. (1992) *Risk Society: Towards a New Modernity*, London: Sage.

Beckerman, W. (1974) *In Defence of Economic Growth*, London: Jonathan Cape.

Bedaux, C. (1917) *The Bedaux Efficiency Course for Industrial Application*, Bedaux Industrial Institute.

Bell, C. and Newby, H. (1976) 'Communion, communalism, class and community action: the sources of new urban politics', in D. Herbert and R. Johnston (eds) *Social Areas in Cities*, vol. 2, Chichester: Wiley.

Bell, D. (1974) *The Coming of Post-Industrial Society*, London: Heinemann.

Bendix, R. (1956) *Work and Authority in Industry*, Chichester: Wiley.

Benenson, H. (1982) 'The reorganisation of US manufacturing industry and workers' experience, 1880–1920: a review of bureaucracy and the labour process by Dan Clawson', *Insurgent Sociologist*, 11: 65–81.

Benjamin, W. (1979) *One-Way Street and Other Writings*, London: Verso.

Benn, S.I. (1976) 'Rationality and political behaviour', in S.I. Benn and G.W. Mortimer (eds) *Rationality and the Social Sciences*, London: Routledge & Kegan Paul.

Benton, T. (1977) *Philosophical Foundations of the Three Sociologies*, London: Routledge & Kegan Paul.

Berger, J. and Offe, C. (1982) 'Functionalism vs rational choice: some questions concerning the rationality of choosing one or the other', *Theory and Society*, 11: 521–6.

Bergson, H. (1910) *Time and Free Will*, London: Swan Sonnenschein.

Berman, M. (1983) *All that Is Solid Melts into Air. The Experience of Modernity*, London: Verso.

Bhabha, H. (ed.) (1990) *Nation and Narration*, London: Routledge.

Bhaskar, R. (1975) *The Realist Theory of Science*, Leeds: Alma.

Bhaskar, R. (1979) *The Possibility of Naturalism*, Hassocks: Harvester.

Bianchini, F. and Schwengel, H. (1991) 'Re-imagining the city', in J. Corner and S. Harvey (eds) *Enterprise and Heritage*, London: Routledge.

Bicknell, P. and Woof, R. (1983) *The Lake District Discovered 1810–1850: The Artists, the Tourists, and Wordsworth*, Grasmere: Trustees of Dove Cottage.

Bird, J., Curtis, B., Putnam, T., Robertson, G. and Tickner, L. (eds) (1993) *Mapping the Futures*, London: Routledge.

Blau, P. and Duncan, O.D. (1967) *The American Occupational Structure*, New York: Wiley.

231

Bledstein, B.J. (1976) *The Culture of Professionalism*, New York: Norton.

Boden, D. (1994) 'Trust, modernity and the interaction order', Mimeo, Dept of Sociology, Lancaster University.

Bottomore, T.B. and Nisbet, R.A. (eds) (1979) *A History of Sociological Analysis*, London: Heinemann.

Boudon, R. (1981) *The Logic of Social Action*, London: Routledge & Kegan Paul.

Bourdieu, P. (1990) 'Time perspectives in the Kabyle', in J. Hassard (ed.) *The Sociology of Time*, London: Macmillan.

Braverman, H. (1974) *Labour and Monopoly Capital*, New York: Monthly Review Press.

Brech, J. (1982) *Strike*, Boston: South End Press.

Brendon, P. (1991) *Thomas Cook: 150 Years of Popular Tourism*, London: Secker & Warburg.

Brenner, R. (1976) 'Agrarian class structure and economic development in pre-industrial Europe', *Past and Present*, 70: 30–75.

Broadbent, T.A. (1977) *Planning and Profit in the Urban Economy*, London: Methuen.

Brody, D. (1980) *Workers in Industrial America*, Oxford: Oxford University Press.

Brown, E.H. and Browne, M.H. (1968) *A Century of Pay*, London: Macmillan.

Brown, E.R. (1980) *Rockefeller Medicine Men*, Berkeley: University of California Press.

Brown, G.C. (1935) 'AFL report on the Bedaux system', *American Federationist*, 42: 936–43.

Brunn, S. and Leinbach, T. (eds) (1991) *Collapsing Space and Time*, London: Harper Collins.

Buck-Morss, S. (1989) *The Dialectics of Seeing: Walter Benjamin and the Arcades Project*, Cambridge, Mass.: MIT Press.

Burawoy, M. (1978) 'Towards a Marxist theory of the labour process: Braverman and beyond', *Politics and Society*, 3–4: 247–312.

Burgess, K. (1980) *The Challenge of Labour*, London: Croom Helm.

Burrage, M. (1972) 'Democracy and the mystery of the crafts', *Daedalus*, fall: 141–62.

Buttrick, J. (1952) 'The inside contract system', *Journal of Economic History*, 12: 205–21.

Buzard, J. (1993) *The Beaten Track. European Tourism, Literature, and the Ways to 'Culture' 1800–1914*, Oxford: Clarendon Press.

Cabinet Office (Enterprise Unit) (1985) *Pleasure, Leisure and Jobs: The Business of Tourism*, London: HMSO.

Cadbury, E. (1914a) 'Some principles of industrial organisation: the case for and against scientific management', *Sociological Review*, 7: 99–125.

Cadbury, E. (1914b) 'Reply to C.B. Thompson', *Sociological Review*, 7: 266–9.

Carney, J., Hudson, R. and Lewis, J. (eds) (1980) *Regions in Crisis*, London: Croom Helm.

Carter, E., Donald, J., Squires, J. (eds) (1993) *Space and Place: Theories of Identity and Location*, London: Lawrence & Wishart.

Castells, M. (1977) *The Urban Question*, London: Edward Arnold.

Castells, M. (1978) *City and Power*, London: Macmillan.

Castells, M. (1983) *The City and the Grassroots*, London: Edward Arnold.

Chambers, I. (1994) *Migrancy, Culture, Identity*, London: Routledge.

Chandler, A.D. (1976) 'The development of modern management structures in the US and UK', in L. Hannah (ed.) *Management Strategy and Business Development*, London: Macmillan.

Chandler, A.D. (1980) 'The United States: seed-bed of managerial capitalism', in A.D. Chandler and H. Daems (eds) *Managerial Hierarchies*, Cambridge, Mass.: Harvard University Press.

Chapman, M. (1993) 'Copeland: Cumbria's best-kept secret', in S. Macdonald (ed.) *Inside European Identities*, Oxford: Berg.

Church, R.L. (1974) 'Economists as experts: the rise of an academic profession in the United States, 1870–1920', in L. Stone (ed.) *The University in Society*, vol. 2, Oxford: Oxford University Press.

Clark, S. (1992) 'Leisure: *jeux sans frontières* or major European industry', in J. Bailey (ed.) *Social Europe*, London: Longman.

Clawson, D. (1980) *Bureaucracy and the Labour Process*, New York: Monthly Review Press.

Clover, C. (1990) '"Tourist honeypot" fears for the Cairngorms', *Daily Telegraph*, 12 September.

Cohen, G.A. (1978) *Karl Marx's Theory of History*, Oxford: University Press.

Cohen, G.A. (1980) 'Functional explanation, reply to Elster', *Political Studies*, 18: 129–35.

Cohen, G.A. (1982a) 'Functional explanation, consequence explanation, and Marxism', *Inquiry*, 25: 27–56.

Cohen, G.A. (1982b) 'Reply to Elster on "Marxism, Functionalism, and Game Theory"', *Theory and Society*, 11: 483–95.

Cohen, P. (1968) *Modern Social Theory*, London: Heinemann.

Coleman, D.C. (1973) 'Gentleman and players', *Economic History Review*, 26: 92–116.

Colson, F. (1926) *The Week*, Westport, Conn.: Greenwood Press.

Connerton, P. (1989) *How Societies Remember*, Cambridge: Cambridge University Press.

Cooke, P. (1981) *Local Class Structure in Wales*, Cardiff: Department of Town Planning, UWIST, Papers in Planning Research no. 31.

Cooke, P. (1983) *Theories of Planning and Spatial Development*, London: Hutchinson.

Cooke, P. (1985) 'Class practices as regional markers', in D. Gregory and J. Urry (eds) *Social Relations and Spatial Structures*, London: Macmillan.

Cooke, P. (1986) *Global Restructuring, Local Response*, London: Economic and Social Research Council.

Cooke, P. (ed.) (1989) *Localities: The Changing Face of Urban Britain*, London: Unwin Hyman.

Copley, F.B. (1923) *Frederick W. Taylor*, 2 vols, New York: Harper & Row.

Corner, J. and Harvey, S. (eds) (1991) *Enterprise and Heritage*, London: Routledge.

Cosgrove, D. (1984) *Social Formation and Symbolic Landscape*, London: Croom Helm.

Coward, R. and Ellis, J. (1977) *Language and Materialism*, London: Routledge & Kegan Paul.

Cowen, H. (1990) 'Regency icons; marketing Cheltenham's built environment', in M. Harloe, C. Pickvance and J. Urry (eds) *Place, Policy and Politics: Do Localities Matter?*, London: Unwin Hyman.

Crawshaw, C. (1994a) *Altered Images*, Tourism and the Environment Working Paper no. 2, Lancaster University.

Crawshaw, C. (1994b) *Romancing the Lake District*, Tourism and the Environment Project Working Paper no. 3, Lancaster University.

Crick, M. (1988) 'Sun, sex, sights, savings and servility', *Criticism, Heresy and Interpretation*, 1: 37–76.

Crook, S., Pakulski, J. and Walters, M. (1992) *Postmodernization*, London: Sage.

Crouch, C. (1982) *Trade Unions: The Logic of Collective Action*, London: Fontana.

Cubitt, S. (1991) *Timeshift. On Video Culture*, London: Routledge.

Culler, J. (1981) 'Semiotics of tourism', *American Journal of Semiotics*, 1: 127–40.

Daniel, W. and Milward, N. (1983) *Workplace Industrial Relations in Britain*, London: HEB.

Daniels, S. and Cosgrove, D. (1988) 'Introduction: iconography and landscape', in D. Cosgrove and S. Daniels (eds) *The Iconography of Landscape*, Cambridge: Cambridge University Press.

Davies, T.M. (1978) 'Capital, state and sparse populations: the context of further research', in H. Newby (ed.) *International Perspectives in Rural Sociology*, Chichester: John Wiley.

Davis, M. (1990) *City of Quartz*, London: Verso.

Deane, P. and Cole, W. (1962) *British Economic Growth 1688–1959*, Cambridge: University Press.

Debray, R. (1981) *Teachers, Writers, Celebrities*, London: Verso.

Derrida, J. (1972) 'Sémiologie et grammatologie', in J. Derrida (ed.) *Positions*, Paris: Editions de Minuit.

Devinat, P. (1927) *Scientific Management in Europe*, Geneva: ILO.

Dickens, P. (1987) *One Nation?: Social Change and the Politics of Locality*, London: Allison & Busby.

Disco, C. (1979) 'Critical theory as ideology of the new class', *Theory and Society*, 8: 159–214.

Dobb, M. (1976) 'A reply', in R. Hilton (ed.) *The Transition from Feudalism to Capitalism*, London: New Left Books.

Donnison, D. and Soto, P. (1980) *The Good City*, London: Heinemann.

Dore, R. (1976) *The Diploma Disease*, London: Allen & Unwin.

Dower, M. (1965) *The Challenge of Leisure: The Fourth Wave*, London: Architectural Press.

Drabble, M. (1991) 'A vision of the real city', in M. Fisher and U. Owen (eds) *Whose Cities?*, Harmondsworth: Penguin.

Dubofsky, M. (1983) 'Workers movement in North America, 1873–1970: a preliminary analysis', in I. Wallerstein (ed.) *Labour in the World Social Structure*, Beverly Hills: Sage.

Dunford, M., Geddes, M. and Perrons, D. (1980) *Regional Policy and the Crisis in the UK: A Long-Run Perspective*, London: City of London Polytechnic, Department of Economics and Banking Working Paper no. 3.

Dunleavy, P. (1980) *Urban Political Analysis*, London: Macmillan.

Durkheim, E. (1968) *The Elementary Forms of the Religious Life*, London: George Allen & Unwin.

Durkheim, E. (1984) *The Division of Labour in Society*, London: Macmillan.

Eco, U. (1986) *Travels in Hyper-Reality*, London: Picador.

Economic Development (undated) *I've Never Been to Wigan, But I Know What it's Like*, Wigan: Economic Development.

Edgar, D. (1987) 'The new nostalgia', *Marxism Today*, March: 30–5.

Elbourne, E.T. (1914) *Factory Administration and Accounts*, London: Longman.

Elias, N. (1992) *Time: An Essay*, Oxford: Blackwell

Elliott, P. (1972) *The Sociology of the Professions*, London: Macmillan.

Ellis, A. and Heath, A. (1983) 'Positional competition, or an offer you can't refuse', in A. Ellis and K. Dumar (eds) *Dilemmas of Liberal Democracies*, London: Tavistock.

Ellis, A. and Dumar, K. (eds) (1983) *Dilemmas of Liberal Democracies*, London: Tavistock.

Elster, J. (1978) *Logic and Society*, Chichester: Wiley.

Elster, J. (1979) *Ulysses and the Sirens*, Cambridge: Cambridge University Press.

Elster, J. (1980a) 'Cohen on Marx's theory of history', *Political Studies*, 18: 121–8.

Elster, J. (1980b) 'Reply to comments', *Inquiry*, 23: 213–32.

Elster, J. (1982a) 'Marxism, functionalism and game theory, the case for methodological individualism', *Theory and Society*, 11: 453–82.

Elster, J. (1982b) 'Roemer vs. Roemer: a comment on "New directions in the Marxian theory of exploitation and class"', *Politics and Society*, 11: 363–73.

Engels, F. (1969) *The Condition of the Working Class in England*, London: Granada.

Evans, D. (1992) *A History of Nature Conservation in Britain*, London: Routledge.

Evans-Pritchard, E. (1940) *The Nuer*, Oxford: Oxford University Press.

Ewen, S. and Ewen, E. (1982) *Channels of Desire*, New York: McGraw Hill.

Featherstone, M. (1991) *Consumer Culture and Postmodernism*, London: Sage.

Fine, B., Kinsey, R., Lea, J., Picciotto, S. and Young, J. (eds) (1979) *Capitalism and the Rule of Law*, London: Hutchinson.

Flatow, S. von and Huisken, F. (1973) 'Zum Problem der Ableitung des bürgerlicken Staates', *Probleme des Klassenkampfs*, 7.

Flynn, A., Lowe, G. and Cox, G. (1990) *The Rural Land Development Process*, ESRC Countryside Change Initiative, Working Paper no. 6.

Folch-Serra, M. (1990) 'Place, voice, space: Mikhail Bakhtin's dialogical landscape', *Environment and Planning D: Society and Space*, 8: 255–74.

Foner, P.S. (1955) *History of the Labour Movement in the United States*, vol. 2, New York: International Publishers.

Fothergill, S. and Gudgin, G. (1979) 'Regional employment change: a sub-regional explanation', *Progress in Planning*, 12: 155–219.

Fothergill, S. and Gudgin, G. (1982) *Unequal Growth*, London: Heinemann.

Foucault, M. (1972) *The Archaeology of Knowledge*, London: Tavistock.

Frank, A. (1969) *Latin America: Underdevelopment or Revolution*, New York: Monthly Review Press.

Frankel, M. (1955) 'Obsolescence and technical change in a maturing economy', *American Economic Review*, 45: 296–319.

Frankenberg, R. (1966) *Communities in Britain*, Harmondsworth: Penguin.

Frankenberg, R. (1988) '"Your time or mine?" An anthropological view of the tragic temporal contradictions of biomedical practice', in M. Young and T. Schuller (eds) *The Rhythms of Society*, London: Routledge.

Frisby, D. (1992a) *Simmel and Since*, London: Routledge.

Frisby, D. (1992b) *Sociological Impressionism*, London: Routledge.

Fröbel, F., Heinrichs, J. and Kreye, K. (1977), *The New International Division of Labour*. Cambridge: Cambridge University Press.

Frölich, N., Oppenheimer, J.A. and Young, O.R. (1971) *Political Leadership and Collective Goods*, New Jersey: Princeton University Press.

Game, A. (1990) 'Nation and identity: Bondi', *New Formations*, 11: 105–21.

Game, A. (1991) *Undoing the Social*, Milton Keynes: Open University Press.

Game, A. (1994) 'Time, space, memory, with reference to Bachelard', in M. Featherstone, S. Lash and R. Robertson (eds) *Global Modernities*, London: Sage.

Gans, H. (1986): 'Urbanism and suburbanism as ways of life', in R. Pahl (ed.) *Readings in Urban Sociology*, Oxford: Pergamon.

Gasson, R. (1966) 'Part-time farmers in south-east England', *Farm Environment*, 11: 135–9.

Gasson, R. (1980) 'Roles of farm women in England', *Sociologia Ruralis*, 20: 165–80.

Gauthier, D. (1982) 'Reason and maximisation', in B. Barry and R. Hardin (eds) *Rational Man and Irrational Society*, Beverly Hills: Sage.

Geertz, F. (1983) *Local Knowledge*, New York: Basic Books.

Gershuny, J. (1978) *After Industrial Society*, London: Macmillan.

Gershuny, J. and Miles, I. (1983) *The New Service Economy*, London: Frances Pinter.

Giddens, A. (1976) *New Rules of Sociological Method: A Positive Critique of Interpretative Sociologies*, London: Hutchinson.

Giddens, A. (1977) *Studies in Social and Political Theory*, London: Hutchinson.

Giddens, A. (1979) *Central Problems in Social Theory*, London: Macmillan.

Giddens, A. (1981) *A Contemporary Critique of Historical Materialism*, London: Macmillan.

Giddens, A. (1982) 'A commentary on the debate', *Theory and Society*, 11: 527–39.

·Giddens, A. (1984) *The Constitution of Society*, Cambridge: Polity.

Giddens, A. (1990) *The Consequences of Modernity*, Cambridge: Polity.

Giddens, A. (1991a) *Modernity and Self-Identity*, Cambridge: Polity.

Giddens, A. (1991b) 'Structuration theory: past, present and future', in C. Bryant and D. Jary (eds) *Giddens' Theory of Structuration*, London: Routledge.

Goldthorpe, J.H. (1980) *Social Mobility and Class Structure*, London: Oxford University Press.

Goldthorpe, J. (1982) 'On the service class, its formation and future', in A. Giddens and G. Mackenzie (eds) *Social Class and the Division of Labour*, Cambridge: Cambridge University Press.

Gorz, A. (1985) *Paths to Paradise*, London: Pluto.

Green, N. (1990) *The Spectacle of Nature*, Manchester: Manchester University Press.

Gregory, D. (1985) 'Suspended animation: the stasis of diffusion theory', in D. Gregory and J. Urry (eds) *Social Relations and Spatial Structures*, London: Macmillan.

Gregory, D. and Urry, J. (eds) (1985) *Social Relations and Spatial Structures*, London: Macmillan.

Grigg, D. (1969) 'Regions, models and classes', in R.J. Chorley and P. Haggett (eds) *Integrated Models in Geography*, London: Methuen.

Haber, S. (1964) *Efficiency and Uplift: Scientific Management in the Progressive Era, 1890–1920*, Chicago: Chicago University Press.

Habermas, J. (1976) *Legitimation Crisis*, London: Heinemann.

Habermas, J. (1979) *Communications and the Evolution of Society*, London: Heinemann.

Habermas, J. (1981) *Theorie des Kommunikativen Handels*, Frankfurt: Suhrkamp.

Hahn, F. (1980) 'Ulysses and the sirens', *Inquiry* 23: 479–82.

Hakim, C. (1987) 'Homeworking in Britain', *Employment Gazette*, February: 92–104.

Halsall, M. (1987) 'Hopeful hint of a renaissance along the Mersey', *Guardian*, 28 January.

Hamilton, A. (1990) 'The enchanted nightmare', *Guardian*, 10 August.

Hannah, L. (1976) *The Rise of the Corporate Economy*, London: Methuen.

Hannerz, U. (1990) 'Cosmopolitans and locals in world culture', *Theory, Culture and Society*, 7: 237–52.

Hardin, R. (1982) *Collective Action*, Baltimore: Johns Hopkins University Press.

Harloe, M., Pickvance, C. and Urry, J. (eds) (1990) *Place, Policy, Politics: Do Localities Matter?*, London: Unwin Hyman.

Harré, R. (1970) *The Principles of Scientific Thinking*, London: Macmillan.

Harré, R. and Madden, E. (1975) *Causal Powers*, Oxford: Basil Blackwell.

Harris, R. (1983) 'Space and class: A critique of Urry', *International Journal of Urban and Regional Research*, 6: 115–21.

Harrison, C. (1991) *Countryside Recreation in a Changing Society*, London: TMS Partnership.

Harvey, D. (1982) *The Limits to Capital*, Oxford: Basil Blackwell.

Harvey, D. (1985) 'The geo-politics of capitalism', in D. Gregory and J. Urry (eds) *Social Relations and Spatial Structures*, London: Macmillan.

Harvey, D. (1989) *The Condition of Postmodernity*, Oxford: Blackwell.

Hassard, J. (1988) *The Sociology of Time*, London: Macmillan.

Heal, F. (1990) *Hospitality in Early Modern England*, Oxford, Clarendon.

Heath, A. (1976) *Rational Choice and Social Exchange*, Cambridge: University Press.

Hebdige, D. (1988) *Hiding in the Light*, London: Routledge.

Hebdige, D. (1990) 'Fax to the future', *Marxism Today*, January: 18–23.

Hefferan, J. (1985) *The Recreation of Landscape*, Hanover: University Press of New England.

Heidegger, M. (1962) *Being and Time*, Oxford: Blackwell.

Held, D. (1990) 'Democracy, the nation-state and the global system', in D. Held (ed.) *Political Theory Today*, Cambridge: Polity.

Henderson, J. and Castells, M. (eds) (1987) *Global Restructuring and Territorial Development*, London: Sage.

Hernes, G. and Selvik, A. (1981) 'Local corporatism', in S. Berger (ed.) *Organising Interests in Western Europe: Pluralism, Corporatism, and the Transformation of Politics*, Cambridge: Cambridge University Press.

Herrmann, E.S. (1981) *Corporate Control, Corporate Power*, Cambridge: Cambridge University Press.

Hetherington, K. (1990) 'The contemporary significance of Schmalenbach's concept of the Bund', *Sociological Review*, 42: 1–25.

Hewison, R. (1987) *The Heritage Industry*, London: Methuen.

Hewison, R. (1993) 'Field of dreams', *Sunday Times*, 3 January.

Hill, S. (1982) *Competition and Control at Work*, London: Heinemann.

Hirsch, F. (1978) *Social Limits to Growth*, London: Routledge & Kegan Paul.

Hirsch, J. (1978) 'The state apparatus and social reproduction: elements of a theory of the bourgeois state', in J. Holloway and S. Picciotto (eds) *State and Capital*, London: Edward Arnold.

Hobsbawm, E. (1964) *Labouring Men*, London: Weidenfeld & Nicolson.

Hobson, J.A. (1913) 'Scientific management', *Sociological. Review*, 6: 197–212.

Hobson, J.A. (1922) *Incentives in the New Industrial Order*, London: Parsons.

Hoffman-Axthelm, D. (1992) 'Identity and reality: the end of the philosphical immigration officer', in S. Lash and J. Friedman (eds) *Modernity and Identity*, Oxford: Blackwell.

Hoggart, K. and Kofman, E. (eds) (1986) *Politics, Geography and Social Stratification*, Beckenham, Kent: Croom Helm.

Hoggett, P. and Bishop, J. (1986) *Organizing Around Enthusiasms*, London: Comedia.

Holderness, G. (1988) 'Bardolatry: or, The cultural materialist's guide to Stratford-upon-Avon', in G. Holderness (ed.) *The Shakespeare Myth*, Manchester: Manchester University Press.

Holloway, J. and Picciotto, S. (eds) (1978) *State and Capital*, London: Edward Arnold.

Hooper, J. (1990) 'The highway to the Spanish by-ways', *Guardian*, 10 August.

Hopkins, A. (1990) 'Fragile Spain', *Sunday Times*, 24 June.

Horne, D. (1969) *God is an Englishman*, Sydney.

Humphries, J. (1977) 'Class struggle and the persistence of the working class family', *Cambridge Journal of Economics*, 1: 241–58.

Ingham, G. (1982) 'Divisions within the dominant class and British "exceptionalism"', in A. Giddens and G. Mackenzie (eds) *Social Class and the Division of Labour*, Cambridge: Cambridge University Press.

Ingham, G. (1984) *Capitalism Divided*, London: Macmillan.

Jameson, F. (1991) *Postmodernism, or the Cultural Logic of Late Capitalism*, London: Verso.

Jay, M. (1992) *Force Fields*, London: Routledge.

Jencks, C. (1991) *The Language of Post-Modern Architecture*, London: Academy Editions.

Jessop, B. (1978) 'Corporatism, fascism and social democracy', ECPR Workshop on Corporatism in Liberal Democracies, Grenoble.

Johnston, B. (1990) 'Chianti turns sour for British expats', *Sunday Times*, 23 September.

Jones, A. (1987) 'Green tourism', *Tourism Management*, December: 354–6.

Josling, T.E. (1974) 'Agricultural policies in developed countries: a review', *Journal of Agricultural Economics*, 25: 229–58.

Kearns, G. and Philo, C. (eds) (1993) *Selling Places*, Oxford: Pergamon.

Keat, R. and Urry, J. (1982) *Social Theory as Science*, second edn, London: Routledge & Kegan Paul.

Keat, R., Whiteley, N. and Abercrombie, N. (eds) (1994) *The Authority of the Consumer*, London: Routledge.

Keeble, D. (1976) *Industrial Location and Planning in the UK*, London: Methuen.

Keith, M. and Pile, S. (eds) (1993) *Place and the Politics of Identity*, London: Routledge.

Kellner, D. (1992) 'Popular culture and the construction of postmodern identities', in S. Lash and J. Friedman (eds) *Modernity and Identity*, Oxford: Blackwell.

Kelly, J. (1990) 'Malta: sink or swim?' *Daily Telegraph*, 29 August.

Kennett, S. (1982) 'Migration between British local labour markets and some speculation on policy options for influencing population distributions', *British Society for Populational Studies Occasional Paper 28*, Conference on Population Change and Regional Labour Markets, OPCS: 35–54.

Kern, S. (1983) *The Culture of Time and Space, 1880–1918*, London: Weidenfeld & Nicolson.

Kettle, M. (1990) 'Slippery slopes', *Marxism Today*, 7 January.

Kocka, J. (1978) 'Entrepreneurs and managers in German industrialisation', in P. Mathias and M. Postan (eds) *Cambridge Economic History of Europe*, vol. 7, Cambridge: Cambridge University Press.

Kocka, J. (1980) *White Collar Workers in America, 1890–1940*, London: Sage.

Kolko, G. (1963) *The Triumph of Conservatism*, New York: Free Press.

Kreckel, R. (1980) 'Unequal opportunity structures and labour market segmentation', *Sociology*, 14: 525–50.

Kuhn, T.S. (1970) *The Structure of Scientific Revolutions*, Chicago: University of Chicago Press.

Laclau, E. (1979) *Politics and Ideology in Marxist Theory*, London: Verso.

Lakatos, I. (1970) 'Falsification and the methodology of scientific research programmes', in I. Lakatos and A. Musgrave (eds) *Criticism and the Growth of Knowledge*, Cambridge: Cambridge University Press.

Lakatos, I. and Musgrave, A. (eds) (1970) *Criticism and the Growth of Knowledge*, Cambridge: Cambridge University Press.

Large, P. (1983) 'Globe trotting computers join the million mile club', *Guardian*, 2 May.

Larson, M.S. (1977) *The Rise of Professionalism: A Sociological Analysis*, Berkeley: University of California Press.

Larson, M.S. (1980) 'Proletarianisation and educated labour', *Theory and Society*, 9: 131–75.

Lasch, C. (1977) 'The siege of the family', *New York Review of Books*, 24: 15–18.

Lasch, C. (1980) *The Culture of Narcissism*, London: Sphere.

Lash, S. (1984) *The Militant Worker, Class and Radicalism in France and America*, London: Heinemann.

Lash, S. (1990a) 'Coercion as ideology: the German case', in N. Abercrombie, S. Hill and B. Turner (eds) *Dominant Ideologies*, London: Allen & Unwin.

Lash, S. (1990b) *Sociology of Postmodernism*, London: Routledge.

Lash, S. (1991) 'Reflexive modernization', Unpublished Paper, Department of Sociology, Lancaster University.

BIBLIOGRAPHY

Lash, S. and Friedman, J. (eds) (1992) *Modernity and Identity*, Oxford: Blackwell.

Lash, S. and Urry, J. (1984) 'The new Marxism of collective action: a critical analysis', *Sociology*, 18: 33–50.

Lash, S. and Urry, J. (1987) *The End of Organized Capitalism*, Cambridge: Polity Press.

Lash, S. and Urry, J. (1994) *Economies of Signs and Space*, London: Sage.

Lawson, A. (1989) *Adultery: an Analysis of Love and Betrayal*, Oxford: Basil Blackwell.

Layton, E. (1974) 'The diffusion of scientific management and mass production from the US in the twentieth century', *International Congress of Historical Science*, 4: 377–86.

Layton, E. (1971) *The Revolt of the Engineers*, Cleveland: Press of Case Western Reserve University.

Lebowitz, M. (1980) 'Capital as finite', paper given at the Marx Conference, University of Victoria, Canada.

Lecourt, D. (1975) *Marxism and Epistemology*, London: New Left Books.

Lefebvre, H. (1991) *The Production of Space*, Oxford: Blackwell.

Lehmbruch, G. and Schmitter, P. (eds) (1982) *Patterns of Corporatist Policy-making*, Sage Modern Politics Series, vol. 7, London: Sage.

Leong, W.-T. (1989) 'Culture and the state: manufacturing traditions for tourism', *Critical Studies in Mass Communication*, 6: 355–75.

Levine, A.L. (1967) *Industrial Retardation in Britain, 1880–1914*, London: Weidenfeld & Nicolson.

Levine, D. (ed.) (1971) *Georg Simmel. On Individuality and Social Forms*, Chicago: Chicago University Press.

Lipietz, A. (1980) 'The structuration of space, the problem of land and spatial policy', in J. Carney, R. Hudson and J. Lewis (eds) *Regions in Crisis*, London: Croom Helm.

Litterer, J. (1963) 'Systematic management: design for organisational recoiling in American manufacturing firms', *Business History Review*, 37: 369–91.

Littlejohn, G., Smart, B., Wakeford, J. and Yuval-Davis, N. (eds) (1978) *Power and the State*, London: Croom Helm.

Littler, C. (1978) 'Understanding Taylorism', *British Journal of Sociology*, 29: 185–202.

Littler, C. (1982a) 'Deskilling and changing structures of control', in S. Wood (ed.) *The Degradation of Work*, London: Hutchinson.

Littler, C. (1982b) *The Development of the Labour Process in Capitalist Societies*, London: Heinemann.

Littler, C. (1980) 'The bureaucratisation of the shop-floor: the development of the modern work-system', Ph.D. thesis, University of London.

Livingstone, P. (1969) 'Stop the stopwatch', *New Society*, 10 July, 49–51.

Lodge, D. (1983) *Small World*, Harmondsworth: Penguin.

Lowe, P. and Flynn, A. (1989) 'Environmental politics and policy', in J. Mohan (ed.) *The Political Geography of Contemporary Britain*, London: Macmillan.

Lowe, P. and Goyder, J. (1983) *Environmental Groups in Politics*, London: Allen & Unwin.

Lowe, P., Cox, G., Goodman, D., Munton, R. and Winter, M. (1990) 'Technological change, farm management and pollution regulation: the example of Britain', in P. Lowe, T. Marsden and S. Whatmore (eds) *Technological Change and the Rural Environment*, London: David Fulton.

Lowenthal, D. (1985) *The Past is a Foreign Country*, Cambridge: Cambridge University Press.

Lowenthal, D. (1991) 'British national identity and the English landscape', *Rural History*, 2: 205–30.

Lowenthal, D. and Binney, M. (1981) *Our Past Behind Us: Why Do We Save It?*, London: Temple Smith.

Lynch, K. (1973) *What Time is this Place?*, Boston: MIT Press.

Lyotard, J. (1984) *The Postmodern Condition*, Manchester: Manchester University Press.

MacCannell, D. (1976) *The Tourist*, London: Macmillan.

MacCannell, D. (1989) *The Tourist*, second edn, London: Macmillan.

MacIntyre, S. (1980) *Little Moscows*, London: Croom Helm.

Mack, J. and Lansley, S. (1985) *Poor Britain*, London: Allen & Unwin.

MacKenzie, J. and Richards, J. (1986) *The Railway Station: A Social History*, Oxford: Oxford University Press.

Macnaghten, P. and Urry, J. (1993) 'Constructing the countryside and the passive body', in C. Brackenbridge (ed.) *Body Matters: Leisure Images and Lifestyles*, Leisure Studies Association, no. 47.

Macnaghten, P. and Urry, J. (1994) 'Towards a sociology of nature', *Sociology* 28 (forthcoming).

Maier, C. (1970) 'Between Taylorism and technocracy: European ideologies and the vision of industrial productivity in the 1920s', *Journal of Contemporary History*, 5: 27–61.

Markus, T. (1993) *Buildings and Power*, London: Routledge.

Marshall, A. (1938) *Principles of Economics*, London: Macmillan.

Marx, K. (1973) *Grundrisse, Foundations of the Critique of Political Economy* (translated by M. Nicolaus), Harmondsworth: Penguin Books.

Marx, K. and Engels, F. (1964) [1848] *Manifesto of the Communist Party*, London: Modern Reader.

Marx, K. and Engels, F. (1976) *Collected Works*, vol. 6, London: Lawrence & Wishart.

Massey, D. (1978) 'Regionalism: some current issues', *Capital and Class*, 6: 106–25.

Massey, D. (1981) 'The UK electrical engineering and electronics industries: the implication of the crisis for the restructuring of capital and locational change', in M. Dear and A.J. Scott (eds) *Urbanisation and Urban Planning in Capitalist Society*, London: Methuen.

Massey, D. (1983) 'Industrial restructuring as class restructuring', *Regional Studies*, 17: 73–89.

Massey, D. (1984) *Spatial Divisions of Labour*, London: Macmillan.

Massey, D. and Meegan, R. (1982) *The Anatomy of Job Loss*, Andover, Hants: Methuen.

Masterman, M. (1970) 'The nature of a paradigm', in I. Lakatos and A. Musgrave (eds) *Criticism and the Growth of Knowledge*, Cambridge: Cambridge University Press.

Mead, G.H. (1959) *The Philosophy of the Present*, La Salle, Ill.: Open Court.

Mellor, A. (1991) 'Enterprise and heritage in the dock', in J. Corner and S. Harvey (eds) *Enterprise and Heritage*, London: Routledge.

Mennell, S. (1985) *All Manners of Food*, Oxford: Blackwell.

Meyrowitz, J. (1985) *No Sense of Place*, Oxford: Oxford University Press.

Middleton, D. and Edwards, D. (eds) (1990) *Collective Remembering*, London: Sage.

Miles, I. (1985) 'The new post-industrial state', *Futures*, December.

Miliband, R. (1970) 'The capitalist state: a reply to Nicos Poulantzas', *New Left Review*, 59: 53–60.

Miliband, R. (1973) 'Poulantzas and the capitalist state', *New Left Review*, 82: 83–92.

Miller, S.M. (1975) 'Notes on neo-capitalism', *Theory and Society*, 2: 1–36.

Milner, D. (1984) 'The art and sport of rock climbing in the English Lake District', in Countryside Commission and Victoria and Albert Museum: *The Lake District;*

A Sort of National Property, London: Countryside Commission and Victoria and Albert Museum.

Mishan, E. (1969) *The Costs of Economic Growth*, Harmondsworth: Penguin.

Montgomery, D. (1979) *Workers' Control in America*, Cambridge: Cambridge University Press.

Moorhouse, B. (1991) *Driving Ambitions*, Manchester: Manchester University Press.

Morgan, D.H.J. (1975) *Social Theory and the Family*, London: Routledge & Kegan Paul.

Morley, D. and Robins, K. (1990) 'No place like *Heimat*: images of home(land) in European culture', *New Formations*, Autumn: 1–23.

Morris, A. (1991) 'Popping the cork: history, heritage and the stately home in the Scottish borders', in G. Day and G. Rees (eds) *Regions, Nations and European Integration*, Cardiff: University of Wales Press.

Morris, M. (1990a) 'Life as a tourist object', World Congress of Sociology, Madrid, July.

Morris, M. (1990b) 'Metamorphoses at Sydney Tower', *New Formations*, 11: 5–18.

Mulhern, F. (1981) '"Teachers, writers, celebrities": intelligentsias and their histories', *New Left Review*, 126: 43–59.

Murdoch, J. (1990) 'A villa in Arcadia', in S. Pugh (ed.) *Reading Landscape. Country–City–Capital*, Manchester: Manchester University Press.

Murgatroyd, L. and Urry, J. (1983) 'The restructuring of a local economy: the case of Lancaster', in J. Anderson, S. Duncan and R. Hudson (eds) *Redundant Spaces in Cities and Regions*, London: Academic Press.

Nadworny, M.J. (1955) *Scientific Management and the Unions 1900–1932*, Cambridge, Mass.: Harvard University Press.

Nelson, D. (1975) *Managers and Workers: Origins of the New Factory System in the United States, 1880–1920*, Madison, Wisc.: University of Wisconsin Press.

Nelson, R. (1959) *The Merger Movement in American Industry, 1895–1956*, Princeton, NJ: Princeton University Press.

Newby, H. (1977) *The Deferential Worker*, London: Allen Lane.

Newby, H. (1978) 'The rural sociology of advanced capitalist societies', in H. Newby (ed.) *International Perspectives in Rural Sociology*, New York: Wiley.

Newby, H. (1979) *Green and Pleasant Land?*, London: Hutchinson.

Newby, H. (1980a) 'Rural sociology', *Current Sociology*, 28: 1–41.

Newby, H. (1980b) 'Urbanisation and the rural class structure: Reflections on a case study', in F. Buttel and H. Newby (eds) *The Rural Sociology of the Advanced Societies: Critical Perspectives*, London: Croom Helm.

Newby, H. (1982) 'Rural sociology and its relevance to the agricultural economist', *Journal of Agricultural Economics*, 33: 125–165.

Newby, H. (1985) *Green and Pleasant Land*, London: Wildwood House.

Newby, H. (1990) 'Revitalizing the countryside: the opportunities and pitfalls of counter-urban trends', *Royal Society of Arts Journal*, 138: 630–6.

Newby, H., Bell, C., Rose, D. and Saunders, P. (1978) *Property, Paternalism and Power*, London: Hutchinson.

Newby, P. (1991) 'Literature and the fashioning of tourist taste', in D. Pocock (ed.) *Humanistic Geography and Literature*, London: Croom Helm.

Nguyen, D. T. (1992) 'The spatialization of metric time', *Time and Society*, 1: 29–50.

Nichols, T. (1969) *Ownership, Control and Ideology*, London: Allen & Unwin.

Nichols, T. and Beynon, H. (1977) *Living with Capitalism*, London: Routledge & Kegan Paul.

Nicholson, N. (1955) *The Lakers: The Adventures of the First Tourists*, London: Robert Hale.

Nicholson, N. (1978) *The Lake District*, Harmondsworth: Penguin.

Noble, D. (1979) *America by Design*, Oxford: Oxford University Press.

Nowotny, H. (1985) 'From the future to the extended present: time in social systems', in G. Kirsch, P. Nijkamp, K. Zimmerman (eds) *Time Preferences: An Interdisciplinary Theoretical and Empirical Approach*, Berlin: Wissenschaftszentrum.

O'Connor, J. (1973) *The Fiscal Crisis of the State*, New York: St Martin's Press.

Offe, C. (1972) 'Political authority and class structures: an analysis of late capitalist societies', *International Journal of Sociology*, 2: 73–108.

Offe, C. (1975) 'Further comments on Müller and Neusüss', *Telos*, 25: 99–111.

Offe, C. and Wiesenthal, H. (1980) 'Two logics of collective action: theoretical notes on social class and organisational form', in M. Zeitlin (ed.) *Political Power and Social Theory* 1, Greenwich: Jai, 67–115.

Olson, M. (1965) *The Logic of Collective Action*, Cambridge, Mass.: Harvard University Press.

Ong, W. (1982) *Orality and Literacy*, London: Methuen.

OPCS (Office of Population Censuses and Surveys) (1991) *1991 Census – Economic Activity: Great Britain*, vol. 2, London: HMSO.

Orwell, G. (1938) *Homage to Catalonia*, London: Secker & Warburg.

Orwell, G (1959) [1937] *The Road to Wigan Pier*, London: Secker & Warburg.

Ousby, I. (1990) *The Englishman's England*, Cambridge: Cambridge University Press.

Oxaal, I. (ed.) (1975) *Beyond the Sociology of Development*, London: Routledge & Kegan Paul.

Pahl, R. (1965) *Urbs in Rure*, London: London School of Economics, Geographical Papers, no. 2.

Pahl, R. (1968) 'The rural–urban continuum', in R. Pahl (ed.) *Readings in Urban Sociology*, Oxford: Pergamon.

Pahl, R. (1975) *Whose City?*, Harmondsworth: Penguin.

Pahl, R. (1980) 'Employment, work and the domestic division of labour', *International Journal of Urban and Regional Research*, 4: 1–20.

Pahl, R. (1984) *Divisions of Labour*, Oxford: Blackwell.

Palmer, B. (1975) 'Class, conception and conflict: the thrust for efficiency, managerial views of labour and the working class rebellion 1903–22', *Review of Radical Political Economy*, 7: 31–49.

Panitch, L. (1978) 'Recent theorization of corporatism: reflections on a growth industry', Ninth World Congress of Sociology, Uppsala, Sweden.

Parkin, F. (1979) 'Social stratification', in T.B. Bottomore and R.A. Nisbet (eds) *A History of Sociological Analysis*, London: Heinemann.

Pashukanis, E. (1978) *Law and Marxism: A General Theory*, London: Ink Links.

Pearce, D. (1989) *Tourist Development*, Harlow: Longman.

Pearce, P. and Moscardo, G. (1986) 'The concept of authenticity in tourist experiences', *Australian and New Zealand Journal of Sociology*, 22: 121–32.

Pemble, J. (1987) *The Mediterranean Passion*, Oxford: Clarendon Press.

Perkin, H. (1961–2) 'Middle-class education and employment in the nineteenth century: a critical note', *Economic History Review*, 14: 122–30.

Perkin, H. (1976) 'The "social tone" of Victorian seaside resorts in the north-west', *Northern History*, XI: 180–94.

Perrot, M. (1974) *Les ouvriers en grève, France 1871–1890*, Paris: Mouton.

Person, H. (1920) *Scientific Management in American Industry*, The Taylor Society, New York: Harper.

Phillips, M. (1990) 'Must do better', *Guardian*, 14 September.

Pichierri, A. (1978) 'Diffusion and crisis of scientific management in European industry', in S. Giner and M. Archer (eds) *Contemporary Europe*, London: Routledge & Kegan Paul.

Pickvance, C. (1985) 'The rise and fall of urban movements and the role of the comparative analysis', *Environment and Planning. D. Society and Space*, 3: 31–53.

Pickvance, C. (1990) 'Introduction', in M. Harloe, C. Pickvance and J. Urry (eds) *Place, Policy and Politics: Do Localities Matter?*, London: Unwin Hyman.

Pillsbury, R. (1990) *From Boarding House to Bistro*, Boston: Unwin Hyman.

Piore, M. and Sabel, C. (1984) *The Second Industrial Divide*. New York: Basic Books

Pocock, D. (1982) 'Valued landscape in memory: the view from Prebends' Bridge', *Transactions of the Institute of British Geographers*, 7: 354–64.

Pollard, S. (1965) 'Trade unions and the labour market 1870–1914', *Yorkshire Bulletin of Economic and Social Research*, 17.

Pollard, S. (1969) *The Development of the British Economy, 1914–67*, London: Edward Arnold.

Poon, A. (1989) 'Competitive strategies for a "new tourism"', in C. Cooper (ed.) *Progress in Tourism, Recreation and Hospitality Management*, vol. 1, London: Belhaven Press.

Popper, K. (1970) 'Normal science and its dangers', in I. Lakatos and A. Musgrave (eds) *Criticism and the Growth of Knowledge*, Cambridge: Cambridge University Press.

Poulantzas, N. (1969) 'The problem of the capitalist state', *New Left Review*, 58: 67–78.

Poulantzas, N. (1973) *Political Power and Social Classes*, London: New Left Books.

Poulantzas, N. (1976) 'The capitalist state: a reply to Miliband and Laclau', *New Left Review*, 95: 68–83.

Przeworski, A. (1977) 'Proletariat into a class: the process of class formation from Karl Kautsky's *The Class Struggle* to recent controversies', *Politics and Society*, 7: 343–401.

Przeworski, A. (1980) 'Material bases of consent: economics and politics in a hegemonic system', in M. Zeitlin (ed.) *Political Power and Social Theory*, 1: 21–66.

Przeworski, A. (1982) 'The ethical materialism of John Roemer', *Politics and Society*, 11: 289–313.

Redfield, R. (1947) 'The folk society', *American Journal of Sociology*, 52: 293–308.

Relph, E. (1976) *Place and Placelessness*, London: Pion.

Renner, K. (1978) 'The service class', in T. Bottomore and P. Goode (eds) *Austro-Marxism*, Oxford: Clarendon Press.

Reynolds, H. (1988) '"Leisure revolutions" – prime engines of regional recovery', *Daily Telegraph*, 2 December.

Riddell, P. (1983) *The Thatcher Government*, Oxford: Martin Robertson.

Rifkin, J. (1987) *Time Wars. The Primary Conflict in Human History*, New York: Henry Holt.

Robins, K. (1991) 'Tradition and translation: National culture in its global context', in J. Corner and S. Harvey (eds) *Enterprise and Heritage*, London: Routledge.

Roemer, J.E. (1981) *Analytical Foundations of Marxian Economic Theory*, Cambridge: Cambridge University Press.

Roemer, J.E. (1982a) 'Methodological individualism and deductive Marxism', *Theory and Society*, 11: 513–20.

Roemer, J.E. (1982b) 'New directions in the Marxian theory of exploitation and class', *Politics & Society*, 11: 253–87.

Romeril, R. (1990) 'Tourism – the environmental dimension', in C. Cooper (ed.) *Progress in Tourism, Recreation and Hospitality Management*, vol. 1, London: Belhaven.

Rorty, R. (1982) *Consequences of Pragmatism*, Brighton: Harvester.

Routh, G. (1980) *Occupation and Pay in Great Britain*, London: Macmillan.

243

Roy, D. (1990) 'Time and job satisfaction', in J. Hassard (ed.) *The Sociology of Time*, London: Macmillan.

Rubinstein, W.D. (1977) 'Wealth, elites and class structure in Britain', *Past and Present*, 76: 99–126.

Rule, J. and Tilly, C. (1975) 'Political processes in revolutionary France, 1830–32', in J.M. Merriman (ed.) *1830 in France*, New York: New Viewpoints.

Sabolo, Y. (1975) *The Service Industries*, Geneva: ILO.

Sack, R. (1993) *Place, Modernity and the Consumer's World*, Baltimore: Johns Hopkins Press.

Samuel, R. (1985) 'Breaking up is very hard to do', *Guardian*, 2 December.

Sargant Florence, P. (1948) *Investment, Location and Size of Plant*, Cambridge: Cambridge University Press.

Sarlvik, B. and Crewe, I. (1983) *Decade of Dealignment*, Cambridge: Cambridge University Press.

Saunders, P. (1980) *Urban Politics*, Harmondsworth: Penguin.

Saunders, P. (1982) *Social Theory and the Urban Question*, London: Hutchinson.

Saunders, P. (1990) *A Nation of Home Owners*, London: Unwin Hyman.

Savage, M. and Warde, A. (1993) *Urban Sociology, Capitalism and Modernity*, London: Macmillan.

Savage, M., Barlow, J., Dickens, P. and Fielding, T. (1992) *Property, Bureaucracy and Culture*, London: Routledge.

Savage, M., Barlow, J., Duncan, S. and Saunders, P. (1987) 'Locality research: the Sussex programme on economic restructuring, social change and the locality', *The Quarterly Journal of Social Affairs*, 3: 27–51.

Saville, J. (1957) *Rural Depopulation in the United Kingdom*, London: Routledge & Kegan Paul.

Sayer, A. (1982) 'Explanation in human geography: abstraction versus generalisation', *Progress in Human Geography*, 6: 68–88.

Sayer, A. (1992) *Method in Social Science*, London: Routledge.

Schivelbusch, W. (1986) *The Railway Journey. Trains and Travel in the Nineteenth Century*, Oxford: Blackwell.

Schmalenbach, H.S. (1977) *Herman Schmalenbach: On Society and Experience*, Chicago: University of Chicago Press.

Schmitter, P. (1974) 'Still the century of corporatism?', *Review of Politics*, 36: 85–131.

Scott, A.J. (1985) 'Location processes, urbanisation and territorial development: an exploratory essay', *Environment and Planning A*, 17: 479–502.

Scott, A.J. and Storper, A. (eds) (1986) *Production, Work, Territory*, Hemel Hempstead, Herts: George Allen & Unwin.

Selbourne, D. (1990) 'Club Yob', *Sunday Times*, 19 August.

Sen, A. (1967) 'Isolation assurance and the social rate of discontent', *Quarterly Journal of Economics*, 80: 112–24.

Sennett, R. (1991) *The Conscience of the Eye*, London: Faber & Faber.

Sewell, R. (1980) *Work and Revolution in France*, Cambridge: Cambridge University Press.

Shadwell, A. (1906) *Industrial Efficiency*, 2 vols, London: Longman.

Shadwell, A. (1916) 'The welfare of factory workers', *Edinburgh Review*, October: 375–6.

Shanks, M. (1963) 'The comforts of stagnation', in A. Koestler (ed.) *Suicide of a Nation?*, London: Hutchinson.

Sharratt, B. (1989) 'Communications and image studies: notes after Raymond Williams', *Comparative Criticism*, 11: 29–50.

Sharrock, D. (1990) 'Rainham's dreams for the future', *Guardian*, 27 July.

Shields, R. (1991) *Places on the Margin*, London: Routledge.

Shoard, M. (1987) *The Land is Our Land*, London: Paladin.

Shurmer-Smith, P. (1990) 'Home is where the heart is? Second home ownership on Ile de Moine, S. Brittany', Mimeo.

Shutt, J. and Whittington, R. (1987) 'Fragmentation strategies and the rise of small units: cases from the north west', *Regional Studies*, 21: 13–24.

Simmie, J. (1981) 'Beyond the Industrial City', Mimeo, Berkeley, California.

Smith, A. (1986) *The Ethnic Origins of Nations*, Oxford: Blackwell.

Smith, N. (1984) *Uneven Development*, Oxford: Basil Blackwell.

Smith, V. (ed.) (1978) *Hosts and Guests*, Oxford: Blackwell.

Soffer, B. (1960) 'A theory of trade union development: the role of the "autonomous" workman', *Labour History*, 1: 141–63.

Soja, E. (1989) *Postmodern Geographies*, London: Verso.

Sontag, S. (1979) *On Photography*, Harmondsworth: Penguin.

Sorokin, P. and Merton, R. (1937) 'Social time: a methodological and functional analysis', *American Journal of Sociology*, 42: 615–29.

Squire, S. (1993) 'Gender and Tourist Experiences: Assessing Women's Shared Meanings for Beatrix Potter', Mimeo.

Stark, D. (1980) 'Class struggle and the transformation of the labour process', *Theory and Society*, 9: 89–130.

Stinchcombe, A.L. (1961) 'Agricultural enterprise and rural class relations', *American Journal of Sociology*, 67: 169–76.

Stinchcombe, A. (1974) 'Merton's theory of social structure', in L. Coser (ed.) *The Idea of Social Structure, Papers in Honour of Robert Merton*, New York: Harcourt, Brace, Jovanovich.

Stinchcombe, A. (1980) 'Is the prisoners' dilemma all of sociology?', *Inquiry*, 23: 187–92.

Stone, K. (1974) 'The origin of job structures in the steel industry', *Review of Radical Political Economy*, 6: 113–73.

Storper, M. (1981) 'Towards a structural theory of industrial location', in J. Rees, G. Hewings, H. Stafford (eds) *Industrial Location and Regional Systems*, London: Croom Helm.

Strathern, M. (1992) *After Nature. English Kinship in the Late Twentieth Century*, Cambridge: Cambridge University Press.

Sweezy, P. (1976) 'A critique', in R. Hilton (ed.) *The Transition from Feudalism to Capitalism*, London: New Left Books.

Taylor, C. (1980) 'Formal theory in social science', *Inquiry*, 23: 139–44.

Taylor, F.W. (1947) *The Principles of Scientific Management*, New York: Harper.

Thayer, R. (1990) 'Pragmatism in landscape: technology and the American landscape', *Landscape*, 30: 1–11.

Thompson, C.B. (1917) *The Theory and Practice of Scientific Management*, Boston: Houghton Mifflin.

Thompson, E.P. (1967) 'Time, work-discipline, and industrial capitalism', *Past and Present*, 38: 56–97.

Thrift, N. (1985) 'Flies and germs: a geography of knowledge', in D. Gregory and J. Urry (eds) *Social Relations and Spatial Structures*, London: Macmillan.

Thrift, N. (1990) 'The making of a capitalist time consciousness', in J. Hassard (ed.) *The Sociology of Time*, London: Macmillan.

Tighe, C. (1990) 'Lake District "has room for more tourists"', *Daily Telegraph*, 9 September.

Tilly, L.A. and Tilly, C. (eds) (1981) *Class Conflict and Collective Action*, London: Sage.

Toffler, A. (1970) *Future Shock*, New York: Random House.

Tönnies, F. (1955) *Community and Association*, London: Routledge & Kegan Paul.

Touraine, A. (1974a) *The Post-Industrial Society*, London: Wildwood House.

Touraine, A. (1974b) *The Academic System in American Society*, New York: McGraw Hill.

Travel Alberta (n.d.) *West Edmonton Mall*, Edmonton: Alberta Tourism.

Tribe, K. (1978) *Land, Labour and Economic Discourse*, London: Routledge & Kegan Paul.

Tuan, Y.F. (1977) *Space and Place*, London: Edward Arnold.

TUC Report (1933) *Bedaux Report*, London: TUC.

Turner, B.S. (1987) 'A note on nostalgia', *Theory, Culture and Society*, 4: 147–56.

Turner, R.H. (1961) 'Modes of social ascent through education: sponsored and contest mobility', in A.H. Halsey, J. Floud and C.A. Anderson (eds) *Education, Economy and Society*, New York: Free Press.

Turner, L. and Ash, J. (1975) *The Golden Hordes*, London: Constable.

Tweedie, J. (1990) 'Abroad thoughts from home: a tourist's taster', *Guardian*, 27 August.

Urry, J. (1973) 'Thomas S. Kuhn as sociologist of knowledge', *British Journal of Sociology*, 24: 462–73.

Urry, J. (1980) 'Sociology: a brief survey of recent developments', in B. Dufour (ed.) *New Perspectives in the Humanities and Social Sciences*, London: Temple Smith.

Urry, J. (1981a) *The Anatomy of Capitalist Societies*, London: Macmillan.

Urry, J. (1981b) 'Localities, regions and social class', *International Journal of Urban and Regional Research*, 5: 455–74.

Urry, J. (1982) 'Duality of structure, some critical issues', *Theory, Culture and Society*, 1: 100–6.

Urry, J. (1983a) 'De-industrialisation, classes and politics', in R. King (ed.) *Capital and Politics*, London: Routledge & Kegan Paul.

Urry, J. (1983b) 'Some notes on realism and the analysis of space', *International Journal of Urban and Regional Research*, 5: 122–7.

Urry, J. (1985) 'Space, time and social relations', in D. Gregory and J. Urry (eds) *Social Relations and Spatial Structures*, London: Macmillan.

Urry, J. (1986) 'The growth of scientific management: transformation in class structure and class struggle', in N. Thrift and P. Williams (eds) *The Making of Urban Society*, London: Routledge & Kegan Paul.

Urry, J. (1987a) *Economic Planning and Policy in the Lancaster District*, Lancaster Regionalism Group Working Paper no. 21, Department of Sociology, Lancaster University.

Urry, J. (1987b) *Holiday-making, Cultural Change and the Seaside*, Lancaster Regionalism Group Working Paper no. 22, Department of Sociology, Lancaster University.

Urry, J. (1988) 'Cultural change and contemporary holiday-making', *Theory, Culture and Society*, 5: 35–55.

Urry, J. (1990) *The Tourist Gaze*, London: Sage.

Urry, J. (1991) 'Time and space in Giddens' social theory', in C. Bryant and D. Jary (eds) *Giddens' Theory of Structuration*, London: Routledge.

Urry, J. (1992) 'The Tourist Gaze "Revisited"', *American Behavioral Scientist*, 36: 172–86.

Urry, J. (1994) 'Sociology of time and space', in B. Turner (ed.) *Companion to Social Theory*, Oxford: Blackwell.

Urwick, L. (1929) *The Meaning of Rationalisation*, London: Nisbet.

Urwick, L. and Brech, E.F.L. (1946) *Management in British Industry*, London: Management Publications Trust.

Veblen, T. (1912) *The Theory of the Leisure Class*, New York: Macmillan.

Venturi, R. (1977) *Learning from Las Vegas*, Cambridge, Mass.: MIT Press.

Vergo, P. (ed.) (1989) *The New Museology*, London: Reaktion.

Virilio, P. (1986) *Speed and Politics*, New York: Semiotext.

Wacquant, L. (1989) 'The ghetto, the state and the new capitalist economy', *Dissent*, Fall: 508–20.

Walby, S. (1986) *Patriarchy at Work*, Cambridge: Polity Press.

Walker, P. (ed.) (1979) *Between Labour and Capital*, New York: Monthly Review.

Walker, R. (1978) 'Two sources of uneven development under advanced capitalism: spatial differentiation capital mobility', *Review of Radical Political Economics*, 10: 28–37.

Walker, R. and Storper, M. (1981) 'Capital and industrial location', *Progress in Human Geography*, 5: 473–508.

Wallace, A. (1993) *Walking, Literature, and English Culture*, Oxford: Clarendon Press.

Walsh, K. (1992) *The Representation of the Past*, London: Routledge.

Walter, J. (1982) 'Social limits to tourism', *Leisure Studies*, 1: 295–304.

Walton, J. (1978) *The Blackpool Landlady*, Manchester: Manchester University Press.

Ward, C. and Hardy, D. (1986) *Goodnight Campers! The History of the British Holiday Camp*, London: Mansell.

Warde, A. (1985) 'Comparable localities: some problems of method', in L. Murgatroyd, M. Savage, D. Shapiro, J. Urry, A. Warde and S. Walby (eds) *Localities, Class and Gender*, London: Pion.

Warde, A. (1986) 'Space, class and voting', in K. Hoggart and E. Kofman (eds) *Politics, Geography and Social Stratification*, Beckenham, Kent: Croom Helm.

Watts, M. (1992) 'Spaces for everything (a commentary)', *Cultural Anthropology*, 7: 115–29.

Webb, S. (1918) *The Works Manager Today*, London: Longman.

Weber, M. (1930) *The Protestant Ethic and the Spirit of Capitalism*, London: Unwin.

Weber, M. (1958) *The City*, New York: Free Press.

Westaway, J. (1974) 'The spatial hierarchy of business organisations and its implication for the British urban system', *Regional Studies*, 8: 145–55.

Wheatcroft, G. (1990) 'We are all caught without escape in the tourist trap', *Daily Telegraph*, 20 November.

Wiebe, R.H. (1967) *The Search for Order*, London: Macmillan.

Wiener, M.J. (1981) *English Culture and the Decline of the Industrial Spirit 1850–1980*, Cambridge: Cambridge University Press.

Williams, R. (1973) *The Country and the City*, London: Chatto & Windus.

Wilson, A. (1992) *The Culture of Nature*, Oxford: Blackwell.

Wilson, E. (1991) *The Sphinx in the City*, London: Virago.

Wilson, E. (1992) 'The invisible flâneur', *New Left Review*, 191: 90–110.

Wilson, W. (1978) *The Declining Significance of Race*, Chicago: University of Chicago Press.

Wilson, W. (1987) *The Truly Disadvantaged: The Inner City, the Underclass and Public Policy*, Chicago: University of Chicago Press.

Winckler, J. (1977) 'The corporatist strategy: theory and administration', in R. Scase, (ed.) *Industrial Society: Class, Cleavage and Control*, London: Allen & Unwin.

Wirth, L. (1938) 'Urbanism as a way of life', *American Journal of Sociology*, 44: 1–24.

Wishart, R. (1991) 'Fashioning the future – Glasgow', in M. Fisher and U. Owen (eds) *Whose Cities?*, Harmondsworth: Penguin.

Wolff, J. (1987) 'The invisible flâneuse: women and the literature of modernity', in A. Benjamin (ed.) *The Problems of Modernity*, London: Routledge.

Wood, M. (1974) 'Nostalgia or never: you can't go home again', *New Society*, 7 November.

Wood, S. and Kelly, J. (1982) 'Taylorism, responsible autonomy and management strategy', in S. Wood (ed.) *The Degradation of Work?*, London: Hutchinson.

Worcester, R. (1993) 'Business and the environment – the weight of public opinion', *Admap*, 325 (January): 1–5.

Wordsworth, W. (1984) *Illustrated Guide to the Lakes*, Exeter: Webb & Bower.

Wright, P. (1985) *On Living in an Old Country*, London: Verso.

Wright, P. (1992) *A Journey Through Ruins*, London: Paladin.

Wright Mills, C. (1959) *The Sociological Imagination*, New York: Oxford University Press.

Yearley, S. (1991) *The Green Case*, London: Harper Collins.

Young, M. and Schuller, T. (eds) (1988) *The Rhythms of Society*, London: Routledge.

Zukin, S. (1991) 'Post-modern landscapes: mapping culture and power', in S. Lash and J. Friedman (eds) *Modernity and Identity*, Oxford: Blackwell.

Zukin, S. (1992a) 'The city as a landscape of power', in L. Budd and S. Whimster *Global Finance and Urban Living*, London: Routledge.

Zukin, S. (1992b) *Landscapes of Power*, Berkeley: University of California Press.

INDEX

shopping mall 123, 148–9
Shurmer-Smith, P. 191
Shutt, J. 121
signs, economy of 2
Simmel, G. 8–9, 20, 141, 144
skiing 185
Smith, A. 27
Smith, N. 69
Smith, V. 185
social, concept of 29
society: concepts of 29, 39–40, 120;
    post-industrial 112–25; relationship
    with nature 2; space and 29, 63–6
Society for the Interpretation of
    Britain's Heritage 223
Society for the Promotion of Scientific
    Management 94
sociology: and the state 35–8; as a
    parasite 33–45; discursive
    organisation 29, 38–42; time and
    space 2–4
Soffer, B. 92
Soja, E. 3, 20, 143
Sontag, S. 143, 146, 176
Sorokin, P. 4, 18
Soto, P. 84
Southey, R. 201
space: brief history 7–11; 1970s
    critique 11–18; relationship with
    society 29, 63–6; social analysis
    18–29; social identities 166; social
    objects 66–73; sociology of 11;
    time-space compression 22–3, 141,
    177–8, 219; time-space distanciation
    15–18
Spain 181–2
Squire, S. 208
Stark, D. 61, 91, 92–3, 98, 107
state, sociology and the 35–8
Stephens, L. 202
Stevenson, R.L. 202
Stinchcombe, A.L. 78
Stone, K. 92
Stonehenge 194
Storper, A. 68
Storper, M. 69, 82, 84–5, 90n
Stourhead Park 137, 180
Stratford-on-Avon 194, 195, 201
Strathern, M. 209
structuralism 40
suburbanisation 135
Sweezy, P. 46
Sydney Tower 178

Tahoe, Lake 133
Taylor, C. 52–3, 59
Taylor, F.W. 93, 94, 96–7, 102–3
Taylor Society 94, 104
Taylorism 105–7
technological change 3
Terry, Q. 177
Thatcherism 115, 211, 220
Thayer, R. 187–8
Theory and Society 46
Thompson, C.B. 96, 103
Thompson, E.P. 4–5, 19–20, 91
Thoreau, H.D. 202
Thrift, N. 19, 68
Tighe, C. 184
Tilly, C. 56, 57
Tilly, L.A. 57
time: approaches to 4–7; scientific
    'discoveries' 18–19; instantaneous
    216–18; social analysis 18–23; social
    identities 166; time-space
    compression 22–3; time-space
    distanciation 15–18
Toffler, A. 177, 217
Tönnies, F. 10
Touraine, A. 98, 114
tourism: consumption of 29, 129–40;
    destinations 168; economic theory
    133–9; end of 147–50; environment
    173–92; environmental
    consciousness 179–84;
    environmental damage 133–4,
    184–7; global developments 173–4;
    travel and the modern subject
    141–51; visual consumption of
    environment 187–92
Transactions of American Society of
    Mechanical Engineers 94
travel: air 130, 134, 179, 192; cars 142,
    179; democratisation 130, 134, 176;
    long-distance 164; modernity and
    identity 29; railways 119, 130, 174,
    179, 199; shift in nature of 195;
    social organisation 142–5; sociology
    of 129–30; time and space 17;
    tourism and the modern subject
    141–51; walking 201–2
Travel Alberta 148
Tuan, Y.F. 66
TUC Report (1933) 104–5
Turkey 184
Turner, B.S. 124
Turner, J.B. 97

256